HI, MY NAME IS

HI, MY NAME IS

Babble's Guide to Choosing the Perfect Name for Your Baby

from the editors of Babble.com

CHRONICLE BOOKS

SAN FRANCISCO

Library of Congress Cataloging-in-Publication Data
  Hi, my name is : Babble's guide to choosing the perfect name for your
baby / from the editors of Babble.com.
      p. cm.
  ISBN 978-0-8118-7059-7 (pbk.)
  1. Names, Personal—Handbooks, manuals, etc. 2. Names,
Personal—Dictionaries. I. Babble (Electronic resource)
CS2377.H5 2011
929.4′4—dc22
                        2010044576

Manufactured in China

Designed by Jennifer Tolo Pierce
Cover photography by Rachel Weill
Typeset by Happenstance Type-O-Rama

10 9 8 7 6 5 4 3 2 1

Chronicle Books
680 Second Street
San Francisco, California 94107

www.chroniclebooks.com

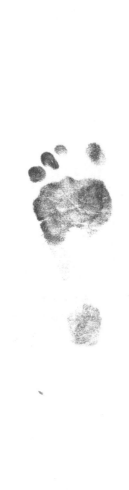

table of contents

introduction

SHAKESPEARE ASKED, WHAT'S IN A NAME? The answer, you can guess, is a whole lot. You are giving your child something they'll carry with them their entire lives, and the difference between Lola and Leila can be considerable. But don't worry; no matter what your perspective, there's a name out there both you and your partner will love. And whatever name you end up choosing, your child will eventually grow into it and make it their own.

Parenting in general is an inexact science, but at least with names, there's a lot you can know. When beginning to select among the thousands of options out there, it pays to think a little about the name's meaning, its popularity, the way it sounds with your last name, and the monogram the initials would form.

Then you might want to think about your family history and ethnicity, whether you want to make a statement (or expressly *not* make a statement), and whether anyone will be made happy or sad because you used (or didn't use) *their* name.

Finally you have to sort through all the associations you have with certain names—Peter, the kid in kindergarten who picked his nose; Sinéad, whose music you love; and Amy, your favorite high school teacher. None of those people will have anything to do with how your child turns out, but the associations you have with a name will affect you—at least until your child gives you all new things to think about.

Since finding a name that fits all your criteria can be a challenge, this introduction will be a how-to guide to walk you through the important factors in baby-naming. It will get you thinking about what matters most to you in a name, help you avoid embarrassing name blunders, and give you advice on how to navigate the social pitfalls of naming—all so that you can choose a name you and your child will love for life.

The rest of this introduction is divided into three categories: *Finding a Name You Love*, *Practical Matters to Contemplate*, and *Dealing with Family and Friends*. Along the way, we've included survey data to give you some perspective on how others feel about the same issues.

Good luck—and don't worry! The perfect name is out there, and we're here to help you find it.

finding a name you love

This section is composed of questions that you should ask yourself to help figure out what you're really looking for in a name. Do you care most about the name's meaning, that the name is popular, or that it *isn't* popular? This is where you get to decide what you like most about names, what features you can't live without, and what you want to avoid like the plague.

How important is everyone *else's* opinion?

Some people aren't concerned with what everyone else thinks about a name. If they want to name their daughter Persephone, they don't care that most of the nonscholars out there will think it's hard to pronounce and spell. Other parents want to strike a balance between names they love and names society will smile upon.

Of course, there's no right answer here, but this is one of those moments where it really pays to be honest with yourself early on. For example, even if you have loved the name Persephone since the third grade, you have to acknowledge that your daughter might get annoyed having to spell and respell the name for strangers her whole life. Is it worth it? If you're in doubt, Persephone might not be the right name. On the other hand, if you're the sort of person who jumps at the chance to talk about Greek mythology (and think your daughter will too), Persephone could be the perfect pick.

Once you know how important it is to you whether others like the name you choose, consider the names on your list and keep names or cross names off accordingly.

Is it important to you that your family members like the name you choose?

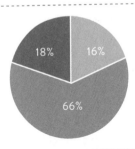

Is it important to you that your friends like the name you choose?

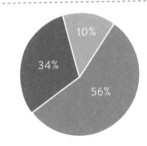

Is it important to you that your work colleagues like the name you choose?

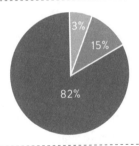

Is it important to you that your child's teacher likes the name you choose?

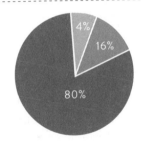

Is it important to you that others like the name you choose?

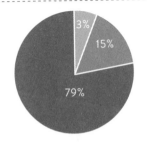

■ THEIR OPINION IS VITAL

■ I CARE, JUST NOT THAT MUCH

■ THEY CAN MIND THEIR OWN BUSINESS

How important is it that the name reflects your cultural background?

In the past, some people Anglicized names in order to "fit in" to American culture. Leonardo became Leonard and Rosa became Rose. Today, many parents head back to their roots and choose culturally relevant names for their children. These days, you'd probably be more surprised to hear the name Leonard on a playground than you would be to hear Leonardo.

Some multicultural families even make an effort to choose names that work in all the family backgrounds. Celebrity parents Tom Brady and Gisele Bündchen factored both their cultural backgrounds into their choice, eventually settling on Benjamin Rein for their son because the name has meaning to them in both English and Portuguese.

Is the name's meaning important to you?

With the exception of a few invented names, all names have meanings. The definitions can be nature-related, religion-inspired, and everything in between. Some names even have funny or negative meanings, for example, Campbell means "crooked mouth" and Regan means "impulsive, angry."

If you're undecided about where you stand, consider specific examples and how your child might feel. Will your Dempsey mind that his name means "proud" or "arrogant"? Would Amy feel a little bit more cherished when she finds out her name means "beloved"?

How important is a name's meaning to you?

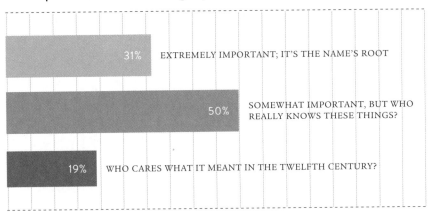

31% EXTREMELY IMPORTANT; IT'S THE NAME'S ROOT

50% SOMEWHAT IMPORTANT, BUT WHO REALLY KNOWS THESE THINGS?

19% WHO CARES WHAT IT MEANT IN THE TWELFTH CENTURY?

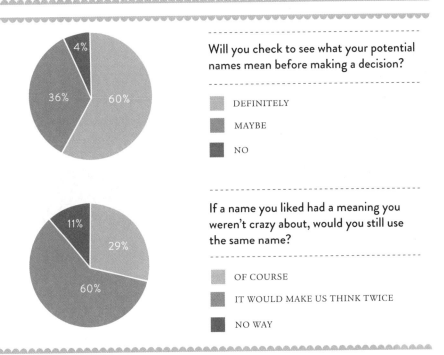

Will you check to see what your potential names mean before making a decision?

DEFINITELY

MAYBE

NO

If a name you liked had a meaning you weren't crazy about, would you still use the same name?

OF COURSE

IT WOULD MAKE US THINK TWICE

NO WAY

How do you feel about naming children after their parents?

In some families, it's a foregone conclusion that the firstborn (usually son) will be named after a parent (usually dad). If you're considering naming a child after yourself or your partner, consider these questions:

* Does the other parent agree?

* Is there an established tradition of naming children after parents in your family?

* Does the name have nickname potential or will two people in the same house be responding to the same name?

* Will the child feel too much pressure to emulate the namesake?

* Will the child struggle to establish a unique identity?

* Will the child be proud to be a part of a family tradition?

* Will sharing a name create a special bond between child and parent?

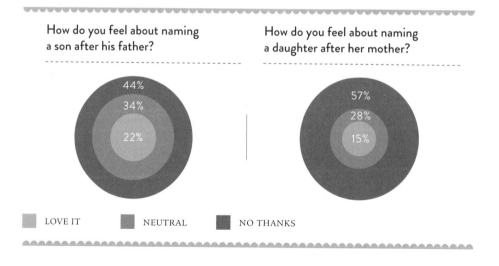

How do you feel about naming a son after his father?

44%
34%
22%

How do you feel about naming a daughter after her mother?

57%
28%
15%

LOVE IT   NEUTRAL   NO THANKS

How do you feel about creatively spelled names?

A Rose is a Roze is a Roaze—or maybe it's not. Few issues in the baby naming world elicit more heated debate than creative spelling. People tend to either love or hate creatively spelled names, and you probably already know which camp you side with.

Some spelling variations have become commonplace. Take Catherine, Katherine, and Kathryn; you wouldn't be surprised to come across any of these spellings and, though you might have a preference, you're unlikely to have a strong reaction one way or the other. On the other hand, there's Madison, Maddison, Madisyn, and Madyson; these variations are all found in the Social Security list of most popular names. The difference with the Madison variations is that because they haven't been a part of our lexicon as long as the Catherine variations have, they don't look familiar to us. Many parents like the newness; many others cringe at it.

Spelling names creatively can be a way to distinguish a child from the more common versions of the same name. Traditionalists, however, argue that these modifications create confusion and sometimes challenge phonetic rules. For example, if you didn't know better, you might think Madyson would be pronounced "Maddy-son" not "Madda-son." Again, the child with the alternate spelling is going to have to do a lot of explaining over the years.

As with most baby naming issues, there is no right answer, but it can't hurt to consider both sides when making your decision.

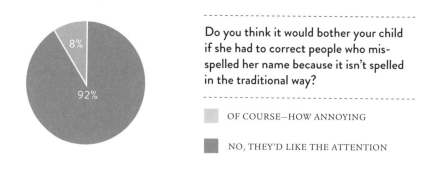

Do you think it would bother your child if she had to correct people who misspelled her name because it isn't spelled in the traditional way?

8% OF COURSE—HOW ANNOYING

92% NO, THEY'D LIKE THE ATTENTION

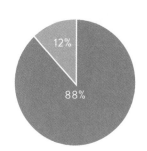

12%

88%

Do you think it would bother your child if he had to correct people who mispronounced his name because of the way it was spelled?

YES, IT'S FRUSTRATING TO HAVE TO KEEP EXPLAINING

NO, PEOPLE WILL GET IT THE SECOND TRY

Choose one:

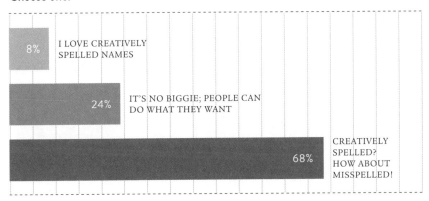

8%   I LOVE CREATIVELY SPELLED NAMES

24%   IT'S NO BIGGIE; PEOPLE CAN DO WHAT THEY WANT

68%   CREATIVELY SPELLED? HOW ABOUT MISSPELLED!

Do you want to give all your children related names?

If you like the idea of giving all your children names that relate to one another somehow, it's best to figure out the connection before you name your first child rather than when you start thinking about names for your second.

Some common ways to relate names are:

* Use names with the same first letter. You can go one step further and choose names with the same monogram.

  Famous example—the Duggar family used *J* as the first letter for all their children's names: Joshua, Jana, John-David, Jill, Jessa, Jinger, Joseph, Josiah, Joy-Anna, Jedidiah, Jeremiah, Jason, James, Justin, Jackson, Johannah, Jennifer, Jordyn-Grace, and Josie.

* Use names with the same meaning—this is great for families who want a more subtle connection.

  Example: All these names mean "beloved"—Cara, Morna, Darrell, and Thaddeus

* Use names with the same theme

  Examples: all biblical names or all names from your family tree

* Use all "nickname" names

  Examples: Beth, Ricky, Charlie, and Addie

Before embarking on a related-name scheme, ask yourself these questions:

* How do you think your kids will feel? Will they love it or hate it? Will they be embarrassed or proud?

* If you use the same initial as one of the parents, will the parent who has a different initial feel left out?

* Do you like enough names within the category? Say you plan on having only three children and decide to name all your children names that start with *Q* because you love the names Quincy, Quinn, and Quentin. But what happens when your third pregnancy turns out to be surprise triplets, and you don't have any other *Q* names to choose from?

Name themes can be a lot of fun, but choose them carefully and plan for the unexpected.

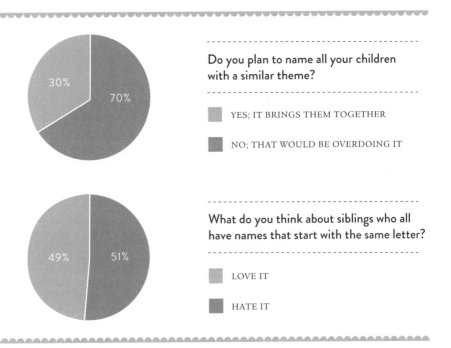

Do you plan to name all your children with a similar theme?

- YES; IT BRINGS THEM TOGETHER
- NO; THAT WOULD BE OVERDOING IT

What do you think about siblings who all have names that start with the same letter?

- LOVE IT
- HATE IT

How would you feel if most people didn't know how to pronounce the name?

Let's face it, if it weren't for *Harry Potter*, most people wouldn't know how to pronounce Hermione. Having to spell and pronounce your name all the time can be an icebreaker or an embarrassing hassle (or both). Will your child mind? Give it some careful thought when choosing a name, particularly if you're thinking outside the box.

If you knew that most people wouldn't be able to pronounce a name, would you still use it?

25% YES; IT WILL MAKE MY CHILD STAND OUT

75% NO; IT WILL MAKE MY CHILD STAND OUT

Do you have a name that's difficult to pronounce? If so, how do you feel about correcting people?

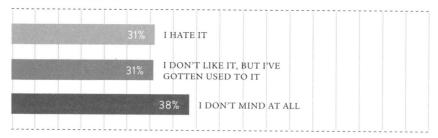

31% I HATE IT

31% I DON'T LIKE IT, BUT I'VE GOTTEN USED TO IT

38% I DON'T MIND AT ALL

Does a name's popularity matter to you?

Some people love names because they're popular; others hate them for the same reason. Parents can be frustrated when they choose a name they think is unique only to discover five years later that there are three other Aidans in the same kindergarten class.

Here are tips for parents on both sides:

▶ **If you like popular names**

Try to avoid choosing a name at the tail end of its popularity. Popular names from two years ago can actually already be unfashionable. Name popularity has a predictable cycle. When a name becomes too common or has been popular for a long time, it doesn't sound as stylish to our ears as it once did and usually decreases in popularity—and can even become uncool. Think about once-popular names like Larry and Janice. Eventually these names will sound cool again, but it takes a couple generations for the cycle to repeat itself.

One way to be ahead of the curve is to look for names that are similar in style to current trendy names, but aren't popular themselves yet. For example, a hot trend today is occupational names—Mason, Cooper, and Carter are all popular, and all originally referred to professions. Some occupational names that haven't reached "popular" status yet are Walker, Sawyer, and Tucker—choose one of those today and you might be ahead of the pack.

A current trend for girls is names that start with the letter A. A isn't just for apple, it's for six of the top 20 girls' names: Ava, Abigail, Addison, Alexis, Alyssa, and Ashley. To get ahead of this trend, look for A names that haven't become too popular yet, like Adelaide, Arabella, Adalyn, Aurora, and Alice.

Here's a list of names that currently aren't especially common but, because there's a celebrity, celebrity child, or popular character who has the name, or because it's due for a bounce back in use, could be headed for trendiness in the future. Choosing one of these names today could put you ahead of the curve:

GIRLS' NAMES	**BOYS' NAMES**
Brielle	August
Isla (actor Isla Fisher)	Colt (Colt McCoy, football
Journey	player)
Juliet	Elliot/Elliott
Malia/Maliyah (daughter of U.S.	Emmett (from *Twilight*)
president Barack Obama)	Graham
Milla (Milla Jovavich)	Jasper (also from *Twilight*)
Nora/Norah (Nora Ephron)	Judah
Paisley	Leon
Penelope (Penélope Cruz)	Paxton
Presley	

► **If you don't like popular names**

You have some homework to do. Consider the sources of the unique names you're attracted to. For example, beware of fresh-sounding names that come from pop culture, like Miley or Addison. These "new" names tend to appeal to a lot of people and skyrocket in popularity. When you have your baby you may have never met a Miley before, but by the time your child goes to kindergarten, you're likely to have met or heard about a few others.

Examples of celebrity-inspired and pop-culture-driven names:

Paris (Paris Hilton)

Miley (Miley Cyrus)

Addison (character on *Grey's Anatomy* and *Private Practice*)

Madison (character in *Splash*)

Brooklyn (Brooklyn Beckham, son of Victoria and David Beckham)

What's the next generation of celebrity-inspired names? Watch out for these names to gain popularity in the future:

GIRLS' NAMES	**BOYS' NAMES**
Audrina	Cash
Harper	Cruz
Kimora	Jude
Rihanna	Kellen
Valentina	Kingston

Does a name's popularity make you:

6% — MORE LIKELY TO CHOOSE IT

94% — LESS LIKELY TO CHOOSE IT

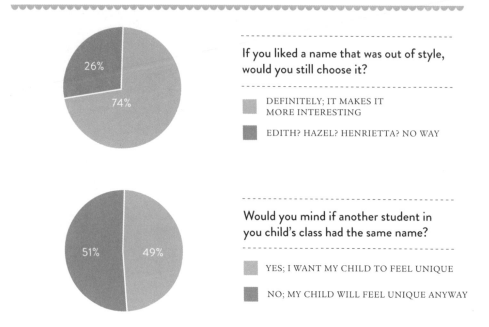

If you liked a name that was out of style, would you still choose it?

26%
74%

DEFINITELY; IT MAKES IT MORE INTERESTING

EDITH? HAZEL? HENRIETTA? NO WAY

Would you mind if another student in you child's class had the same name?

51%
49%

YES; I WANT MY CHILD TO FEEL UNIQUE

NO; MY CHILD WILL FEEL UNIQUE ANYWAY

What do you think about unisex names?

Unisex names have no preconceived gender attached to them. That makes them attractive to some parents, but it can also pose a challenge. When you have to write a business letter to a Taylor whom you've never met, do you address it to Mr. or Ms.?

In America today, name-sharing isn't equal. A girl named Ryan might be seen as unique and interesting, but a boy named Sue (as the song says) doesn't fare as well. For this reason, unisex name trends typically start with girls being given a traditionally male name. That name eventually becomes a girl's name exclusively as parents stop using the name for boys.

How would you feel if there was a boy in your daughter's class with the same name?

How would you feel if there was a girl in your son's class with the same name?

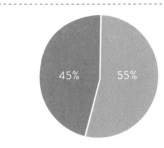

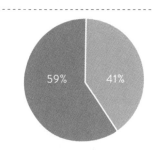

| IT WOULD BOTHER ME— AND MAYBE HER OR HIM | IT WOULD BE OKAY, AND IF SHE OR HE WAS TEASED, I'D HELP HER OR HIM UNDERSTAND |

How do you feel about unisex names?

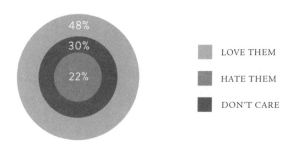

LOVE THEM

HATE THEM

DON'T CARE

Some examples of once male names that are now usually girls' names:

Ashley, Carol, Evelyn, Hillary, Kelly, Leslie, Shannon, Shirley

Current unisex names that may become exclusively girls' names in the future:

Avery, Bailey, Brooklyn, Cameron, Dakota, Hayden, Jaden, Jordan, Logan, Morgan, Paris, Peyton, Reese, Riley, Skylar, Taylor

How do you feel about nicknames?

If you name your son Edward, someone's bound to call him Eddie. Would that be okay with you? If you don't like certain nicknames, there are things you can do:

* Choose a name with no built-in nicknames, like Ethan

* Choose a nickname you like and start using it early on

* Resign yourself to the fact that your son will always be Edward to you but may be Eddie to someone else

Some people like a nickname so much that they bypass the traditional name and use the nickname as the full name—Beth, Jim, and Johnny. This is one way to ensure your child gets the nickname you love. If you do this, know that most people will assume that Johnny is a nickname and your son will likely be called John now and again.

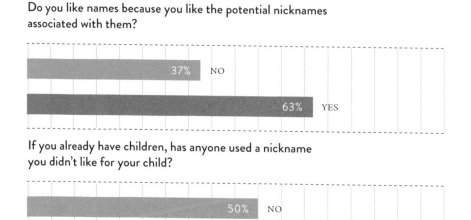

Do you like names because you like the potential nicknames associated with them?

37% NO

63% YES

If you already have children, has anyone used a nickname you didn't like for your child?

50% NO

50% YES

Hi, My Name Is

What will you do if someone starts using a nickname you don't like? To ward off unwanted nicknames, a little diplomacy may be in order. The very first time you hear a nickname you don't like, respond quickly so it never has a chance to catch on. The best approach is usually friendly but direct. Say something like, "Oh! You love nicknames, too. Please don't call her Sammy, we've already decided her nickname will be Sam."

If it persists, you may need to address the behavior again. Beware though, the harder you push, the more incentive it may give a troublemaker to frustrate you. Sometimes ignoring annoying behavior is the best way to stop it.

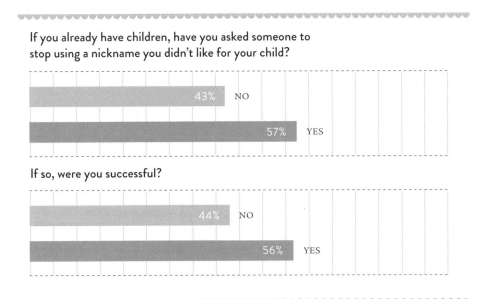

If you already have children, have you asked someone to stop using a nickname you didn't like for your child?

43% NO
57% YES

If so, were you successful?

44% NO
56% YES

How important is it that both parents love the name?

Mom loves the name Shelby for a boy, but Dad hates it. Dad has always liked the name Brian, but it reminds Mom of the class bully in elementary school. Most healthy relationships involve both parties agreeing to disagree over certain topics, but when it comes to naming a baby, that's not really an option.

Needless to say, agreeing on baby names can be very challenging. Couples deal with the situation in different ways: maybe Mom names the girls and Dad the boys (or vice versa) or maybe you flip a coin and leave it up to chance.

If you and your partner have a hard time agreeing on names, how will you handle it? It might be a good idea to set up some ground rules early on to prevent potential conflicts down the road.

Remember the goal: to choose the best name for your baby. The bottom line is that you're not the most important person in this decision—your child is—and keeping that in mind should inspire a team attitude.

Who should have the final say on baby's name?

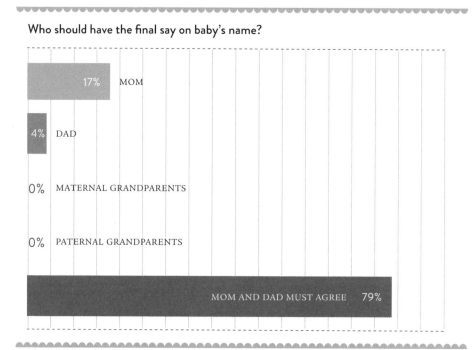

17%	MOM
4%	DAD
0%	MATERNAL GRANDPARENTS
0%	PATERNAL GRANDPARENTS
MOM AND DAD MUST AGREE	79%

Hi, My Name Is

Have you and your partner been fighting over baby names?

45% 55%

NO; IT'S BEEN A NON-ISSUE

YES; IT'S BEEN A PROBLEM

Do you like the idea of inventing a name for your baby?

In a time when more and more parents are using unique and unusual names, some parents go the extra mile and create an original name to make sure they stand out. If you like this idea, here are ways to invent names:

* Combine established names

    Example: Olympic cross-country skier Kikkan Randall—Kikkan is a combination of the names Kiki and Megan. Kikkan's dad liked the name Kiki because he admired successful Alpine skier Kiki Cutter. Kikkan's mom liked the name Megan, but worried that it was too popular. They decided to combine the names and came up with Kikkan.

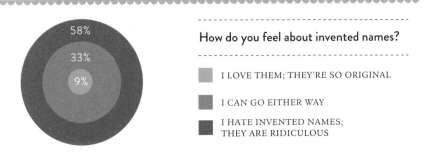

How do you feel about invented names?

58%

33%

9%

I LOVE THEM; THEY'RE SO ORIGINAL

I CAN GO EITHER WAY

I HATE INVENTED NAMES;
THEY ARE RIDICULOUS

* Adding letters or syllables to established names
  Examples of this from the top 1,000: Jamarcus, Keshawn, Deshawn, Deangelo

* Using words not traditionally used as names
  Examples: singer Jewel, and Apple Martin, the daughter of Gwyneth Paltrow and Chris Martin. Here are some of the word names in the top 1,000—Essence, Tiara, Princess, Lyric, Precious, King, and Blaze.

There's usually a good story behind invented names, but they're not everyone's cup of tea.

How do you feel about "virtue" names like Angel, Chastity, or Faith?

Hoping to raise an angel? What better way to ensure that than by naming your child Angel? Not so fast. Instead of giving a child a nice goal to reach for, a virtue name can create burdensome or even unattainable expectations (we know a child named Messiah!).

More than one teacher has joked that students named Angel rarely act like angels. If it weren't for Angel's name, though, the comparison wouldn't be made. It's possible that teachers (and people in general) have higher expectations for children with virtue names or pay greater attention when these children's behavior departs from the name's meaning.

So, while a child named Hope may always see the silver lining in a situation, and a girl named Prudence could prove to be wise, how the child responds to the virtue name will obviously vary case by case, and the parent's attitude likely makes a considerable difference.

Virtue names such as
Charity, Faith, and so on:

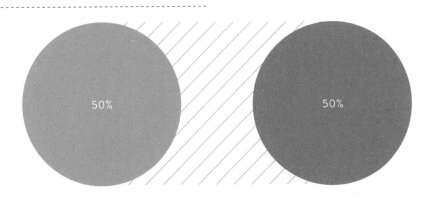

50%　　　　50%

■ GIVE CHILDREN AN ADMIRABLE GOAL TO STRIVE TOWARD

■ CREATE TOO MUCH PRESSURE FOR THE CHILD

What name features are important to you?

Now that you've gone over the factors in a name, it's time to rank what's most important to you.

Here are the factors for you to consider:

* Family members like the name

* Friends like the name

* The name reflects cultural background

* The name has a good meaning

* The name has important family history

* The way the name is spelled

* The way the name works with sibling names

* How unique the name is

* How popular the name is

* The name's nickname potential

* Both parents love the name

* The way the name sounds with the last name

* The monogram created by the first, middle, and last initials

* The letter the name starts with

* Availability of the domain name

* Other

You and your partner might want to rank these features from most to least important and add any other considerations that you'd like. Once you do that, you'll have guidelines you can use to evaluate names.

What's the most important feature in a name?

5%	IT REFLECTS THE FAMILY'S CULTURAL BACKGROUND
5%	IT HAS A GOOD MEANING
5%	IT HAS IMPORTANT FAMILY HISTORY
5%	HOW UNIQUE IT IS
5%	ITS NICKNAME POTENTIAL
38%	BOTH PARENTS LOVE IT
16%	THE WAY IT SOUNDS WITH THE LAST NAME
5%	THE MONOGRAM
12%	THE LETTER IT STARTS WITH
4%	AVAILABLE DOMAIN NAME

practical matters to contemplate

This section focuses on the practical details of baby-naming—unfortunate rhymes and monograms, notorious namesakes, and the like. You may have to channel your most creative and cruel third-grade sense of humor here, but doing that now might save your child embarrassment later on. You can't prevent all teasing just by choosing the right name, but you don't want to make it easy for school-yard bullies either. And with a little forethought, you won't.

The questions in this section will guide you through common issues and help you avoid most pitfalls.

Does the name have another meaning when spoken out loud?

We've all heard stories about people named Ima Hogg and Robin Banks; names like these are punch lines to jokes, but typically aren't good baby names. Sift through your name choices and say them out loud. Be sure and try all combinations—first and last; middle and last; first, middle, and last; nickname and last name; you get the idea.

Bad Baby Names: The Worst True Names Parents Saddled Their Kids With, and You Can Too! by Michael Sherrod and Matthew Rayback chronicles some of the "worst" baby names of all time. Here are a few:

* Travel Loggin

* Church Bell

* Baker Bread

* Park Walker

* June Moon

* Valentine Day

Suffice it to say, these are *not* recommended.

Does the monogram spell something?

What could be embarrassing about your initials? Well, if your name is Penelope Inez Garcia you may have a lovely name, but your initials spell PIG. Aidan Sebastian Smith is an ASS. These aren't the most flattering of monograms and would almost certainly be fodder for playground bullies.

Write out the initials to see if they spell anything. Again, try all combinations of names. Beatrice Tessa Sanders might be BTS, but when you cut out the middle name, you have BS.

If you like the idea of a clever monogram, consider spelling something positive with the name's initials, like Lily Ursula Vance: LUV.

Have you checked to see whether the initials of your potential names spelled anything?

50% NO

50% YES

Does the name rhyme with something embarrassing?

Remember that episode of *Seinfeld* where Jerry can't remember his current fling's name, but knows it rhymes with a female body part? Jerry and friends go through a list of options—Celeste, Aretha, Bovary, Mulva, Loliola. Her name? Dolores. It's hilarious on a sitcom, but your child might not think it's quite as fun if it's his or her name being used as a punch line.

You'll have to be creative, but take some time to figure out whether your preferred names rhyme with anything embarrassing. Your child will thank you!

Have you checked to see whether your name picks rhyme with anything embarrassing?

NO; I'M NOT WORRIED

YES; KIDS ARE CRUEL

Do you plan to give your child a middle name?

Giving children middle names is fairly standard today—and some parents even give more than one—but of course they're not necessary.

Having multiple middle names can create trouble with passports or other official IDs that have limited space for names. On the other hand, if you opt out of using a middle name, your child will likely have to spend some time explaining that every now and then.

NAME FACTOID

The *S* in President Harry S. Truman's name is not short for anything.

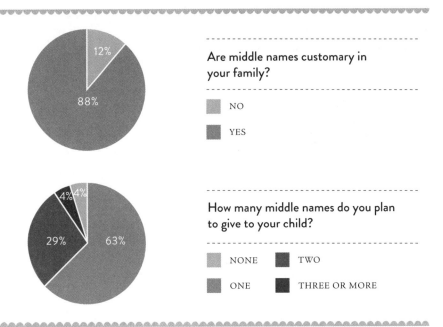

Are middle names customary in your family?

- NO
- YES

How many middle names do you plan to give to your child?

- NONE
- ONE
- TWO
- THREE OR MORE

Do you want to have the baby's name decided in advance or do you want to meet your baby first?

There are parents who have names chosen long before the birth (or even before they're pregnant!); others have two or three top candidates and then make the final decision after they meet the baby; still others go in cold and let the baby "tell" them what his or her name is.

Keep in mind that hospitals don't like parents to be discharged until a name has been added to the birth certificate. With most discharges happening within a couple days after birth, you won't have long to make a final decision.

If you already have a child, how certain were you at birth about what your baby would be named?

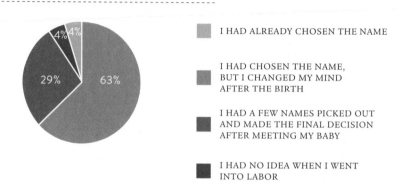

- I HAD ALREADY CHOSEN THE NAME
- I HAD CHOSEN THE NAME, BUT I CHANGED MY MIND AFTER THE BIRTH
- I HAD A FEW NAMES PICKED OUT AND MADE THE FINAL DECISION AFTER MEETING MY BABY
- I HAD NO IDEA WHEN I WENT INTO LABOR

Is the domain name available?

Modern parents have technology concerns to consider that previous generations never faced. In the age of personal Web sites, Facebook, and Twitter, having a unique name and owning the related digital real estate can give your child a technological head start.

Many parents register their child's name as a domain name. Of course, technology is constantly evolving and no one knows what the Internet will be ten or twenty years from now. Even so, some parents go so far as making their final name decisions based on domain name availability.

There's also something to be said for online anonymity. John Smith will be harder to find online than Apollo Smith, which isn't necessarily a bad thing.

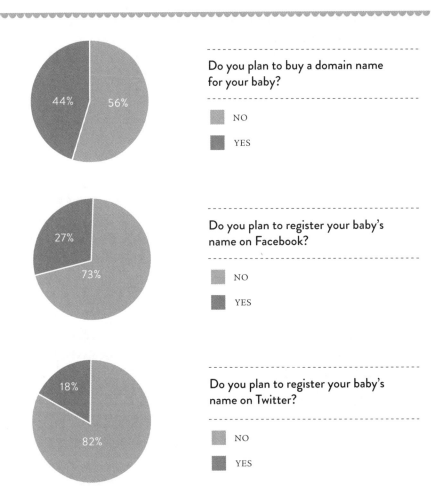

Do you plan to buy a domain name for your baby?

☐ NO
■ YES

44% 56%

Do you plan to register your baby's name on Facebook?

☐ NO
■ YES

27% 73%

Do you plan to register your baby's name on Twitter?

☐ NO
■ YES

18% 82%

How would you feel if someone famous (or infamous) had the same name as your child?

For better or worse, the Internet has made the world a much smaller place, but at least it's easy to do an Internet search to see if anyone famous or infamous has already put a stamp on the names you're considering.

If you're not familiar with current pop culture, you might never have heard of Emma Roberts or Jaden Smith, but a quick Internet search would tell you that these names are already strongly associated with celebrities.

It's safe to say that most parents would be wary of naming children the same name as a notorious criminal. The name Theodore is great, but not if your last name is Bundy. Also be careful of soundalike names. Having the name Ted Lundy would be nearly as problematic as having the name Ted Bundy.

To be safe, head to the Internet and do a search on the names you're considering and see what pops up.

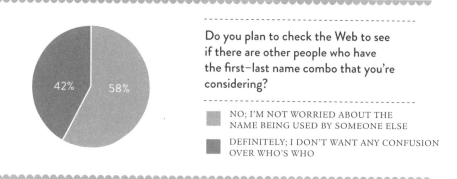

Do you plan to check the Web to see if there are other people who have the first–last name combo that you're considering?

▢ NO; I'M NOT WORRIED ABOUT THE NAME BEING USED BY SOMEONE ELSE

■ DEFINITELY; I DON'T WANT ANY CONFUSION OVER WHO'S WHO

How will the name look on applications and résumés?

Like it or not, people are judged by their names. When people see the name Rainbow, do they think investment banker? Maybe they should, but the reality is that most people won't. If the possibility of name prejudice concerns you, think fifteen or twenty years down the road to college applications and résumés and consider what impression your baby's name will give.

The good news is that more and more people are being given less traditional names, and as that happens, name stereotyping will likely decrease. However, if you find yourself concerned about unfair prejudice but also desperately love a name like Rainbow, you can pair it with a more traditional name so that your child will have options. Your daughter could then decide for herself what name she wants to go by professionally. Maybe she'll be the Rainbow that shines on Wall Street.

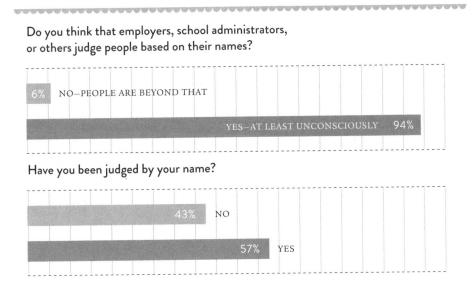

Do you think that employers, school administrators, or others judge people based on their names?

6% NO—PEOPLE ARE BEYOND THAT

YES—AT LEAST UNCONSCIOUSLY 94%

Have you been judged by your name?

43% NO

57% YES

Do you judge people by their names?

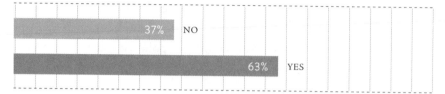

37% NO

63% YES

dealing with family and friends

It takes only two people to make a baby, so who knew that coming up with a name would be a family affair? This section discusses some common problems parents face from family and friends during the baby-naming process and gives you tips on how to diffuse the sticky situations you might come across.

Do you plan to share your name ideas with family
and friends before the birth?

This is a very important decision! If you tell people the names you're considering, you run the risk of having someone tell you they don't like your picks and even lobbying for you to change your mind. If you're willing to make decisions with a group, then this won't be a problem and it's safe to share your ideas.

On the other hand, if you don't want to make your choice based on whether family and friends like the name or not, then hearing others' opinions before the baby's born might be annoying. If you fall into this category, keep your ideas to yourself until after the baby's born.

Hi, My Name Is

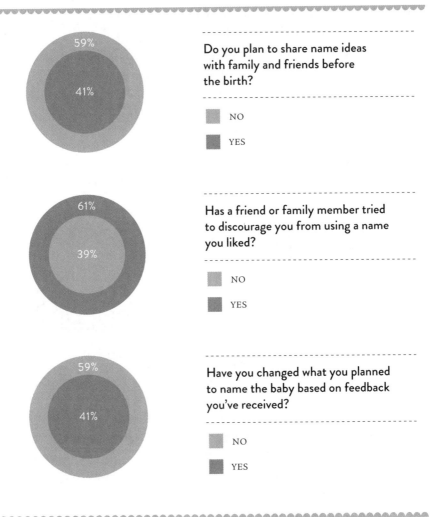

59%

41%

Do you plan to share name ideas
with family and friends before
the birth?

◼ NO

◼ YES

61%

39%

Has a friend or family member tried
to discourage you from using a name
you liked?

◼ NO

◼ YES

59%

41%

Have you changed what you planned
to name the baby based on feedback
you've received?

◼ NO

◼ YES

What would you say if a relative or friend asked you to name your child after him or her?

A lot of people like the idea of passing their name on to another generation, and some won't be shy about asking you to be the parent that bestows them the honor. Be ready with a polite response so you're not caught off guard—maybe something like, "We're still considering lots of names and will be sure to add it to our list."

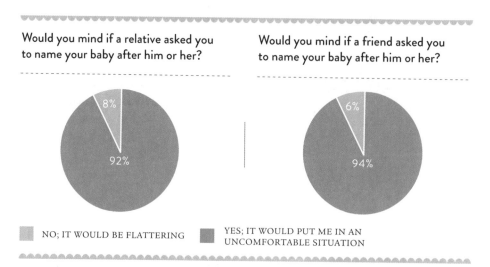

Would you mind if a relative asked you to name your baby after him or her?

8%

92%

Would you mind if a friend asked you to name your baby after him or her?

6%

94%

NO; IT WOULD BE FLATTERING

YES; IT WOULD PUT ME IN AN UNCOMFORTABLE SITUATION

Should older siblings have a say in baby's name?

A new baby can elicit many feelings from older siblings: excitement, anxiety, jealousy, joy, and everything in between. To help with the transition, get them involved in preparations for the new baby's arrival. One way to do this is by getting input on the baby's name (input—not final decision, unless you want a name like Unicorn!). You could share a list of top names and then let everyone in the family vote, or you could go through this book together and let everyone choose

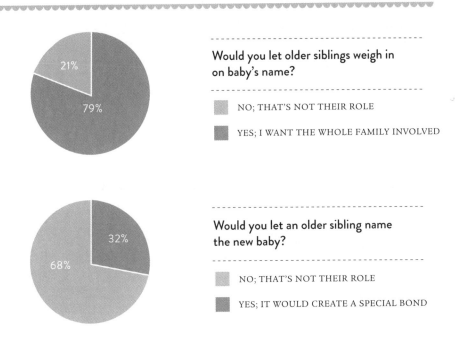

Would you let older siblings weigh in on baby's name?

21%

79%

NO; THAT'S NOT THEIR ROLE

YES; I WANT THE WHOLE FAMILY INVOLVED

Would you let an older sibling name the new baby?

32%

68%

NO; THAT'S NOT THEIR ROLE

YES; IT WOULD CREATE A SPECIAL BOND

two or three favorites. Then the parents can make the final decision based on the compiled list. If you don't want to do that for the first name, it might work for the middle name, where you can be more flexible.

Jennifer Love Hewitt's older brother reportedly played a big role in naming her. As the story goes, he had a crush on a girl named Jennifer and suggested the name for his little sister. If you don't want to go as far as sharing naming duties, you could get a doll and encourage your child to name it using this book—just like you're doing for the new baby.

Is it okay to name a baby after a pet?

91% NO; IT'S WEIRD

9% YES; IT'S PASSING ON THE NAME OF A LOVED ONE

Would you consider using a name you'd previously given to a pet?

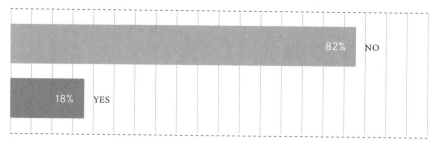

82% NO

18% YES

How would you feel if you found out you were named after a pet?

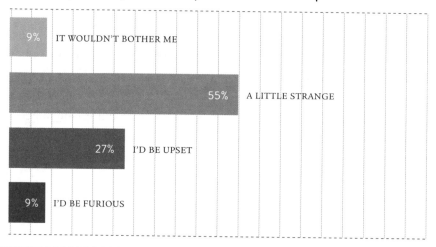

9% IT WOULDN'T BOTHER ME

55% A LITTLE STRANGE

27% I'D BE UPSET

9% I'D BE FURIOUS

How do you feel about using a name you previously gave a pet?

Pets are members of the family, but should you name children after them? On the one hand, should a great name be off-limits just because when you were twelve you named your parakeet Chloe? On the other hand, will your son be happy to learn that he was named after a Chihuahua that's been dead for six years?

There is no right answer here, but give it some careful consideration before resurrecting a name previously used for a pet. And don't count on keeping secret the history of your baby's name from your child. You just may run into your best friend from junior high who spills the beans.

Is it okay to use a name that a family member or friend wants for their own future child?

Now we're getting into really dangerous territory—name theft. There's no law on the subject, so we need to muddle through using our best judgment. The right answer may depend on how close you are to the relative or friend—and how close you want to be in the future.

Here are both sides of the argument:

Use the name

You're the one having the baby now and you should be able to use any name you like. There's no guarantee that your family member or friend would even use the name in the future because they could change their mind at any time. It's a matter of timing; if they had a baby before you, they'd have the right to choose any name they wanted—even a favorite of yours.

Don't use the name

There are many, many wonderful names to choose from, but only a limited number of wonderful family members and friends in a lifetime.

Why risk making them mad? Most importantly, the person at the center of the controversy will be an innocent bystander: your child.

Think carefully before using another's favorite name and be prepared to deal with possible negative consequences if you do.

Is it okay to use a name you know a family member or friend wants for their child?

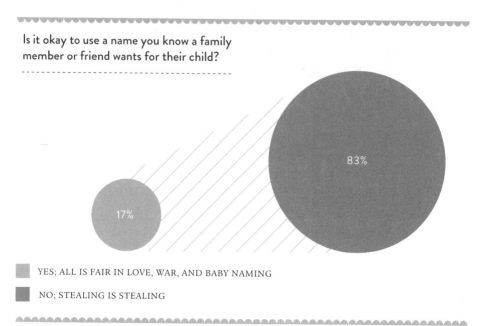

83%

17%

■ YES; ALL IS FAIR IN LOVE, WAR, AND BABY NAMING

■ NO; STEALING IS STEALING

Is it okay to use a name that a family member or friend has already used? Using a name that a family member or friend has already used can be tricky. Your decision will likely depend on how close your relationship is and will continue to be. For example, do you spend holidays together? How close do you live to one another? How often do you get together and how close are the children in age? Two Williams fifteen years apart is different from two Williams six months apart in the same town.

Other issues to consider are:

* How the first parent who used the name will feel—honored or betrayed?

* How the children involved will feel

If you love a name that's already been taken and you've decided not to use it for yourself, one solution is to pick a related or similar name. Instead of using George for your son, you can use Georgia for your daughter. Instead of a second Charlotte, consider Chara. There are plenty of ways to be creative with naming. With some careful thought, you're sure to find something you love.

Is it okay to choose a name that another family member or friend has already used for a baby?

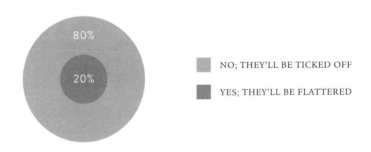

80%

20%

NO; THEY'LL BE TICKED OFF

YES; THEY'LL BE FLATTERED

about this book

Now that you have a clearer sense of how to go about choosing a name, you could probably use a few suggestions, right?

Don't worry; we won't leave you hanging. Instead, turn the page to find a comprehensive list of 500 of the most beloved and interesting boys' and girls' names, some up-and-coming in popularity, others with a long, historical track record. We also tell you each name's original meaning and origin, whether it has any related names or variant spellings, and what famous people in history have had the name. You're sure to find lots of options you'll love from that excellent group.

But in case you need a little more help, we've also included dozens of Top 10 lists to draw names from, including everything from advice columnists to weathermen. Want to name your child after an astronaut? No problem. How about a best-selling author? We've got you covered.

So enjoy the rest of *Hi, My Name Is*. And whether you ultimately decide to go with Aaliyah, Zach, or anything in between, have fun choosing.

BOYS' NAMES

The popularity analysis is based on the Social Security
data on first names from card applications for births.
The data is first recorded for the year 1880.

Aa

Aaron

Meaning: Exalted; high mountain

Origin: Egyptian or Hebrew

Related names and spelling variations: *Aron, Eron, Eryn, Erin, Aeryn*

Despite its biblical roots—and a slew of famous Aarons from Moses's brother to a Neville brother—the origins of the name Aaron are a bit of a mystery. Some say the name has Egyptian roots and some say it has Hebrew roots. What we know for sure is that in the Bible, God appointed Aaron to be Moses's spokesman (who knew they had PR in the old days?). And clearly the PR for the name itself has stayed strong, as Aaron has ranked in the top 50 for all but a couple years since 1971.

THIS NAME IN HISTORY

Aaron Burr (politician who dueled with Alexander Hamilton)

Aaron Carter (singer)

Aaron Copland (composer)

Aaron Eckhart (actor)

Aaron Neville (singer)

Aaron Sorkin (producer)

Aaron Spelling (film and TV producer)

Elvis Aaron Presley (singer)

Hank Aaron (baseball player)

Abraham

Meaning: Father of a multitude of nations

Origin: Hebrew

Related names and spelling variations: *Abram, Abraham, Ibrahim, Abe, Bram, Avraham*

Not that we want to dissuade you from picking it, but isn't Abraham a tough name for a boy to live up to? From Honest Abe, one of the most iconic presidents in U.S. history, to one of the heroes of the Bible, to almost two dozen saints, Abrahams have made their mark on history. The Book of Genesis tells us Abraham means "father of a multitude of nations," but clearly those were the days before child support. Because of (or perhaps despite) its highfalutin history, Abraham has been a popular name for centuries, though it's never reached the top 100, so your son is still likely to be the only Father of a Multitude of Nations in his kindergarten class.

THIS NAME IN HISTORY

Abraham (biblical figure)

Abe Burrows (humorist and author)

Abraham Lincoln (U.S. president)

Abraham Maslow (psychologist)

Bram Stoker (author)

Abe Vigoda (actor)

F. Murray Abraham (actor)

Adam

Meaning: Mankind; earth

Origin: Babylonian, Phoenician, Hebrew

Related names and spelling variations:
Adamo, Addam, Addem, Adom, Adim

In the Bible, of course, Adam was the earth's first man, created when God blew the breath of life into a lump of clay. The name itself is something of an etymological marvel, mixing the roots of two languages to represent God's action, blending the Hebrew word *adama* (earth) with the Assyrian *adamu* (to build).

Not surprisingly, the name has been popular since the seventh century (when Christianity also gained popularity), especially for firstborns, as it makes a little less sense for the second to come along. Adam peaked in 1983 and 1984 at #18, and has been sliding slowly downward since.

THIS NAME IN HISTORY

Adam (biblical figure)

Adam Ant (musician)

Adam Arkin (actor)

Adam Clayton (musician)

Adam Curry (MTV VJ)

Adam Dunn (baseball player)

Adam Horovitz (musician)

TOP TEN: MOVIE ACTION HEROES

1. James Bond
2. Indiana Jones
3. Luke Skywalker
4. Batman (*Dark Knight*)
5. Rambo
6. Jason Bourne
7. Terminator (*Judgement Day*)
8. William Wallace (*Braveheart*)
9. John McClane (*Die Hard*)
10. Neo (*Matrix*)

Adam Lambert (*American Idol* finalist)

Adam Sandler (actor)

Adam Smith (philosopher and economist)

Adam West (actor)

Adrian

Meaning: From the Adriatic Sea; black

Origin: Latin

Related names and spelling variations: *Adrien, Adriano, Adrián*

Yo, Adrian! (Yes, if the film *Rocky* retains popularity, your son will be hearing a lot of that.) But of course the name was famous long before Stallone made it so. Adrian was originally used to denote someone from the Adriatic Sea region, which borders the eastern coast of Italy and is part of the Mediterranean. One famous Adrian was the Roman emperor Publius Aelius Hadrinaus, who built Hadrian's Wall across northern England during his rule from 117 to 138 B.C.E. Despite its ancient roots, Adrian has been becoming more popular now than ever before. Adrian has forms in a dozen languages, including Italian (Adriano) and Spanish (Adrián). And even though Adrian is spelled differently than the girl's version of the name, Adrienne, the pronunciation is identical.

THIS NAME IN HISTORY

Adrian Brody (actor)

Adrian Grenier (actor)

Adrian Paul (actor)

Adrian Peterson (football player)

Adrian Smith (musician)

Aiden, Aidan

Meaning: Fiery one

Origin: Irish

Related names and spelling variations: *Aden, Aaden, Ayden, Aidan, Adan, Aydan, Aydin, Aidyn, Aedan*

Consider yourself warned—Aiden comes from the Irish name Aidan, meaning "fiery one." Historically, however, it's belonged to some very gentle people, including several Irish monks and saints in the seventh century—especially a bishop who was noted for his kindness and generosity and St. Aidan, who brought Christianity to the people of northeast England. As part of the recent Irish name explosion, Aiden went from near obscurity in 1990 to one of the most popular names in the U.S. just a decade later. The most popular spelling is Aiden, but all of these different spellings also appear on the charts: Aidan, Ayden, Aden, Aaden, Adan, Aydan, Aydin, Aidyn, and Aedan.

THIS NAME IN HISTORY

Ayden Callaghan (actor)

Aidan Quinn (actor)

Aidan Shaw (character on *Sex and the City*)

Alan

Meaning: Handsome; harmonious; rock

Origin: Celtic

Related names and spelling variations: *Allan, Allen, Alann, Alen, Alin, Allin*

Alan is a Celtic name from antiquity and has a variety of meanings, including "handsome," "harmonious," and "rock"—a nice range of associations to choose from. In recent U.S. history, Alan was at its prime between the late 1930s and early 1970s, when it ranked in the top 100. The Allen spelling was more popular in the 1800s, but Alan eventually took over and is still more popular today.

THIS NAME IN HISTORY

Alan Alda (actor)

Alan Arkin (actor)

Alan Greenspan (former Federal Reserve chairman)

Allen Iverson (basketball player)

Alan Jackson (singer)

Alan Moore (graphic novel writer)

Alan Rickman (actor)

Alan Shepard (astronaut)

Albert

Meaning: Noble, bright

Origin: German

Related names and spelling variations: *Bert, Alberto, Al*

Albert is of Germanic origin and means "noble and bright"—clearly a nice aspiration to pass on to a child (better do that homework!). Many notable figures have possessed the name, including Albert Einstein and Prince Albert (though associations with the latter are no longer so positive). Albert would be a good choice

TOP TEN: MALE CELEBS WHO DIED TOO SOON

❶ Heath (Ledger)

❷ Michael (Jackson)

❸ Kurt (Cobain)

❹ John (Belushi; Lennon; F. Kennedy Jr.)

❺ James/Jim/Jimi (Dean; Morrison; Hendrix)

❻ Buddy (Holly)

❼ Andy (Kaufman)

❽ River (Phoenix)

❾ Bruce (Lee)

❿ Chris/Christopher (Farley; Wallace)

for you if you like old-fashioned sounding names that have fallen out of recent popularity. Albert reached its peak in the late 1880s and early 1900s, and has been on a steady decline since then, while the Spanish version, Alberto, has been becoming more popular.

THIS NAME IN HISTORY

Prince Albert (husband of Queen Victoria)

Albert Camus (philosopher)

Albert Einstein (physicist)

Al Gore (former U.S. vice president)

Alexander

Meaning: Mankind's defender

Origin: Greek

Related names and spelling variations: *Alex, Alejandro, Xander, Zander, Alec, Alexis, Alessandro, Alexzander*

Want to give your little boy a name to live up to? How about Alexander the Great? The name Alexander comes from the Latin form of the Greek name Alexandros, meaning "mankind's defender," and has been the moniker of a slew of heroes and leaders. In Greek mythology it was another name for the hero Paris and it's also been the name used by dozens of monarchs, rulers, and popes. Alexander has spent much of the time since the 1880s in the top 100. Even with that long history, Alexander is currently at its most popular. Also popular are Alex, Alejandro, Alexis, Xander, Zander, Alec, and Alessandro.

THIS NAME IN HISTORY

Alexander the Great (ancient Greek ruler)

Alec Baldwin (actor)

Alexander Graham Bell (inventor)

Sir Alec Guinness (actor)

Alexander Hamilton (American statesman)

Alejandro Gonzá (director)

Alejandro Ingelmo (shoe designer)

Alex P. Keaton (character on the TV show *Family Ties*)

Alexander McQueen (fashion designer)

Alex Rodriguez (baseball player)

Alejandro Toledo (former Peruvian president)

Alfred

Meaning: Elf counselor

Origin: English

Related names and spelling variations: *Al, Alfie, Fred, Freddie, Alfredo*

Ready for this? Alfred, the consummate old-fashioned-sounding name, has an unexpectedly whimsical definition: "elf counselor." Although the meaning is a bit odd, its longevity through the nineteenth and twentieth centuries proves the name's viability (or the surprisingly high number of elves who need therapy). As of late, it's been on a steady decline. These days, Alfredo, the Italian and Spanish version (famed also for the fettuccine dish), is actually more popular.

Hi, My Name Is

Alfred Hitchcock (director)

Freddie Mercury (musician)

Alfred Molina (actor)

Alfred Nobel (creator of the Nobel Prize)

Fred Segal (clothing retailer)

Alfred, Lord Tennyson (poet)

Andrew

Meaning: Manly

Origin: Greek

Related names and spelling variations: *Drew, Andres, Andre, Andy, Andreas*

Andrew is the English form of the Greek name Andreas, which means "manly," and it has also been linked to "warrior." (Keep that in mind when your little Andy whacks the mailman with his toy sword.) It's also one of the most popular boys' names of all time, dating back to the New Testament, and has the appealing nicknames of Andy and Drew. With its classic and timeless identity, Andrew has been in the U.S. top 100 since the 1880s.

THIS NAME IN HISTORY

Prince Andrew (Duke of York)

Andrew Carnegie (entrepreneur)

Andy García (actor)

Andrew Jackson (U.S. president)

Andrew Johnson (U.S. president)

Andy Roddick (tennis player)

Andy Warhol (artist)

Andrew Lloyd Webber (composer)

Andrew Weil (author and doctor)

Andrew Wyeth (painter)

Angel

Meaning: Messenger of God

Origin: Greek

Related names and spelling variations: *Angell, Anjel, Angelo*

Angel comes from the Greek root *angelos* and, no surprise, means "messenger of God." For girls, Angel has been in the top 100 in terms of popularity since the 1970s. For boys, it is rather common in Latino cultures, but has also slowly gotten more popular in the U.S. as a whole since 1997 (when it was #86). Of course, if you give your kid the name Angel, it creates a lot to live up to—and we've heard some teachers say that a lot of Angels exhibit less than angelic behavior—but plenty of parents are still doing it, keeping Angel on the list for both boys and girls.

THIS NAME IN HISTORY

Angel (character on the TV shows *Buffy the Vampire Slayer, Angel*, and *Dexter*)

Angel Clare (character in Thomas Hardy's novel *Tess of the D'Urbervilles*)

Angel Di Maria (soccer player)

Angel "Robinson" Garcia (boxer)

Ángel Pagán (baseball player)

"Angel" (code name for Air Force One)

TOP TEN: MALE REALITY TV STARS

1. Spike (*Top Chef*)
2. Ruben (*American Idol*)
3. Brody (*The Hills*)
4. Theo (*Road Rules*)
5. Jon/Jonny (*Jon & Kate Plus 8, Survivor*)
6. Rudy (*Survivor*)
7. Santino (*Project Runway*)
8. Spencer (*The Hills*)
9. Clay (*American Idol*)
10. Evan (*Joe Millionaire*)

Anthony

Meaning: Worthy of praise

Origin: Latin

Related names and spelling variations: *Antonio, Tony, Antoine, Antony, Anton*

Want your kid to grow up to be a saint? Naming him Anthony might increase the chances—or at least give him some historical precedents. Anthony is the English form of the Roman family name Antonius. The name's fame grew in the Christian world due to St. Anthony the Great, a third-century hermit who founded Christian monasticism, then continued in the Middle Ages thanks to St. Anthony of Padua. Anthony has been in the top 50 U.S. names almost continually for the past century, breaking into the top 10 for the first time in 2003.

THIS NAME IN HISTORY

Tony (character in the musical *West Side Story*)

Antonio Banderas (actor)

Tony Bennett (singer)

Tony Blair (former British prime minister)

Anthony Bourdain (celebrity chef)

Anton Chekhov (author)

Tony Danza (actor)

Tony Dungy (football coach)

Anthony Michael Hall (actor)

Sir Anthony Hopkins (actor)

Anthony Kiedis (singer)

Tony Romo (football player)

Marc Antony (ancient Roman statesman)

Marc Anthony (singer)

Arthur

Meaning: Bear; rock

Origin: Gaelic

Related names and spelling variations: *Art, Artie, Arturo*

Arthur has been a popular boy's name since the Middle Ages, helped at the time by the popularity of King Arthur and the Knights of the Round Table (if your kid triumphed at sports or other popular things, King Arthur would be a likely schoolyard nickname—not so good if it's being used sarcastically). Arthur has somewhat disputed etymology, but may be derived from words meaning "bear" or "rock." For a while, Arthur was certainly a rock of constancy, spending all but one year at the end of the 1800s ranked #14. It has slowly been on the decline since then, falling out of the top 100 in 1970; the Spanish version, Arturo, has stayed close to its English brother on the list.

THIS NAME IN HISTORY

Arthur (children's book series and TV show)

King Arthur (legendary figure)

Arthur Ashe (tennis player)

Arthur C. Clarke (author)

Sir Arthur Conan Doyle (author)

Arthur Miller (playwright)

Arturo Sandoval (musician)

Artie Shaw (musician)

Art Spiegelman (artist)

Asa

Meaning: Healer; born in the morning

Origin: Hebrew; Japanese

Related names and spelling variations: *None*

Asa, curiously, has roots in both the Hebrew and Japanese languages—it's not too often that those lexicons overlap. Asa may become a fresh alternative to other more popular short and cool boys' names like Max, Leo, and Sam. The highest Asa has ever ranked was #178 back in 1881, and it didn't even make the charts in the 1950s and 1960s. It crept back on the list in the mid-1970s, but has never been too widely used.

THIS NAME IN HISTORY

Asa Brainard (baseball player)

Asa Buchanan (character on the soap opera *One Life to Live*)

Asa Griggs Candler (founder of Coca-Cola)

Ashton

Meaning: Ash tree settlement

Origin: English

Related names and spelling variations: *Ashtun, Ashtin, Ash*

1. Hamlet (1,422)

2. Richard III (1,124)

3. Iago (1,097)

4. Henry V (1,025)

5. Othello (860)

6. Vincentio (820)

7. Coriolanus (809)

8. Timon of Athens (795)

9. Antony (766)

10. Richard II (753)

With only one famous Ashton in the world today, it's hard to think of the name without calling to mind the handsome actor: Demi Moore's husband, the creator of *Punk'd*. Mr. Kutcher's parents were clearly ahead of their time, as the name hadn't been anywhere near the top 100 until his celebrity put it there in 2003. Ashton was once a surname and it traces its origins to a place in England that was referred to as "ash tree settlement." In Old English, *aesc* means "ash tree" and *tun* means "enclosure, settlement, or town."

THIS NAME IN HISTORY

Ashton B. Carter (undersecretary of defense)

Ashton-Drake (collectible doll company)

Ashton Holmes (actor)

Ashton Kutcher (actor)

Alan Ashton (businessman)

John Ashton (musician)

August

Meaning: Great, magnificent; the month of August

Origin: Latin, German, English

Related names and spelling variations: *Augie, Auggie, Gus, Augustus, Augustine, Augusto, Augustino*

August comes from the Latin name Augustus, a title used by Roman emperors, so it's no surprise that it means "great" and "magnificent" (and, yes, there's also the month. You've probably heard of it). August was a top 100 name in the 1880s and then started to decline in popularity. The name started to make a comeback in the 1990s and has continued to rise. August would be a great pick if you're looking for familiar names that don't sound common. Gus is also a cool nickname—probably a little cooler than Auggie (one of the Busches of brewing company Anheuser-Busch).

THIS NAME IN HISTORY

St. Augustine (theologian and author)

Gus (character in Disney's *Cinderella*)

Auggie Busch (former president of brewing company Anheuser-Busch)

Augustus McCrae (character in Larry McMurtry's *Lonesome Dove* books)

Gus Van Sant (director)

August Wilson (playwright)

Gaius Julius Caesar Augustus (first ruler of the Roman Empire)

Austin

Meaning: Great one, magnificent

Origin: English, Latin

Related names and spelling variations: *Austyn, Ostin, Austen*

Austin these days is likely to call to mind either Austin Powers—and who doesn't want to name their son after a spoof of James Bond?—or the Texan cultural hotbed (another fun association—South by Southwest, anyone?), but originally Austin was a shortened form of the Latin name Augustinus, meaning "great one, magnificent." Austin can be traced back to the Middle Ages and was formed perhaps due to the notoriety of church father St. Augustine. In the U.S. it enjoyed moderate popularity throughout the 1900s, but had a major surge in the mid-1990s, even reaching the top 10 for four years. Austin's popularity was helped by a couple hot trends. It was originally a surname, and parents have been using more surnames as first names recently, plus location names have also been trendy, putting Austin up there with names like Paris, London, and Brooklyn.

THIS NAME IN HISTORY

Austin Pendleton (actor)

Austin Powers (movie character)

Brian Austin Green (actor)

Jane Austen (author)

Kurt Austin (character in Clive Cussler's books)

"Stone Cold" Steve Austin (wrestler)

Bb

Beau

Meaning: Handsome

Origin: French

Related names and spelling variations: *Bo, Beauregard*

Beau began as a nickname for a good-looking man. One of the most famous Beaus in history was Beau Brummell, a nineteenth-century dandy whose given name was George, but whose fashion sense earned him the handsome handle (he advised polishing your boots with champagne).

In the U.S., parents started picking Beau as a first name in the early 1900s, boosted by a couple literary references, including Beau Wilks in Margaret Mitchell's *Gone with the Wind*. Beau made the top 1,000 for the first time in 1967. It was at its most popular in 1980 at #203. It declined in the following years, but has been on a slight uptick recently. The Bo spelling has been on the charts from the late 1970s, perhaps inspired by Bo Duke of the 1970s TV show *Dukes of Hazzard*.

THIS NAME IN HISTORY

Bo Bice (*American Idol* finalist)

Beau Biden (politician, son of U.S. vice president Joe Biden)

Beau Bridges (actor)

Bo Derek (actor)

Bo Diddley (musician)

Bo Jackson (football and baseball player)

Bo Obama (first dog)

Benjamin

Meaning: Son of my right hand; son of the south

Origin: Hebrew

Related names and spelling variations: *Binyamin, Ben, Benji, Benjy, Benny*

The origins of the name Benjamin (according to the Old Testament) are kind of a downer, but here goes: Rachel, in the throes of death, gives birth to her twelfth son, and names him Benoni or "son of my sorrow." Dad (aka Jacob) realizes this is really pretty depressing and changes it to Benyamin, which means "son of the right hand," or "son of the south," in honor of the geographic location of his birth.

Creepily, Benjamin hung on to its morbid reputation and it was a name frequently given to sons whose mothers died in childbirth in the Middle Ages, but that was a loooooong time ago so don't worry about it. On a brighter note, in the U.S., not only has Benjamin been on the charts since the 1880s, but it's also been in the top 50 since 1974 and is only getting more popular. Celebrity couple Gisele Bündchen and Tom Brady used the name for their son in 2009.

THIS NAME IN HISTORY

Ben Affleck (actor)

Ben Bernanke (Federal Reserve chairman)

Benjamin Bratt (actor)

Ben Cohen (cofounder of Ben & Jerry's)

Benjamin Franklin (American politician, inventor, and diplomat)

Benny Goodman (musician)

Ben Harper (musician)

Benjamin Harrison (U.S. president)

Benjamin Netanyahu (prime minister of Israel)

Benjamin Rein Brady (son of Gisele Bündchen and Tom Brady)

Ben Stiller (actor)

Blake

Meaning: Black; white

Origin: English

Related names and spelling variations: *None*

Want to pass on a sense of balance and equilibrium—a yin and a yang, a little Michael Jackson ebony and Paul McCartney ivory—to your child? Then choose the English name Blake. It means both "black" and "white." Blake was on the charts infrequently between the

TOP TEN: *AMERICAN IDOL* FINALISTS AND WINNERS

1. Kelly (Clarkson)

2. Carrie (Underwood)

3. Chris (Daughtry)

4. Jordin (Sparks)

5. Adam (Lambert)

6. David (Cook)

7. David (Archuleta)

8. Jennifer (Hudson)

9. Clay (Aiken)

10. Kris (Allen)

TOP TEN: MALE INVENTORS

1. George (Washington Carver; Stephenson; Eastman)
2. Benjamin (Franklin; Chew Tilghman)
3. Alexander (Graham Bell; Fleming)
4. Thomas (Edison)
5. Louis (Daguerre; Braille; Lumière)
6. Henry (Ford)
7. Eli (Whitney)
8. Orville (Wright)
9. Auguste (Lumière)
10. Kia (Silverbrook)

late 1880s and mid-1940s, but eventually became a steady presence. It reached its peak in 2002 at #76.

THIS NAME IN HISTORY

Blake Carrington (character on the TV series Dynasty)

Blake Edwards (screenwriter, producer, and director)

Blake Griffin (basketball player)

Blake Lewis (singer)

Blake Shelton (singer)

William Blake (poet)

James Blake (tennis player)

Bradley

Meaning: Broad meadow

Origin: English

Related names and spelling variations: *Brad*

Like most names that end in -*ley*, Bradley's definition refers to a meadow, specifically a "broad meadow." Over the years, Bradley has been more popular in the U.S. than in other countries, hitting the charts most years since 1880. Perhaps that's a reflection of Americans' love of wide open spaces. Or maybe it's just a nice name. Bradley broke into the top 100 in 1960 and stayed there until the late 1990s. Bradley's got a friendly feel to it and is a good option if you like the name Brad, but prefer to use it as a nickname.

THIS NAME IN HISTORY
Bradley Cooper (actor)
Bradley Nowell (musician)
Brad Paisley (musician)
Brad Pitt (actor)
Bradley Whitford (actor)

Brady

Meaning: Descendant of Brádach; broad eyes; broad island

Origin: Irish, English

Related names and spelling variations: *Bradey*

Brady's definition is somewhat unclear, but it's generally thought to be a reference to someone who has broad-set eyes or lives on a broad island. (Don't let your teenage son tell anyone it means he "likes broads.") The name sounds very fresh, but it actually hit the U.S. charts for the first time way back in 1883. The name got a big boost in 1993, one year after a character was given the name on the soap *Days of Our Lives*. It's continued to gain in popularity since then. Brady is a good example of the recent surname name trend.

THIS NAME IN HISTORY
Brady Black (character on the soap opera *Days of Our Lives*)
Brady Corbet (actor)
Tom Brady (football player)

Wayne Brady (comedian)
The Brady Bunch (TV show)

Brandon

Meaning: Gorse hill

Origin: English

Related names and spelling variations: *Brand, Brandyn, Branden*

Brandon is one of the many names inspired by nature and location. An English name, Brandon means "gorse hill." (For all you nonbotanical types, gorse is a shrub.) Brandon entered the top 1,000 in 1950 at #936. It continued to grow in popularity and spent 1992 through 1998 in the top 10, possibly due to the character Brandon Walsh (Jason Priestley) on *Beverly Hills, 90210*, dude.

THIS NAME IN HISTORY
Brandon Jennings (basketball player)
Brandon Lee (martial artist, actor, and son of Bruce Lee)
Brandon Marshall (football player)
Brandon Sanderson (author)
Brandon Walsh (Jason Priestley on *Beverly Hills, 90210*)

Brayden

Meaning: Salmon; broad valley

Origin: Irish; English

Related names and spelling variations: *Braden, Brady, Bradyn, Braedon, Braeden, Braiden, Braydon*

TOP TEN: ASTRONAUTS

1. Neil (Armstrong)
2. Buzz (Aldrin)
3. John (Glenn)
4. James (Irwin)
5. Mae (Jemison, M.D.)
6. Kathryn (Sullivan)
7. Robert (Crippen; Lawrence)
8. David (Scott)
9. Susan (Still Kilrain; Helms)
10. Thomas (Patten Stafford; Reiter)

Brayden is another way to spell the name Braden, which comes from an Irish surname that means "salmon"—perhaps a good name for a Pisces baby? It's also linked to an English name meaning "broad valley." On the U.S. charts, Braden goes back to 1970, but Brayden is a relative newcomer, entering the top 1,000 for the first time in 1991. It's also a favorite name for parents who like creative spellings. You, too, can pick from Braden, Braydon, Braeden, Braiden, Bradyn, and Braedon. Currently, the Brayden spelling is most popular. Just don't get all crazy and start adding extra vowels like Braayden. Promise?

THIS NAME IN HISTORY

Braden Bacha (reality TV star)
Braden Looper (baseball player)
Braden Murray (hockey player)
Brayden Quinn (football player)
Brayden Schenn (hockey player)

Brendan

Meaning: Prince

Origin: Irish

Related names and spelling variations: *Brenden, Brendon*

Brendan would be an excellent pick if you're looking for an Irish name that is easy to spell and pronounce, unlike its quirkier cousins Bronwyn and Seamus. Brendan dates back at least to the sixth century, means "prince," and famous Brendans include Catholic saints, but Mommy and Daddy can still put little Brendan on time-out for flushing his Power Rangers down the potty. In the U.S., Brendan made the top 1,000 for the first time in 1941. It steadily gained popularity until 1999, reaching its peak at #96.

THIS NAME IN HISTORY
Brendan Benson (musician)
Brendan Fraser (actor)

Brennan

Meaning: Moisture; little drop

Origin: Irish

Related names and spelling variations: *Brennen*

Brennan is an Irish surname that means "moisture." Maybe a good choice if you like water or rain? Brennan may also appeal to you if you like the sound of other Irish names such as Brendan, Brayden, and Brandon, but want something more unique. Brennan entered the top 1,000 in 1966 at #1,000. It has slowly crept up the charts since then, but has never been overly popular.

THIS NAME IN HISTORY
Brennan Boesch (baseball player)
Brennan Mejia (actor)

Brent

Meaning: Person who lives near a hill

Origin: English

Related names and spelling variations: *None*

Brent is an English name that has a very specific geographical meaning—"person who lives near a hill." If by some chance you actually live near a hill, it would be a shame for you not to name your son Brent. After one appearance on the charts at the end of the 1800s, Brent dropped out of the top 1,000 until 1933. It slowly worked its way up and was at its peak in the 1970s, but it has been on the decline since then. Brent would be a good pick if you're looking for names with no built-in nicknames.

THIS NAME IN HISTORY
Brent Jones (football player)
Brent Musburger (sportscaster)
Brent Spiner (actor)
Brent Weinbach (comedian)

1. Jack (Kerouac)
2. Allen (Ginsberg)
3. William (S. Burroughs)
4. Neal (Cassady)
5. Peter (Orlovsky)
6. Edie (Parker)
7. Lawrence (Ferlinghetti)
8. Gregory (Corso)
9. Joan (Vollmer)
10. Herbert (Huncke)

Brett

Meaning: Breton

Origin: English

Related names and spelling variations: *Bret*

Brett means "Breton" and was originally used in the Middle Ages to refer to one of the Bretons who came to England after the Norman Conquest. It may be a nice choice today for Anglophiles. Cheerio! In the U.S., Brett landed in the top 1,000 for the first time in 1946. It made it to the top 100 in 1969 and was there most years until 1993. Brett is another good choice if you like names that do not have built-in nicknames.

THIS NAME IN HISTORY

Brett Dennen (musician)
Brett Favre (football player)
Bret Harte (author)
Bret Michaels (musician)
Brett Ratner (director)

Brian

Meaning: High, noble

Origin: Celtic

Related names and spelling variations: *Bryan, Brien, Bry, Bri*

Brian is a classic Celtic name with truly ancient roots. Famous namesakes date back as far as the year 1002 and include

Brian Boru, the king of Ireland, who some credit with driving Vikings out of Ireland (Tell that to your Brian when he defends his little sister). So who wins on the Brian vs. Bryan smackdown? Depends on how you look at it. Bryan has a longer history on the charts, but Brian has reached the highest rank. Brian was in the top 10 from the end of the 1960s through the 1970s, but Bryan is just slightly more popular these days. This may be due to the popularity of other "y" names like Brayden, Cayden, and Jayden. No matter how you spell it, this is a great choice if you're looking for Celtic names.

THIS NAME IN HISTORY

Bryan Adams (musician)

Brian Boitano (figure skater)

Bryan Cranston (actor)

Brian Eno (musician)

Brian Austin Green (actor)

Bryan Greenberg (actor)

Brian McKnight (musician)

Bryan Singer (producer and director)

Bryan Trottier (hockey player)

Brian Wilson (musician)

William Jennings Bryan (politician)

Brody

Meaning: Muddy place

Origin: Scottish

Related names and spelling variations: *Brodie*

Brody comes from the Scottish surname Brodie, which means "muddy place." Given how much most little boys like muddy places, this name could prove prophetic. In the U.S., Brody is a new favorite with parents. It wasn't seen on the charts before 1976 but has been steadily rising since it appeared. Brody's current popularity has probably been helped by reality TV star Brody Jenner from *The Hills*.

THIS NAME IN HISTORY

Brodie Croyle (football player)

Brody Hutzler (actor)

Brody Jenner (reality TV star)

Adam Brody (actor)

Adrien Brody (actor)

Bruce

Meaning: Woods

Origin: Scottish

Related names and spelling variations: *None*

Bruce means "woods" and is a great pick for parents looking for a classic Scottish name. The most legendary ancient namesake is Robert the Bruce, who became the king of Scotland in 1306 and is called "the Hero King." The name also has a long history here in the U.S., making the top 1,000 every year since the 1880s. It was at its most popular in the 1940s and 1950s and has been on the decline since then, despite several notable kick-ass Bruces (Lee, Springsteen).

THIS NAME IN HISTORY

Bruce Hornsby (musician)

Bruce Jenner (athlete and TV personality)

Bruce Lee (martial artist and actor)

Bruce Springsteen (musician)

Bruce Wayne (Batman's alter ego)

Bruce Willis (actor)

Robert the Bruce (king of Scotland)

Bryce

Meaning: Strength; freckled

Origin: Celtic; Welsh

Related names and spelling variations: *Bry, Bri, Brice*

Bryce has Celtic and Welsh origins and means, oddly enough, both "strength" and "freckled." It's also another name with dueling spellings. "Brice" was the first to appear on the U.S. charts in 1882. "Bryce" didn't show up until 1918, but it has been consistently more popular ever since. Bryce is a good pick if you like the "y" trend with names like Brayden, Cayden, and Jayden, but also want a name that sounds a little less made up.

THIS NAME IN HISTORY

Brice Beckham (actor)

Bryce Davison (figure skater)

Brice Marden (painter)

Bryce Salvador (hockey player)

Mr. Brice (character in Dr. Seuss's *The Pop-Up Mice of Mr. Brice*)

Cc

Caden

Meaning: Son of Cadán

Origin: Gaelic

Related names and spelling variations: *Caiden, Cayden, Kaden, Kadin, Kaiden, Kaeden, Kayden, Kadyn*

Caden may be a shortened form of the Gaelic surname McCadden, which means "son of Cadán." (Cadán, by the way, is linked to the name Cathan, which means battle—an appropriate name for rough-and-tumble boys.) As a first name, Caden didn't hit the U.S. charts for the first time until 1992, but it's already quite popular. Caden is part of a current trend that includes the similar sounding names Aiden, Brayden, and Jayden.

THIS NAME IN HISTORY

Cayden Boyd (actor)

Caden Cotard (character in the film *Synecdoche, New York*)

Caden Lane (baby accessory company)

Caleb

Meaning: Dog; courageous

Origin: Hebrew; Arabic

Related names and spelling variations: *Kaleb*

Caleb is a biblical name with an old-fashioned charm to it. In Hebrew, Caleb is related to the word "dog," considered to be a symbol of loyalty and, considering the biblical context, especially loyalty to God (it does not mean that baby Caleb's big sister should feed him dog food as a joke). The Arabic meaning is "courageous." Both definitions are great sentiments to pass on to a non-dog-food-eating child. After moderate popularity in the 1800s, Caleb dropped off the charts in the mid-1920s and didn't reappear until the 1960s.

THIS NAME IN HISTORY

Caleb Carr (author)

Caleb Deschanel (cinematographer)

Caleb Followill (singer)

Caleb Hanie (football player)

1. Bill (Gates)

2. Oprah (Winfrey)

3. Donald (Trump)

4. Steve (Jobs)

5. Mark (Zuckerberg)

6. Ralph (Lauren)

7. Warren (Buffet)

8. Michael (Bloomberg)

9. J. K. (Rowling)

10. Steven (Spielberg)

Calvin

Meaning: Little bald one

Origin: Latin

Related names and spelling variations: *Cal, Kalvin*

Calvin technically means "little bald one" and is one of many names that refer to physical characteristics. John Chauvin (*chauve* means bald) was a fourteenth-century French theologian and one of the leaders of the Protestant Reformation. His name was Latinized as Calvinus and he became known as John Calvin—and the name was used in his honor around the early nineteenth century. In the U.S., Calvin has been in the top 1,000 since 1880. It was at its most popular in the 1920s, when Calvin Coolidge was president. While most names go up and down the charts over time, Calvin has stayed remarkably steady, ranking in the 100s for most years since then. Calvin would be a great choice if you're looking for familiar names that are not overly popular. Cal makes a great nickname, too.

THIS NAME IN HISTORY

Calvin Coolidge (U.S. president)

Calvin Klein (fashion designer)

John Calvin (Protestant theologian)

Calvin & Hobbes (comic strip)

Cameron

Meaning: Crooked nose

Origin: Scottish

Related names and spelling variations:
Camren, Camron, Kameron, Kamren, Kamron, Camryn

Cameron is a Scottish surname that means "crooked nose," but you might not want your little Cameron's teasing classmates to know this. Despite the less-than-attractive meaning, Cameron has become an incredibly popular name in recent years and is one of those names that inspires parents to break out their creative spellings. Each of these versions are popular among U.S. parents: Cameron, Kameron, Camron, Camren, Camryn, Kamron, and Kamryn.

In the last decade, Cameron has become a unisex name, boosted by celebrities like Cameron Diaz and Camryn Manheim. The recent popularity of the name for girls may eventually cause parents to stop using it for their sons, often the result for unisex names.

THIS NAME IN HISTORY

Cameron Crowe (director)

Cameron Diaz (actor)

Camryn Manheim (actor)

Cameron Mitchell (entrepreneur)

Cameron Tucker (character on the
TV show *Modern Family*)

Cameron Wake (football player)

James Cameron (director)

Kirk Cameron (actor)

Mike Cameron (baseball player)

Carl

Meaning: Free man; farmer

Origin: German

Related names and spelling variations: *Carlo, Carlito, Karl, Karol, Carlos*

Carl is the German form of the name Charles and it means "free man" or "farmer." The traditional German spelling is Karl, but Carl has been more popular in the U.S., and quite popular at that. Carl was a top 50 name from 1880 through the late 1950s. It remained in the top 100 through the 1970s, but has been on the decline since then, making it attractive if you want a name with an old-fashioned ring. Carl has been dropping in popularity recently, while Carlos, the Spanish version, has taken the opposite path, reaching the top 100 for the first time in 1970. Olé!

THIS NAME IN HISTORY

Carl Jung (psychologist)

Karl Lagerfeld (fashion designer)

Karl Marx (philosopher)

Karl Rove (political consultant)

Carl Sagan (astronomer)

Carl Sandburg (author and poet)

Carlos Santana (musician)

Carl's Jr. (restaurant)

Carson

Meaning: Unknown

Origin: English, Scottish

Related names and spelling variations: *Carsen, Carsan, Karson*

Carson is the perfect example of the surname name trend. It hovered near the bottom of the charts for decades, but shot to the top in the early 2000s. Without a doubt, the popularity of TV host Carson Daly in the late 1990s played a role in the meteoric rise, too. A new celebrity on the scene and the surname trend were enough to turn Carson into a new favorite with parents.

THIS NAME IN HISTORY

Carson Daly (TV personality)

Carson Drew (character in Carolyn Keene's *Nancy Drew* series)

Carson Kressley (fashion critic)

Carson McCullers (author)

Carson Palmer (football player)

Johnny Carson (TV personality)

Kit Carson (frontiersman)

Rachel Carson (author)

Carter

Meaning: Cart maker, cart driver

Origin: English

Related names and spelling variations: *Karter*

Carter, an English name, was used for someone who made or used . . . carts (duh). Carter is also an example of the surname-for-first-name trend as well as the occupational name trend (See Cooper, Parker, and Spencer). When one name falls into more than one current trend category, it's no surprise that it gains popularity quickly. The name's popularity could also have been boosted by the character Dr. John Carter on the TV show *ER*, who was usually called "Carter."

THIS NAME IN HISTORY

Carter Beauford (musician)

Carter Braxton (signer of the Declaration of Independence)

Carter Stanley (musician)

Carter G. Woodson (historian and founder of a celebration that became Black History Month)

Jimmy Carter (U.S. president)

Dr. John Carter (character on the TV show *ER*)

Linda Carter (actor)

Casey

Meaning: Alert, brave

Origin: Irish

Related names and spelling variations: *Case, Kasey*

Casey is a classic Irish name with a great meaning—"alert, brave,"—even though your little Casey may not feel so brave on the first day of kindergarten. Casey is also a popular unisex name. Casey first made the boys' chart in 1888. It reached the top 100 ninety years later in 1978 and stayed there until 1991. Casey has been on the girls' list since 1967. It broke into the top 100 for three years in the 1980s and has been declining since then. While most unisex names tend to become less popular for boys as they become more popular for girls, Casey has stayed strong for boys.

THIS NAME IN HISTORY

Casey Affleck (actor)

Kasey Kahne (race car driver)

Casey Kasem (radio personality)

John Casey (character on the
TV show *Chuck*)

Cedric

Meaning: War chief

Origin: English

Related names and spelling variations: *Cedrick*

Cedric comes from the name of a Saxon king in England in the early sixteenth century, so it might work if you're looking to inspire a warrior. But it might be just as good if you're more bookish parents. Cedric of Rotherwood appeared in Sir Walter Scott's *Ivanhoe*. Cedric Errol Fauntleroy is the title character in Frances Hodgson Burnett's *Little Lord Fauntleroy*. Most recently, Cedric Diggory is a hero in J. K. Rowling's *Harry Potter* series. Cedric was off and on the U.S. charts from the end of the 1800s through the 1930s. It was at its peak in the 1970s and early 1980s when it ranked in the mid-200s.

THIS NAME IN HISTORY

Cedric the Entertainer (comedian and actor)

Cedric Benson (football player)

Cedric Diggory (character in J. K. Rowling's
Harry Potter series)

Cedric Errol Fauntleroy (character in *Little Lord Fauntleroy*)

Cedric of Rotherwood (character in *Ivanhoe*)

Chad

Meaning: Warrior

Origin: English, Celtic

Related names and spelling variations: *None*

Chad's origin is somewhat unclear, but it's often attributed to English or Celtic origins with the meaning "warrior." (Given how many action figures you're going to be stepping on in coming years, this could be prophetic.) Chad is one of those great one-syllable names that could appeal to you if you have longer last names. It's also a good pick if you don't like nicknames. Chad first appeared in the top 1,000 in 1945. It was a top 100 name between 1969 and 1990, peaking at #25.

THIS NAME IN HISTORY

Chad Hedrick (speed skater)

Chad Hurley (cofounder of YouTube)

Chad Kroeger (singer)

Chad Michael Murray (actor)

Chad Ochocinco (football player)

Chandler

Meaning: Candle maker

Origin: English

Related names and spelling variations: *Chan*

Chandler is an English occupational name that means "candle maker," but since candles are not the hot manufacturing item

TOP TEN: BRITISH KINGS

1. Edward
2. Henry
3. George
4. William
5. Richard
6. Charles
7. James
8. John
9. Stephen
10. Arthur

they once were, the name's popularity in the 1990s was likely attributable to something else. When the TV show *Friends* debuted in 1994 (featuring Chandler Bing, played by Matthew Perry), the name Chandler was ranked #348. The following year it jumped to #177.

THIS NAME IN HISTORY

Chandler Bing (character on the
    TV show *Friends*)
Chandler Massey (actor)

Charles

Meaning: Free man; farmer

Origin: French, German

Related names: *Carlos, Charlie, Carlo, Chuck, Chuckie*

Charles has German and French roots and means "free man" and "farmer." The name goes back centuries and has long been popular for royalty, but don't let it go to your little Charlie's head. Charlemagne was the Holy Roman Emperor in 800 C.E. and his name translates to "Charles the Great." The name also made its mark on the British royal family—Mary, Queen of Scots, named her son Charles James in 1566 and he went on to become king of Scotland and king of England. The name is still part of the British royal family today—Prince Charles is next in line for the throne. Charles has been one of the most popular boys' names of all time in the U.S. It was in the top 10 from 1880 through 1954 and didn't fall out of the

Hi, My Name Is

top 50 until 2000. It's dropped slightly since then, but the classic name is still a perennial parental favorite.

Charles Barkley (basketball player)

Charles Bronson (actor)

Charlie Chaplin (silent film star)

Charles Darwin (scientist)

Charles de Gaulle (French president and general)

Charles Dickens (author)

Charles Lindbergh (aviator)

Charles Schulz (cartoonist)

Charlie Sheen (actor)

Chuck E. Cheese (restaurant)

Chase

Meaning: To hunt

Origin: English

Related names and spelling variations: *Chace, Chayce, Chayse*

Chase is an English occupational surname that dates back to the Middle Ages and means "to hunt," or "to chase," as in what you'll be doing with your toddler boy on the playground. Chase didn't make a splash in the baby name world until the early 1980s, when it broke into the Top 150 for the first time. Chase has a cool, modern feel to it, and that, in combination with the occupational surname trend, has caused the name to grow in popularity. And, ohmigod . . . it, like, can't hurt that the name is totally shared by *Gossip Girl* hottie Chace Crawford.

THIS NAME IN HISTORY

Chase Blackburn (football player)

Chace Crawford (actor)

Chase Ellison (actor)

Chase Utley (baseball player)

Chevy Chase (actor)

David Chase (screenwriter, director, and producer)

Christian

Meaning: Christian

Origin: Latin

Related names and spelling variations: *Cristian, Kristian*

The name Christian holds an obvious appeal if you're religious parents. It started being used as a first name for boys in England after the Norman Conquest, which began all the way back in good old 1066. In Denmark, the name has been used for ten kings since the fifteenth century. Despite the name's holy and regal origins, you can tell your Christian he'd better stop pulling his sister's hair. Or else.

In the U.S., Christian has been moderately popular since the 1880s, but has become much more stylish since the 1990s. Even though it's a name with a long history, it doesn't sound outdated. It is rarely used for girls today and hasn't made the girls' chart since 2004.

THIS NAME IN HISTORY

Kristian Alfonso (actor)

Christian Bale (actor)

Christian Dior (fashion designer)

Christian Ehrhoff (hockey player)
Christian Hosoi (pro skateboarder)
Christian Lacroix (fashion designer)
Christian Lous Lange (Nobel prize winner)
Christian Louboutin (footwear designer)
Christian Slater (actor)
Hans Christian Andersen (author)

Christopher

Meaning: Bearer of Christ

Origin: Greek

Related names and spelling variations:
Cristofer, Cristopher, Kristofer, Kristopher, Chris, Kris, Topher

Some names are new and trendy (see the Jayden/Cayden repertoire). Christopher, a Greek name that means "bearer of Christ," has got some serious history, dating all the way back to the 1500s. In the Middle Ages, the name was associated with St. Christopher, the patron saint of travelers, and at the time many inns were given the name to attract customers (perhaps a good name then if you tend to have wanderlust).

In the 1960s in the U.S., Christopher started an incredible forty-plus-year run in the top 10. Most traditional names start to sound overused before too long, but Christopher still manages to sound classic and fresh.

THIS NAME IN HISTORY

Christopher Columbus (explorer)
Topher Grace (actor)

Kris Kristofferson (singer-songwriter)
Christopher Lee (actor)
Christopher Moore (author)
Christopher Reeve (actor)
Christopher Robin (character in
    A. A. Milne's *Winnie-the-Pooh*)
Chris Rock (comedian and actor)
Christopher Walken (actor)

Clark

Meaning: Scribe, clerk

Origin: English

Related names and spelling variations: *Clarke*

Clark is an English surname and occupational name that means "scribe" or "clerk," making it a good choice if you're wordsmiths. In a time when few people were literate, the name Clark was used to denote people who earned a living by their ability to read and write, often as part of a religious order. Records of Clark being used as a first name date back to the 1600s in England. In the U.S., the highest Clark has ever ranked is #176 and that was in 1881. It saw a small boost in the 1940s, perhaps influenced by Superman's Clark Kent, who first revealed his alter ego's blue tights on the comics page in 1938. Clark would be a good choice if you want a familiar name that is not too common.

THIS NAME IN HISTORY

Clark Gable (actor)
Clark Kellogg (sports analyst)
Clark Kent (Superman's alter ego)

Hi, My Name Is

TOP TEN: BRITISH PRINCES

1. William
2. George
3. Edward
4. Albert
5. Ernest
6. Alfred
7. Henry
8. John
9. Charles
10. Richard

Clayton

Meaning: Clay town

Origin: English

Related names and spelling variations: *Clay, Klayton, Klay*

Some definitions of names are steeped in mystery. Clayton is not one of them. It literally means "clay town." The related name Clay has been used for a long time as well in the U.S., dating all the way back to 1880. It took a steep drop in the early 2000s, as Clayton surged ahead. Clayton has been in the top 100 and 200 since 1880! Clayton is probably seeing more popularity these days because the *-on* sound at the end is similar to the *-en* sound of trendy names like Brayden, Jayden, and Cayden. Also, you have more options with Clayton—you can use the full name or use Clay as a nickname.

THIS NAME IN HISTORY

Clay Aiken (singer)
Clay Matthews (football player)
Clay Walker (singer)

Cody

Meaning: Helpful

Origin: Irish; English

Related names and spelling variations: *Codey, Codie, Kody, Kodie*

TOP TEN:
MALE *TITANIC* SURVIVORS

1. Alfred (Evans)

2. Walter (Perkis)

3. Charles (Joughin)

4. Ralph (Wells)

5. William (White)

6. Joseph (Boxhall)

7. Johan (Sundman)

8. George (Symons)

9. John (Thayer)

10. Frank (Mason)

Despite Irish and English roots, Cody has an Americana cowboy appeal today, likely due to the association with legendary frontiersman "Buffalo Bill" Cody. (While the Western showman rocketed to fame in the late 1800s, the name Cody wasn't regularly on the list of popular names in the U.S. until 1951.) Cody hit its prime in the early 1990s, when it ranked in the top 25. Other names with the same Western feel are Chase, Colton, and Wyatt.

THIS NAME IN HISTORY

Cody Banks (character in the movie
   Agent Cody Banks)
Cody Gifford (actor and son of Kathy
   Lee and Frank Gifford)
Cody Linley (actor)
Cody Ransom (baseball player)
Cody Ross (baseball player)
Cody Willard (financial journalist)
William Frederick "Buffalo Bill" Cody
   (frontiersman)

Colby

Meaning: Coal town

Origin: English

Related names and spelling variations: *Kolby*

Pittsburgh parents, pay attention! Colby is an English location name probably meaning "coal town." It entered the charts at #842 in 1968. It gained some popularity over the decades, but made a big leap to #99 in 2001—perhaps not coincidentally the same year Colby Donaldson won hearts (but not the million dollars) in *Survivor: The Australian Outback*. The name has dropped nearly to #300 since then. With the popularity of female singer Colbie Caillat, the name has the potential to become unisex, as well.

THIS NAME IN HISTORY

Colbie Caillat (singer)
Colby Donaldson (reality TV star)
Colby Lewis (baseball player)
The Colbys (TV show)

Cole

Meaning: Coal; black

Origin: English

Related names and spelling variations: *Kole*

Cole is an English surname name with an obvious meaning, "coal," and was probably used to denote someone with a dark, swarthy appearance (perhaps the perfect name for a son you hope to one day be tall, dark, and handsome). Cole made its debut on the U.S. charts in 1886, but didn't reappear as a consistent pick until the 1950s. Cole's popularity peaked at #69 in the early 2000s. Cole is a great one-syllable choice if you have a longer last name. Cole is also sometimes used as a nickname for Nicholas.

THIS NAME IN HISTORY

Cole Haan (fashion designer)
Cole Hamels (baseball player)
Cole Hauser (actor)
Cole Porter (musician)
Cole Sprouse (actor)

Kenneth Cole (fashion designer)
Nat King Cole (musician)
Natalie Cole (musician)

Colin

Meaning: Cub; people's victor

Origin: Celtic; Greek

Related names and spelling variations: *Collin, Colyn*

Colin is a Celtic name and also has roots in the name Nicholas. The dual origins give it two appealing meanings—"cub" and "people's victor"—making it friendly and fierce at the same time. Colin was popular during the Middle Ages and again beginning in the 1800s. It wasn't until the 1930s that Colin became a regular on the name charts in the U.S. It broke into the top 200 in the early 1980s and remains there today, along with the Collin spelling. It's not too popular or too old-fashioned, making it a good pick if you like names that everyone knows, but that haven't been overused.

THIS NAME IN HISTORY

Colin Baker (actor)
Colin Dunne (dancer)
Colin Farrell (actor)
Colin Firth (actor)
Colin Greenwood (musician)
Colin Hanks (actor)
Colin Montgomerie (golfer)
Colin Powell (U.S. general and former secretary of state)
Colin Quinn (comedian)

TOP TEN: MATHEMATICIANS

1. Blaise (Pascal)
2. Paul (Erdős)
3. August (Möbius)
4. Étienne (Bézout)
5. Jules (Henri Poincaré)
6. Hermann (Minkowski)
7. Ada (Lovelace)
8. Niels (Henrik Abel)
9. René (Descartes)
10. Gottfried (Leibniz)

Colton

Meaning: Coal town

Origin: English

Related names and spelling variations: *Colten, Kolton, Kolten, Colt*

Colton is an English surname that means "coal town." Colton is a recent chart-topper that broke into the top 100 for the first time in 2008. It didn't appear on the U.S. charts at all until 1982. Like other *C* names, such as Caden and Cameron, it's much more popular than its rank suggests because of creative parental spellers. Some of the imaginative variations are Colton, Colten, Kolton, and Kolten.

NAME FACTOID

The name Colt was one of the biggest movers in 2009. It jumped 164 spots in just one year and ranked #370.

THIS NAME IN HISTORY

Colt Cabana (wrestler)

Colton Gillies (hockey player)

Colton James (actor)

Colt McCoy (football player)

Colton Orr (hockey player)

Connor

Meaning: Hound lover

Origin: Irish

Related names and spelling variations: *Conor, Konor, Konner, Conner, Konnor*

Connor is an Irish surname from a Gaelic name that may mean "hound lover." If your first "baby" was of the canine variety, this might be the perfect name for your son. Connor was a popular name in Ireland and eventually started to expand to other countries. It first found its way onto the U.S. charts in 1981 and a decade later it became a top 100 staple. Like other *C* names, creative parents have been spelling it many different ways, including Conner, Conor, Konner, and Konnor.

THIS NAME IN HISTORY

Conor Jackson (baseball player)

Conor Oberst (musician)

Connor Trinneer (actor)

John Connor (character in the *Terminator* movies)

Sinéad O'Connor (singer)

Conrad

Meaning: Daring advisor

Origin: German

Related names and spelling variations: *Conrado, Konrad*

Conrad is a German name that means "daring advisor," a cool combination of action and academics, despite the name's somewhat nerdy sound. Conrad was sometimes used in the Middle Ages, but didn't become popular in English-speaking countries until the 1800s. In the U.S., Conrad was at its peak of popularity in 1931 at #215. Conrad would be a great pick if you like established, but uncommon, names.

THIS NAME IN HISTORY

Conrad Birdie (character in the musical *Bye Bye Birdie*)

Conrad Hilton (hotelier)

Joseph Conrad (author)

Cooper

Meaning: Barrel maker

Origin: English

Related names and spelling variations: *Kooper, Coop*

Cooper is an English occupational surname that was used for barrel makers. (If we named people now for what they do, it would be John Financial Consultant. Not nearly as catchy as Cooper.) Cooper was first on the U.S. charts in the 1880s, but then disappeared for one hundred years. It came back in 1982, but really came into vogue in the early 2000s. Look for Cooper to maintain its popularity—it sounds friendly and fresh, which should continue to appeal to parents. The cool nickname Coop has charm, too.

Cooper (character on the TV show
  Hannah Montana)

Cooper Pillot (actor)

Alice Cooper (musician)

Chris Cooper (actor)

Gary Cooper (actor)

Corey

Meaning: Valley, hollow

Origin: Irish

Related names and spelling variations:
Korey, Cory

Corey is an Irish name that may mean "valley" or "hollow." Corey had a skateboarder-cool feel to it in the 1980s and it retains that outsider cachet today. It's also one of the most accessible Irish names. Corey first made the U.S. charts in 1949. It was a top 100 pick from 1969 through 1996. Corey also spent twenty-five years on the girls' chart between the late 1960s and mid-1990s, when it dropped off entirely. It's unusual that a name goes from boys, to unisex, and then back to boys again.

THIS NAME IN HISTORY

Corey Feldman (actor)

Corey Haim (actor)

Corey Maggette (basketball player)

Corey Hart (musician)

Korey Stringer (football player)

Craig

Meaning: Steep rock

Origin: Gaelic

Related names and spelling variations: *Kraig*

Craig is a Gaelic name that means "steep rock," one of several rough-and-tumble rock-themed names (See Peter and Alan). It was originally given as a nickname to people who lived near steep rocks, eventually coming into vogue as a first name. Craig has been particularly popular in Scotland. In the U.S., Craig was on and off the charts at the turn of the last century, but eventually reached the top 100 in 1947. It stayed there for several decades, but has been quickly declining recently. Craig would make a great pick if you want a name without a ready-made nickname.

THIS NAME IN HISTORY

Craig David (musician)

Craig Ferguson (TV personality)

Craig James (sports analyst)

Craig Robinson (actor)

Craigslist (popular Web site)

Curtis

Meaning: Courteous

Origin: French

Related names and spelling variations: *Curt, Kurt, Kurtis*

Hoping to have a polite little boy? Choose Curtis—a French name that means "courteous." It began in the Middle Ages as a nickname for someone who minds his manners and eventually became a first name. Curtis has been on the U.S. charts since the 1880s and has a pretty impressive record, spending most of that time in the top 200. Curtis will appeal to you if you're looking for nontrendy names with vintage charm. It has a similar feel to names like Duncan, Felix, and Asa.

Dd

Dakota

Meaning: Ally, friend

Origin: Native American

Related names and spelling variations: *Dakotah*

Hoping to avoid sandbox spats? Perhaps the name Dakota will put your boy in the right mood. Dakota has Native American origins and means "ally" or "friend." Dakota is a rare unisex name that's equally popular for boys and girls. As a boy's name, Dakota first appeared on the charts in 1985. It ranked in the top 100 between 1993 and 2001 and has been on the decline since then. As a girl's name, Dakota didn't enter the charts until 1990, with actor Dakota Fanning boosting its popularity. Dakota has also become one of the most popular location names, along with other hot spots Kingston, Memphis, Houston, and Austin.

THIS NAME IN HISTORY

Dakota Fanning (actor)

Damian

Meaning: To tame

Origin: Greek

Related names and spelling variations: *Damien, Damion*

Damian has origins in a Greek word that means "to tame" (this is no guarantee that your little Damian won't be a wild child). One of the most popular namesakes is St. Damian, a fourth-century Christian who was martyred with his brother, St. Cosmas. Before their deaths, the brothers gained fame for providing free medical care, which is why St. Damian is the patron saint of pharmacists. The name Damian entered the U.S. charts for the first time in the early 1950s. Surprisingly, the Damien spelling got a boost in the late 1970s, when it was used for the spooky boy in the horror flick *The Omen*.

THIS NAME IN HISTORY

Damien (character in *The Omen*)

Damien Duff (soccer player)

Damian Lewis (actor)

TOP TEN: BRITISH ROYALTY

1. Henry
2. George
3. Edward
4. William
5. Elizabeth
6. Mary
7. Charles
8. Victoria
9. Catherine
10. Anne

Damian Marley (musician)
Damian McGinty (singer)
Damien Rice (musician)
Damian Woetzel (dancer)

Dane

Meaning: Dane

Origin: English

Related names and spelling variations: *None*

Dane is an English name that simply means "Dane," a person from Denmark, making the name a good pick if you want to acknowledge Danish ancestry. (Calling your kid, say, Ohio just doesn't have the same ring.) It's also a good choice if you like names without built-in nicknames. Dane debuted on the U.S. charts in 1945. It was at its most popular in the 1980s, where it peaked at #220. After declining for several years, Dane is having a bit of a comeback. Dane has a simple but sophisticated sound that should appeal to a lot of parents.

THIS NAME IN HISTORY
Dane Cook (comedian)
Dane Reynolds (surfer)

Daniel

Meaning: God is my judge

Origin: Hebrew

Related names and spelling variations:
Danyel, Dan, Danny

Daniel is a biblical name meaning "God is my judge" that dates back as far as the Book of Daniel in the Old Testament. Daniel was a slave who gained favor with the king by interpreting dreams, only to be thrown into a den of lions, where he was saved by God (maybe it's a good name if you envision your son emerging unscathed from playground scrapes). The name Daniel has been popular since the 1500s. It's been especially popular with parents in the U.S., spending most of its time in the top 50 since 1880. Daniel is one of those names that works as well for a floppy newborn as it does for a middle-aged man. Since 1972, Daniel has never strayed from the Top 15. The nickname Danny has also become fairly popular on its own.

THIS NAME IN HISTORY

Daniel Boone (frontiersman)

Dan Brown (author)

Daniel Craig (actor)

Daniel Day-Lewis (actor)

Daniel Defoe (author)

Daniel Handler (author)

Daniel Radcliffe (actor)

Daniel Webster (American statesman)

"Daniel" (song by Elton John)

"Danny Boy" (Irish ballad)

Darius

Meaning: King

Origin: Persian; Greek

Related names and spelling variations:
Darian, Darien, Dario, Dorian

Darius is an ancient name that comes from the Greek name Dareios. The name means "king" because it was borne by several Persian kings named Darius, including Darius I, who ruled in the sixth century B.C.E. Darius might be a great choice if you enjoy royalty-inspired names like Prince and Kingston, but want something a little more subtle. Darius was in the top 1,000 for three years in the 1880s and then dropped off the charts until 1952. Its highest rank was #152 in the early 1990s.

NAME FACTOID

The most outrageous royalty-inspired celebrity baby name? Jermajesty, the son of Jermaine Jackson.

THIS NAME IN HISTORY

Darius I (ruler of Persia)

Darius McCrary (actor)

Darius Rucker (singer)

Darrell

Meaning: Beloved

Origin: English

Related names and spelling variations: *Darryl, Daryl, Darrel*

Darrell is an English name that means "beloved" (this doesn't prevent you from

1 Julie (Andrews)		**6** Bill ("Bojangles" Robinson)	
2 Chita (Rivera)		**7** Alfred (Drake)	
3 Bebe (Neuwirth)		**8** Harvey (Fierstein)	
4 Patti (LuPone)		**9** Jerry (Orbach)	
5 Fanny (Brice)		**10** Bernadette (Peters)	

losing your cool now and then with your beloved boy, like when he strips off his diaper in the cereal aisle). Darrell has made the U.S. charts with a couple different spellings. The Darrell spelling has the longest history and is currently the most popular. The name Daryl was on the girls' chart in the 1940s and 1950s, which may have been what inspired Daryl Hannah's parents. The name never really caught on as a unisex name and is considered a boy's name today.

THIS NAME IN HISTORY

Darrell Green (football player)
Daryl Hall (singer)
Darrell Hammond (actor)
Daryl Hannah (actor)
Darrell Steinberg (politician)
Darryl Strawberry (baseball player)
Darryl Worley (singer)

Darren

Meaning: Rocky hill

Origin: English

Related names and spelling variations: *Darran, Darin, Darrin, Daryn*

Darren is the quintessential 1960s name. It has somewhat uncertain roots, though some consider it to be an English name that means "rocky hill." (What's up with all those rock-inspired names? See Peter, Craig, Allen.)

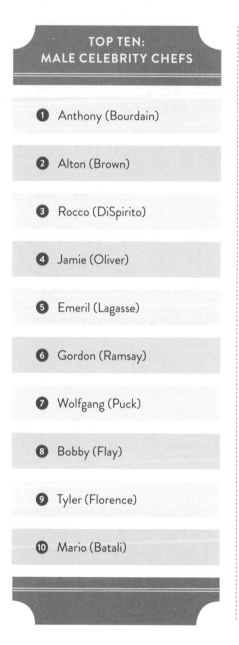

TOP TEN:
MALE CELEBRITY CHEFS

1. Anthony (Bourdain)

2. Alton (Brown)

3. Rocco (DiSpirito)

4. Jamie (Oliver)

5. Emeril (Lagasse)

6. Gordon (Ramsay)

7. Wolfgang (Puck)

8. Bobby (Flay)

9. Tyler (Florence)

10. Mario (Batali)

Darren became a regular on the U.S. charts in 1957 when it ranked #888. One year later it had skyrocketed to #381 and by 1965 it ranked #52. When names rise quickly, they tend to fall quickly, but Darren beat the odds and has had some staying power. The Darrin spelling got a boost in the 1960s with the character Darrin Stephens on *Bewitched*. Female news anchor Daryn Kagan could create some appeal for Daryn as a girl's name, but it hasn't caught on just yet.

THIS NAME IN HISTORY

Darren Aronofsky (director)
Daryn Kagan (TV personality)
Darren McGavin (actor)
Darrin Stephens (character on the
  TV show *Bewitched*)
Bobby Darin (singer)

David

Meaning: Darling

Origin: Hebrew

Related names and spelling variations:
Dave, Davy

Wanna give your boy an edge on the playground bully? Consider David, the little guy who went up against that badass Goliath with a slingshot and wound up as the second king of Israel, ruling in the tenth century B.C.E. Booh-yah! The name is also a classic Hebrew name that means "darling" —a sweet sentiment, too.

After being a top 10 name in the U.S. from 1936 to 1992, David has fallen only slightly. Another plus? David is also one of those ageless names that works equally well for your boy from tot to teen and beyond. Similar classics are Alexander, Benjamin, and Michael.

THIS NAME IN HISTORY

David Beckham (soccer player)

David Bowie (musician and actor)

David Byrne (musician)

David Copperfield (title character from Charles Dickens's novel *David Copperfield*)

David Copperfield (magician)

Davy Crockett (frontiersman)

David Duchovny (actor)

David Letterman (TV personality)

David Livingstone (explorer)

David Lynch (screenwriter, director, and producer)

Dawson

Meaning: David's son

Origin: English

Related names and spelling variations: *Dawsen*

Dawson is an English name that means "David's son." Despite a modern ring, Dawson first made the U.S. charts in 1885. From then until 1911 it was off and on the popular list of names, but then disappeared. It didn't become truly popular until the teen drama *Dawson's Creek* hit the airwaves in the 1990s. Dawson reappeared in 1994 and by 1999 (one year after *Dawson's Creek* debuted) it ranked

#136. The only hurdle you'll face with Dawson is that when some people hear it, they probably still think of Dawson Leary. That will likely change over time as everyone gets obsessed with *Twilight*-inspired names like Cullen and Bella.

THIS NAME IN HISTORY

Dawson Leary (character on the TV show *Dawson's Creek*)

Dean

Meaning: Dean; valley dweller

Origin: English

Related names and spelling variations: *Deane*

Dean is an English name that means both "dean" and "valley dweller," making it an occupational name and location name all rolled into one. You can still use it, even if you're not a dean and don't live in a valley. Dean is simple and no-frills, making it an easy fit for a wide variety of last names. It has been on the U.S. charts since 1880. It was in the top 100 from the late 1950s through the 1960s, but never ranked above #78, and has been on the decline ever since. It's a rarely used name despite some super-cool namesakes (James Dean, Dean Martin, etc.).

THIS NAME IN HISTORY

Dean Cain (actor)

Dean Forester (character on the TV show *Gilmore Girls*)

Dean Kamen (inventor)

Dean Koontz (author)

Dean Martin (singer)

Dr. Dean Ornish (doctor and author)

James Dean (actor)

Dean & DeLuca (store)

Dennis

Meaning: Follower of Dionysius

Origin: Greek

Related names and spelling variations: *Denny, Denis*

Dennis is a Greek name that's perfect if you're oenophiles—its definition is a reference to the Greek god of wine and general good-time guy Dionysius. The name was also popularized by several saints named Denis, dating back as far as the third century. (If you like irony, there is something amusing about a name associated with both saints and partying.) Dennis has been on the U.S. charts since 1880. In 1934, it broke into the top 100, where it stayed through the mid-1980s. It has been on the decline since then. Denny makes for a cool, retro nickname. And it's also a great place to get eggs at 3 A.M.

THIS NAME IN HISTORY

Denny Crane (character on the TV
   series *Boston Legal*)

Denny Hamlin (NASCAR driver)

Dennis Hopper (actor)

Dennis Kucinich (politician)

Dennis Miller (comedian)

Dennis Quaid (actor)

Dennis Rodman (basketball player)

Dennis the Menace (comic strip)

Denny's (restaurant chain)

Derek

Meaning: Ruler of the people

Origin: Dutch

Related names and spelling variations: *Derik, Derrick, Dereck, Deric, Derick*

Derek is a Dutch name with Germanic origins and a regal definition—"ruler of the people," or as Kindergarten Derek will see it: "ruler of the playground twisty slide." The name came to England in the Middle Ages, when it was typically spelled Derrick and used as a surname. Both Derek and Derrick entered the U.S. charts for the first time in the 1940s. The name was at its most popular between the 1970s and 1990s, with Derek trumping Derrick. Derrick is a creative way to get to the nickname Ricky if you aren't thrilled with Richard.

THIS NAME IN HISTORY

Derek Anderson (football player)

Derek Hough (dancer and TV personality)

Derek Jeter (baseball player)

Derek Morris (hockey player)

Derek Shepherd (character on the TV
   series *Grey's Anatomy*)

Derek and the Dominos (Eric Clapton's
first band)

Devin

Meaning: Poet

Origin: Celtic

Related names and spelling variations:
Devinn, Devon, Devyn, Devynn, Deven, Devan

Devin is one of the hottest Celtic names right now and means "poet," which certainly adds to its romantic appeal. It's yet another name that inspires parents to break out their creative spelling skills, leading to entries on the popular names list for Devin, Devon, Deven, Devan, and Devyn. Devin is one of those rare instances where a boy's name flirted with popularity as a girl's name and then dropped off the girls' chart entirely while still remaining popular with boys. Devin ranked as high as #238 for girls in 1991, but hasn't been on the girls' list at all since 2005, although alternate spelling Devyn seems to be positioning itself for a comeback.

THIS NAME IN HISTORY

Devin Harris (basketball player)

Devin Hester (football player)

Devin Scillian (author)

Devin Setoguchi (hockey player)

Devin Thomas (football player)

Devin Townsend (musician)

Devon Woodcomb (character on the TV show *Chuck*)

Dexter

Meaning: Dexterous, right-handed

Origin: Latin

Related names and spelling variations: *Dex*

Dexter is one of those names that sounds like its definition, "dexterous." (Imagine if there were a name inspired by the ability to pee in a potty?) For all but a handful of years since 1880, Dexter has been in the top 1,000 in the U.S., spending most of that time in the middle of the pack. It's seen a recent spike in popularity, probably thanks to the TV show *Dexter*, which debuted in 2006. Perhaps a show chronicling the adventures of a serial killer is an unlikely inspiration for sweet baby boys, but the renewed interest in Dexter may also be an example of how names become more popular despite less than stellar inspirations.

THIS NAME IN HISTORY

Dexter Gordon (singer)

Dexter (TV show and book series)

Dexter's Laboratory (cartoon)

Dominic

Meaning: Lord

Origin: Latin

Related names and spelling variations: *Dominick, Dominik, Dominique, Dom*

Dominic is a Latin name that means "lord," making it one of many holy-, regal-, or mighty-sounding names that could lead older siblings to howl with outrage. One popular namesake, St. Dominic, was a Spanish saint who was born in 1170 and founded the Dominican Order of Catholic monks, which is still active today. That connection initially made the name popular among Catholics, but it has since shed the strict Catholic connection and appeals to parents from a wide variety of backgrounds. Dominic first entered the U.S. charts in 1885

TOP TEN: CHAIN RESTAURANTS

1. Wendy ('s)

2. Carl ('s Jr.)

3. Jack (in the Box)

4. Bob (Evans)

5. Denny ('s)

6. Howard (Johnson's)

7. Logan ('s Roadhouse)

8. Ruby (Tuesday)

9. Moe ('s Southwest Grill)

10. Chuck (E. Cheese's)

and was only moderately popular until 2002, when it broke into the top 100 for the first time.

THIS NAME IN HISTORY

Dominick "Dom" DeLuise (actor)
Dominick Dunne (journalist and author)
Dominic Frontiere (composer)
Dominic Hasek (hockey player)
Dominic Monaghan (actor)
Dominic Purcell (actor)
Dominic Sena (director)
Dominic West (actor)

Donovan

Meaning: Black

Origin: Irish

Related names and spelling variations: *Donavan*

Donovan is a distinguished Irish surname that means "black" and sounds a little mysterious. Donovan entered the U.S. charts for the first time in 1900. The name grew in popularity in the 1960s, perhaps thanks to the folk-rock singer with the same name. (Remember "Mellow Yellow"?) Donovan is a great pick if you're looking for familiar Irish names that are not yet trendy. If you want to go with a familiar nickname, you could choose Don or Donnie. If you like more unusual nicknames, consider Van.

Donovan Leitch (singer)

Donovan McNabb (football player)

Donovan Patton (actor)

Landon Donovan (soccer player)

Douglas

Meaning: Black stream

Origin: Scottish

Related names and spelling variations:
Doug, Dougie, Doogie, Douglass

Ever considered naming your daughter Douglas? If you lived in England in the 1600s or 1700s, you might have. It's certainly not considered a unisex name these days. Douglas is a classic Scottish surname name that means "black stream," and it has been on the U.S. charts since 1880. It was a top 100 name between 1929 and 1989, but has been on the decline since then. Douglas would be a great pick if you're looking for classic Scottish names with an old-fashioned sound.

THIS NAME IN HISTORY

Douglas Adams (author)

Douglas Fairbanks (actor)

Doug Flutie (football player)

Douglas "Doogie" Howser (character on the TV show *Doogie Howser, M.D.*)

General Douglas MacArthur (military leader)

Michael Douglas (actor)

Douglas fir (tree)

Doug (cartoon)

Drake

Meaning: Snake, dragon, male duck

Origin: German; Latin

Related names and spelling variations: *None*

In Old English, Drake was a surname that meant "dragon" or "snake" (from the word *draca*, which refers to the fiery beast). By the time Middle English rolled around, it referred to a less ferocious creature—a male duck. Not sure how a fire-breathing beast gets turned into a quacker, but either way, Drake as a name for boys in the U.S. was pretty much absent from the list of popular names until it first appeared in 1961. (If you want to avoid the ducky reference, you can always say you named your son for the famous explorer Sir Francis Drake, too.)

The name has grown more popular in recent years. Drake is a one-syllable name that will flow nicely with a variety of last names.

THIS NAME IN HISTORY

Drake (musician)

Drake Bell (actor)

Drake Hogestyn (actor)

Sir Francis Drake (explorer)

Duncan

Meaning: Dark warrior

Origin: Gaelic

Related names and spelling variations:
Dun, Dunn, Dunc

TOP TEN: CHAMPION BOWLERS

1. Earl (Anthony)
2. Billy (Welu)
3. Mark (Roth)
4. Dick (Weber)
5. Walter (Ray Williams Jr.)

6. Marshall (Holman)
7. Kirsten (Penny)
8. Don (Carter)
9. Mika (Koivuniemi)
10. Wes (Malott)

Duncan is a Gaelic name that sounds sweet, but has an unexpectedly fierce meaning—"dark warrior." The name goes back for centuries in Scotland and has royal roots. King Duncan I ruled Scotland in the eleventh century. He's also the guy who gets whacked in *Macbeth*. In the U.S., there's been only one year since 1880 that Duncan hasn't made the top 1,000. Despite the long history, it has never ranked very high. Its highest position was #377 in 1997. That makes it the perfect choice if you like unique names with antique charm.

THIS NAME IN HISTORY

Duncan I of Scotland (king of Scotland)
Duncan Hines (dessert company)
Duncan Jones (director)
Duncan Phyfe (furniture maker)
Duncan Sheik (singer)
King Duncan (character in Shakespeare's *Macbeth*)

Dustin

Meaning: Thor's stone

Origin: Norse

Related names and spelling variations: *Dusty*

Dustin is a Norse name with a sense of destiny—the meaning "Thor's stone" gives the name power and mystique. Combine that with the fact that "Thor's stone" sounds like one of the five thousand action figure accessories you'll be stepping on in your living room in the years to come, and that makes Dustin a perfect name. In the U.S., Dustin first entered the top 1,000 in 1968 at #368. It was a top 50 name during the 1980s and has been declining in popularity since then. Dusty makes for a cute, unique nickname.

THIS NAME IN HISTORY

Dustin Lance Black (screenwriter and director)

Dustin Diamond (actor)

Dustin Farnum (actor)

Dustin Hoffman (actor)

Dustin Moskovitz (cofounder of Facebook)

Dustin Nguyen (actor)

Dustin Pedroia (baseball player)

Dylan

Meaning: Sea

Origin: Welsh

Related names and spelling variations:
Dillon, Dylin, Dylen, Dillan

Dylan is a beautiful Welsh name that probably means "sea," making it a perfect pick if you're water-lovers. It's also a name that sounds modern but has truly ancient roots. Dylan is a figure in the *Mabinogion*, a collection of Welsh tales that were written down for the first time in the Middle Ages, but have a long oral tradition prior to that. Dylan made it onto the charts for the first time in 1966. The name got a huge boost in 1991—ohmigod!—the year after *Beverly Hills, 90210* debuted with popular character Dylan McKay. (In 1981 it was #283; by 1991 it was #46.) Dylan still sounds as cool today as Dylan McKay made it seem on the TV show.

THIS NAME IN HISTORY

Dylan Baker (actor)

Dylan Bruce (actor)

Dyllan Christopher (actor)

Dylan McDermott (actor)

Dylan McKay (character on the TV show *Beverly Hills, 90210*)

Dylan Ratigan (reporter)

Dylan Sprouse (actor)

Dylan Thomas (poet)

Bob Dylan (singer)

Ee

Edward

Meaning: Rich guardian

Origin: English

Related names and spelling variations:
Eduard, Eduardo, Eddie, Ed, Ned, Ted, Teddy

Want a name that implies wealth? Edward is a traditional English name that means "rich guardian," something we all wish our kids had. It was popular as far back as the first and second centuries in England, when two kings bore the name—Edward the Martyr and Edward the Confessor. In the U.S., Edward has been on the charts since the 1880s. It stayed in the top 15 through the 1930s and very slowly dropped over time. One of the best things about the name Edward is the wide variety of nickname potential—do you prefer Ed, Ned, or Ted? Maybe Eddie or Teddy? If you're looking for modern inspiration, the vampire hero of Stephenie Meyer's *Twilight* series is named Edward Cullen.

NAME FACTOID

Stephenie Meyer's *Twilight* series has had an impact on baby naming. The name Cullen was the biggest mover in the boys' chart in 2009, rising 297 spots in just one year.

THIS NAME IN HISTORY

Edward Cullen (character in Stephenie Meyer's *Twilight*)

Eduardo Fernandez (musician)

Eduardo Galeano (author)

Edward Hopper (artist)

Edward "Ted" Kennedy (U.S. senator)

Ed Norton (actor)

Ed McMahon (TV personality)

Eddie Murphy (comedian and actor)

Robert Edward "Ted" Turner (media mogul)

Ned Yost (baseball manager)

Eli

Meaning: Ascent

Origin: Hebrew

Related names and spelling variations: *Ely*

Eli is a small name with big appeal. It has Hebrew origins and can be found in the Old Testament Book of Samuel. It means "ascent," which could be quite inspiring for your little one. Eli was a favorite of Puritan parents back in the 1600s and it has been a consistent front-runner on the U.S. charts for years. Interestingly, other than its top 100 spots in the last couple years, the highest Eli ever ranked was #121 in 1881. That's quite a long gap, making Eli one of the old-time classics to come back into vogue in recent years.

THIS NAME IN HISTORY
Eli Manning (football player)
Eli Roth (director)
Eli Wallach (actor)
Eli Whitney (inventor)

Elias

Meaning: Yahweh is God

Origin: Greek

Related names and spelling variations: *Elijah*

Elias is a Greek version of the biblical name Elijah, which means "Yahweh is God." If Elias feels like an old-fashioned name, that's because the last time it was even close to as popular on the U.S. charts as it is today was in 1880, when James Garfield was president and the hot new innovation was electric streetlights. Elias spent most of the 1900s in the middle of the top 1,000. It broke into the top 200 in 2005 and has been on an upward path since. Elias is a great choice if you like biblical names. Similarly old-fashioned biblical names coming back into style are Abraham and Caleb.

THIS NAME IN HISTORY
Elias Ayuso (basketball player)
Elias Canetti (author)
Elias Howe (inventor)
Elias Koteas (actor)

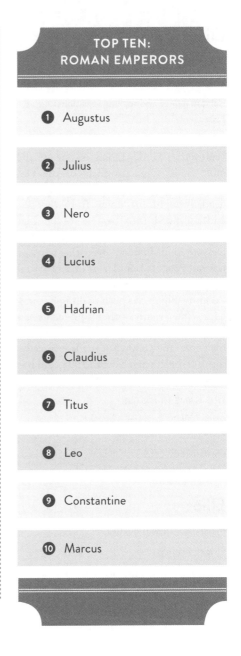

TOP TEN: ROMAN EMPERORS

1. Augustus
2. Julius
3. Nero
4. Lucius
5. Hadrian
6. Claudius
7. Titus
8. Leo
9. Constantine
10. Marcus

ALAMEDA FREE LIBRARY

Elijah

Meaning: Yahweh is God

Origin: Hebrew

Related names and spelling variations: *Alijah, Elias*

Elijah is a Hebrew name that means "Yahweh is God." Elijah is one of the most well-known prophets of the Old Testament and reportedly raised the dead, brought fire down from the sky, and ascended into heaven. (Take that Big Sister, who can poop on the potty!) Despite that history, over the years it has not been as popular as other biblical favorites like David, Daniel, and Adam. Recently, Elijah has been making a comeback, like many other old-fashioned names. The name was a top 200 name at the end of the 1800s, but made it into the top 100 for the first time in 1995, and has continued to climb.

THIS NAME IN HISTORY

Elijah Dukes (baseball player)

Elijah McCoy (inventor)

Elijah Wood (actor)

"Elijah" (composition by Mendelssohn)

Elliot

Meaning: Yahweh is God

Origin: French

Related names and spelling variations: *Eliot, Elliott*

Elliot is French and is part of the family of names derived from the Hebrew name Elijah, which means "Yahweh is God." Despite a long history on the U.S. charts, Elliot has never been very common. The name did get a small boost in the early 1980s from the movie *E.T.: The Extra-Terrestrial*, which featured the cute human boy Elliott. It has been slowly rising since 2000. Elliot is the perfect pick if you like names that are familiar, but not overused. Also, consider Elliot if you don't like nicknames.

THIS NAME IN HISTORY

Elliott (character in the movie *E.T.: The Extra-Terrestrial*)

Elliott Gould (actor)

Elliot Ness (law enforcement agent)

Eliot Pattinson (author)

Elliot Smith (musician)

Elliot Yamin (singer)

George Eliot (author)

Ellis

Meaning: Yahweh is God; kind

Origin: English; Welsh

Related names and spelling variations: *Elias, Elijah*

Ellis is a surname name with dual origins. It is an English version of the names Elias and Elijah, which mean "Yahweh is God," and it's also derived from a Welsh surname that means "kind." (This does not mean your little Ellis will always be nice to his little brother.) Ellis was used as a first name all the way back in the 1400s. After being a top 200 name in the U.S. for most of the late 1800s and early 1900s, Ellis has steadily declined in popularity. This friendly-sounding name may be ready for a comeback.

THIS NAME IN HISTORY

Ellis Dove (character on the TV show
    The Beast)
Brett Easton Ellis (author)
Ellis Grey (character on the TV show Grey's
Anatomy)
Ellis Island (New York landmark)

Eric

Meaning: Constant ruler

Origin: Norse

Related names and spelling variations: *Erik, Eryk, Erick*

Eric is a variation of the traditional Norse name Eirik, which means "constant ruler." (Or for your son, Ruler of the Highchair!) Even today when many people hear the name, they think of first-century Viking explorer and all-around badass Erik the Red. Eric has been on the U.S. charts since 1880. It fluctuated in popularity over the years, but eventually reached its peak in the top 20 in the 1970s, and has been losing ground since.

THIS NAME IN HISTORY

Erik (character in Gaston Leroux's novel
    The Phantom of the Opera)
Prince Eric (character in the Disney
    movie The Little Mermaid)
Erick Avari (actor)

TOP TEN: NASCAR DRIVERS

1. Jeff (Gordon)
2. Dale (Earnhardt)
3. Richard (Petty)
4. Terry (Labonte)
5. Darrell (Waltrip)
6. Tony (Stewart)
7. Jimmie (Johnson)
8. Mark (Martin)
9. Bobby (Allison)
10. Bill (Elliott)

1. Christian (Dior, Lacroix)
2. Jean-Paul (Gaultier)
3. Giorgio (Armani)
4. Valentino
5. Givenchy
6. Donatella (Versace)
7. Karl (Lagerfeld)
8. Oscar (de la Renta)
9. Nina (Ricci)
10. Cristóbal (Balenciaga)

Eric Bana (actor)
Eric Carle (children's book author and illustrator)
Eric Chavez (baseball player)
Eric Clapton (musician)
Erick Dampier (basketball player)
Erik Erikson (developmental psychologist)
Eric Holder Jr. (U.S. attorney general)
Erik the Red (Viking explorer)

Ethan

Meaning: Stable, long-lived

Origin: Hebrew

Related names and spelling variations:
Ethen, Athan, Aitan, Eitan

Ethan is a Hebrew name from the Bible that means "stable, long-lived." Despite that positive-sounding definition, Ethan didn't regularly make the top 1,000 names in the U.S. until the 1950s. (Ethan did appear a handful of times in the 1880s, likely due to patriot Ethan Allen.) It made a huge leap in popularity in 1989, going from #263 in 1988 to #87 the next year, perhaps due to actor Ethan Hawke, who started making movies around that time. The name has continued to gain popularity in recent years. This is a great pick if you don't like nicknames.

THIS NAME IN HISTORY

Ethan Albright (football player)
Ethan Allen (Revolutionary War figure)

Ethan Allen (baseball player)

Ethan Coen (director)

Ethan Embry (actor)

Ethan Hawke (actor)

Ethan Kilmer (football player)

Ethan Moreau (hockey player)

Ethan Zohn (winner of reality TV
show *Survivor: Africa*)

Ethan Frome (novel by Edith Wharton)

Evan

Meaning: God is gracious

Origin: Welsh

Related names and spelling variations: *Evyn*

Evan is an Anglicization of the perennially popular name John, which means "God is gracious." If you like John but want something a little more unique, Evan's a great choice. Though it's been on the U.S. charts since 1880, Evan has only recently started to gain popularity. Evan hit the top 100 in the early 1980s and has been climbing ever since. Evan is also a great option if you do not like names with ready-made nicknames.

THIS NAME IN HISTORY

Evan Bayh (U.S. senator)

Evan Dando (singer)

Evan Longoria (baseball player)

Evan Lysacek (figure skater)

Bill Evans (pianist)

Evan Almighty (movie)

Ff

Felix

Meaning: Fortunate, happy

Origin: Latin

Related names and spelling variations:
Feliciano

Felix is a Latin name with one of the best meanings ever—"fortunate, happy." Who doesn't want a fortunate, happy kid? Combine that with the retro-chic Felix the Cat thing and you've got baby name *gold*. The name was used among Romans and early Christians, but surprisingly has not been especially popular in modern history. In the U.S., Felix was a top 200 name from 1880 through 1920. It has undergone a very slow but steady decline since then.

THIS NAME IN HISTORY

Felix the Cat (cartoon character)

Félix Hernández (baseball player)

Felix Jones (football player)

Felix Mendelssohn (composer)

Felix Unger (character in Neil Simon's
 The Odd Couple)

José Feliciano (singer)

Finn

Meaning: White

Origin: Irish

Related names and spelling variations:
Finnegan, Fionn

So way back in ancient Ireland, Fionn mac Cumhaill was a mythical warrior-hunter who gained all the knowledge in the world by tasting a magical fish, and killing a fire-breathing fairy monster. He supposedly still sleeps today in a cave below Dublin, waiting to defend his homeland. Can you imagine the chicks your Finn can pick up when he's in college by invoking his mythical namesake?

For what it's worth, Finn is also an Irish name that means "white." As part of the recent enthusiasm for Irish names, Finn entered the charts for the first time in 2000 at #834 and rose quickly. The character Finn on the hit TV show *Glee* may give the name another boost in years to come.

THIS NAME IN HISTORY

Finn Hudson (character on *Glee*)

Huckleberry Finn (character in Mark Twain's
 The Adventures of Tom Sawyer and
 Adventures of Huckleberry Finn)

Finnegans Wake (novel by James Joyce)

TOP TEN: COWBOYS

1. Willis (McCutcheon)
2. Burt (Mossman)
3. Abel (Head "Shanghai" Pierce)
4. Montford (T. Johnson)
5. Nat (Love)
6. Wilber (Emery "W. E." Campbell)
7. William ("Bill" Pickett)
8. Oliver (Loving)
9. Zachary (Taylor Miller)
10. John (Ware; Chisum; King Fisher)

Francis

Meaning: Frenchman

Origin: English; Spanish; Portuguese

Related names and spelling variations:
Francisco, Francesco, Frank, François

If the first "baby" in your house was of the four-legged variety, perhaps Francis is a good choice for a little (human) offspring. One of its most famous namesakes is St. Francis of Assisi—the patron saint of animals. It's also a good choice for Francophiles—it's an English name that means "Frenchman."

Francis is not a very widespread name these days, which may appeal to you if you like uncommon names. Today, Francisco, the Spanish version of the name, is much more popular in the U.S. than Francis itself.

THIS NAME IN HISTORY

St. Francis of Assisi (Catholic saint)

Francis Bacon (philosopher)

Francisco de Goya (artist)

Francis Ford Coppola (director)

Francisco Liriano (baseball player)

Francisco Pizarro (Spanish conquistador)

Francisco Rodriguez (baseball player)

Francis "Frank" Sinatra (singer)

Francisco Vásquez de Coronado
   (Spanish conquistador)

Frank

Meaning: Free person, landholder; Frenchman

Origin: French; English

Related names and spelling variations: *Franklyn, Frankie, Franco, Franklin*

Looking for a name with both cool origins and cool namesakes? Consider Frank. Frank is the English version of Francis, which means "Frenchman." The country of France takes its name from the Franks, some pretty tough warriors who settled that region of the world.

Frank's also got French roots and is related to the name Franklin, which means "free person," or "landholder." And we all want our kids to invest in real estate eventually, right? But then you've got the famous Franks: Sinatra! Zappa! What about the related name Franklin? There's Roosevelt and Benjamin! (Just forget all about Franklin, that annoying, whiny cartoon turtle.)

Frank has been a hugely popular name in the U.S. Between 1880 and 1970 it ranked in the top 50. It's been steadily declining since then.

THIS NAME IN HISTORY

Benjamin Franklin

Frankie Avalon (actor and singer)

Frankie Muniz (actor)

Franklin Pierce (U.S. president)

Franklin D. Roosevelt (U.S. president)

Franklin Templeton (investment company)

Frankie Valli (singer)

Frank Lloyd Wright (architect)

Frank Zappa (musician)

Frederick

Meaning: Peaceful leader

Origin: German

Related names and spelling variations: *Fred, Freddie, Freddy, Fritz, Frederik, Federico*

Frederick (and the nickname Fred) is somewhat confusing. Despite incredibly cool namesakes—Frederick Douglass, Fred Rogers, Fred Flintstone—the names are rarely picked by parents, with Frederick ranking #536 and Fred not making the list at all since 2002.

That's too bad, because the name's also got a wonderful meaning. It's a classic German moniker that means "peaceful leader," something the world needs plenty of, right? The name has been popular in Europe for quite a long time and it was common in the U.S. from 1880 through 1957, when it ranked in the top 100. We think it's time for a Frederick renaissance.

THIS NAME IN HISTORY

Fred Astaire (actor)

Frederick Douglass (statesman and abolitionist)

Fred Flintstone (cartoon character)

Frederick the Great (king of Prussia)

Freddie Mercury (musician)

Fred Rogers (TV personality)

Freddy Sanchez (baseball player)

Fred Segal (clothing retailer)

Hi, My Name Is

Gg

Gabriel

Meaning: God has given me strength; man of God

Origin: Hebrew

Related names and spelling variations: *Gabe*

Gabriel is a Hebrew name from the Bible that means "God has given me strength; man of God." The archangel Gabriel's most famous biblical appearance is as a sort of New Testament home pregnancy test, when he visits the Virgin Mary to tell her she's pregnant with Jesus. Despite the biblical connection, Gabriel has only recently become fashionable. Gabriel entered the top 100 for the first time in 1976 and has been gaining popularity since. If you like angels, another classic biblical archangel (and Ninja Turtle) is Raphael.

THIS NAME IN HISTORY

Gabriel Aubry (model)

Gabriel Byrne (actor)

Gabriel Elorde (boxer)

Gabriel Fauré (composer)

Gabriel García Márquez (author)

Gavin

Meaning: White hawk

Origin: Welsh

Related names and spelling variations: *Gavyn, Gavynn, Gavan, Gaven, Gawain*

Gavin may come from a Welsh name that means "white hawk." But an even better backstory for the moniker comes from an older version of the name, Gawain. A character from Arthurian legend, Gawain was pretty much the baddest knight of the Round Table. He was loyal to his king and family, a protector of the poor, a defender of women, and a healer with great knowledge of medicinal herbs.

But back to the more commonly used Gavin: The name debuted on the charts in 1954 and was only modestly popular until the late 1990s, when it reached the Top 150. It's quickly climbed the charts, likely due to the popularity of musicians Gavin DeGraw and Gavin Rossdale.

THIS NAME IN HISTORY

Gavin DeGraw (rock singer)

Gavin Floyd (baseball player)

Gavin MacLeod (actor)

TOP TEN: EIGHTIES CARTOON CHARACTERS

1. Kermit (*Muppet Babies*)
2. Optimus Prime (*Transformers*)
3. Ariel (*The Little Mermaid*)
4. Slimer (*Ghostbusters*)
5. Jem

6. G.I. Joe
7. She-Ra
8. Pac-Man
9. Raphael (*TMNT*)
10. Papa Smurf

Gavin Maxwell (naturalist)
Gavin Newsom (politician)
Gavin Rossdale (musician)
John Gavin (actor)

George

Meaning: Farmer

Origin: Greek

Related names and spelling variations: *Jorge, Georgios, Giorgio*

George is a name with a humble meaning but royal namesakes. George comes from the Greek name Georgios and means "farmer," but the six King Georges who have ruled England over the past few centuries were certainly not men of the soil. There are a number of other impressive namesakes to inspire parents, including the dragon-slayer and patron saint of England, St. George; U.S. presidents Washington and the Bushes; the Beatle (Harrison); actor Clooney; and even the loveable monkey Curious George. After being a top 10 name in the U.S. from the 1880s through 1937, George started a slow slide down the charts. Recently, Jorge, the Spanish George, has become the most popular version of the name in the U.S.

George H. W. Bush and George W. Bush
(former U.S. presidents)

George Carlin (comedian)

George Washington Carver (inventor
and scientist)

George Clooney (actor)

George Harrison (musician)

George Washington (first president of
the United States)

Boy George (singer)

Curious George (character in H. A.
and Margret Rey's *Curious George*)

St. George

Gerald

Meaning: Spear ruler

Origin: German

Related names and spelling variations: *Gerry, Geraldo, Jerold*

The name Gerald sounds like a pocket-protector-wearing science whiz, but the German name actually has a tough-guy meaning: "spear ruler." Over the last several centuries, the name Gerald has gone through quite a few cycles of popularity and obscurity in England. It has had a shorter, but similar, path here in the U.S. In 1880, Gerald ranked #586. Then it went through a period of popularity, ranking as high as #19, but started to decline again, finding its way back to the middle of the pack. The nickname Jerry is far more common today.

Gerald Ford (U.S. president)

Gerald Levert (singer)

Geraldo Rivera (commentator)

Gerald Wallace (basketball player)

Gilbert

Meaning: Bright pledge

Origin: German

Related names and spelling variations: *Gil, Bert, Gilby, Gilberto*

If Gilbert sounds a tad old-fashioned, that might be because it was popular waaay back in the Middle Ages. A German name that means "bright pledge," Gilbert was fairly popular in the U.S. at the end of the nineteenth century. At its peak, Gilbert ranked #91 in 1929 and 1930. Many old-fashioned names have gotten so popular that they don't really sound vintage anymore (Henry, for example). Gilbert still sounds a little antique, which is charming, and Gil is a cute, retro nickname to boot.

THIS NAME IN HISTORY

Gilbert Arenas (basketball player)

Gilbert Blythe (character in L. M.
Montgomery's *Anne of Green Gables*)

Gilbert Gottfried (actor)

Gil Hodges (baseball player)

W. S. Gilbert (musical composer, half of
the Gilbert and Sullivan team)

What's Eating Gilbert Grape (movie)

Grady

Meaning: Noble

Origin: Irish

Related names and spelling variations: *None*

While it doesn't guarantee future greatness, a name like Grady can't hurt. A name that comes from the Irish surname, Grady means "noble." Grady has had its ups and downs on the list of popular names in the U.S. It ranked #717 in 1888 and jumped to #298 the following year and spent the next five decades in the 200s and 300s. It was less popular from the 1950s to the early aughts and is now on the rise. It would be a great choice if you want to be on the early side of a possible name trend.

THIS NAME IN HISTORY

Grady Jackson (football player)

Grady Sizemore (baseball player)

Graham

Meaning: Gravelly place

Origin: Scottish

Related names and spelling variations:
Grahame, Graeme

Graham is a classic Scottish surname that means "gravelly place." The name goes back to at least the eleventh century. In the U.S., it's one of those names that has always been around, but has never been especially popular—until now, that is. Graham has been one of the fastest rising names on the boys' chart recently. It still has room to grow before it becomes truly popular, making it a great pick if you want to be ahead of the curve. If that's not enough, think of famed inventor Alexander Graham Bell. Similar dashing Scottish surname names are Grady, Brody, and Maxwell.

THIS NAME IN HISTORY

Graham Greene (author)

Graham Nash (singer)

Graham Norton (actor)

Graham Watanabe (snowboarder)

Kenneth Grahame (author)

Grant

Meaning: Large

Origin: Scottish

Related names and spelling variations: *None*

If you're hoping to have a larger-than-life kid, consider Grant. It's a surname with Scottish origins and it means "large." Maybe the "large" refers to his bank account, his trust fund from his great-aunt Gertrude, his sizable intellect, or his giant vintage vinyl collection.

Either way, this name might give him the cosmic boost he needs. In the U.S., Grant has spent most of the time since the 1880s hovering between the 200s and 300s. It made a leap up into the 100s in the 1980s and it's stayed there since then. Grant is a great one-syllable choice if you have longer last names or are looking for nickname-proof names.

Grant Balfour (baseball player)

Grant Green (musician)

Grant Hill (basketball player)

Grant Show (actor)

Grant Wood (artist)

Cary Grant (actor)

Ulysses S. Grant (U. S. general and president)

Grayson

Meaning: Son of the steward

Origin: English

Related names and spelling variations: *Graysen, Graysin, Greyson, Greysen, Greysin, Grey, Gray*

Grayson is an English surname that means "son of the steward." Historically, a steward was someone employed by a large estate to manage property or finances. Grayson would be a hip name if you're comic book fans, thanks to Dick Grayson, Robin's alter ego in *Batman*.

Today, Grayson is being used by parents as a stylish first name. The name has come full circle. In the U.S., Grayson appeared on the charts for the first time in 1984. The Greyson spelling appeared for the first time in 1995 and remains less common, but has been gaining popularity pretty quickly. Grayson is one of the coolest surname names today. Other similar picks are Carter, Brady, and Chase.

Grayson Capps (musician)

Grayson McCouch (actor)

Dick Grayson (Robin's alter ego in *Batman*)

Gregory

Meaning: Watchful

Origin: Greek

Related names and spelling variations: *Greg, Gregor*

There have been sixteen—count 'em—sixteen Pope Gregorys in the Catholic Church over the years, which might make your little Gregory an angel (or a holy terror). The name comes from the Greek Gregorios and means "watchful." The name was popular among early Christians and throughout the Middle Ages. In the U.S., Gregory has been consistently on the charts since 1892. It became a real favorite in 1950, when it reached the top 25. Gregory is a solid, classic name that doesn't sound stodgy. If you like something a little more offbeat, consider the German version Gregor or the Scottish McGregor.

Greg Brady (character on the TV show *The Brady Bunch*)

Gregory Hines (actor)

Greg Kinnear (actor)

Gregor Mendel (scientist)

Gregory Peck (actor)

1. Axl Rose (Guns N' Roses)

2. Nikki Sixx (Mötley Crüe)

3. Brett Michaels (Poison)

4. Jon Bon Jovi

5. Eddie Van Halen (Van Halen)

6. Freddie Mercury (Queen)

7. Tommy Lee (Mötley Crüe)

8. Rick Savage (Def Leppard)

9. C. C. DeVille (Poison)

10. Dee Snider (Twisted Sister)

Griffin

Meaning: Mythical creature

Origin: Greek

Related names and spelling variations: *Grif, Griffith*

In Greek mythology, a griffin is a creature with the body of a lion and the head and wings of an eagle. The association turned Griffin into a nickname for a fierce person, but the name sounds pretty cute today. As a name it certainly sounds sweeter than most other mythological creatures, such as the minotaur (half man, half bull) or the centaur (half man, half horse).

In the U.S., Griffin showed up on the charts for a few years at the end of the 1800s and the beginning of the 1900s. Then it dropped off the charts entirely until 1983. It peaked in 1998 at #215—the popular TV show *Party of Five* and the character named Griffin almost certainly helped there.

THIS NAME IN HISTORY

Griffin Dunne (actor)

Griffin Holbrook (character on the TV show *Party of Five*)

Griffin McIntyre (son of singer Joey McIntyre)

Kathy Griffin (comedian)

Griffin and Sabine (novel by Nick Bantock)

Hi, My Name Is

Hh

Harold

Meaning: Army leader

Origin: English

Related names and spelling variations: *Hal, Harry*

Harold is a traditional English name that means "army leader." It went through bouts of popularity, but never really caught on until the 1800s in England. The same happened here in the U.S. Harold was a top 100 name from 1884 through 1966. At its peak, it ranked #12 for a few years in the early 1900s, but has dropped quite a bit since then. Many vintage names like Charles and Henry are coming back into vogue these days. Maybe Harold is ready for a similar comeback? The nickname Hal *is* quite cool.

THIS NAME IN HISTORY

Hal 9000 (character in the *Space Odyssey* movies)

King Harold (king of England)

Harold Bloom (author)

Harold Ford Jr. (politician)

Hal Holbrook (actor)

Harry Potter (protagonist in J. K. Rowling's *Harry Potter* series)

Harry S. Truman (U.S. president)

Harold and Maude (movie)

Harold and the Purple Crayon (book by Crockett Johnson)

Hayden

Meaning: Hay valley

Origin: English

Related names and spelling variations: *Haiden, Haydan*

Hayden is one of those names in the middle of a boys vs. girls smackdown. The first year it made the list of popular names in the U.S. for girls, in 1998, it debuted at #836. That same year, it was #160 for boys, but the gap has closed considerably since then.

Although the name is still more widely used for boys, it remains to be seen how big an impact will come from female actor Hayden Panettiere, who starred in the TV show *Heroes* in 2006. Historically, for boys, Hayden had limited popularity on the U.S. charts at the end of the 1880s through the mid-1900s and then dropped off the charts entirely until 1986. It made a huge leap from 1989 to 1990 and has been increasing in popularity ever since.

For what it's worth, Hayden is an English location name that means "hay valley."

THIS NAME IN HISTORY

Hayden Carruth (poet)

Hayden Christensen (actor)

Hayden Panettiere (actor)

Hayden Turner (National Geographic Channel presenter)

Heath

Meaning: Wild land

Origin: English

Related names and spelling variations: *Heathcliff*

Heath is a rugged English habitation name that was given to people who lived near heaths—uncultivated, wild land. Perhaps the perfect name for free spirits? Heath first entered the U.S. charts in 1966. It peaked in 1974 at #181 and has decreased in popularity since then, although it may be on an upswing. Undoubtedly, the most famous Heath today is deceased actor Heath Ledger, and it is unclear what effect his untimely death will have on the name's popularity. Despite the fact that Heath is commonly used as a nickname for Heathcliff, that name has never ranked in the top 1,000 in the U.S.

THIS NAME IN HISTORY

Heath Ledger (actor)

Heathcliff (character in Emily Brontë's *Wuthering Heights*)

Heathcliff the Cat (cartoon character)

Henry

Meaning: Household ruler

Origin: German

Related names and spelling variations: *Henri, Enrique, Harry, Hank, Hal*

Just because the name Henry means "household ruler," doesn't mean you can't put little Hank on time-out for finger-painting the cat. The name has impressive royal cred, having been borne by eight kings of England. The most notorious namesake was King Henry VIII, who worked his way through six wives in pursuit of a son and inspired songs ("I'm Henry the VIII, I Am"), plays (*Henry VIII* by Shakespeare), and even modern TV shows (*The Tudors*).

Henry was a top 30 name in the U.S. from the 1880s through most of the 1930s. It went through a nerdy phase, but is now coming on strong and back in the top 100. Look for Henry to continue to rise up the charts as old-fashioned names continue to come back into vogue. Henry boasts a variety of cool nicknames too, including Hank, Harry, and Hal.

THIS NAME IN HISTORY

King Henry (king of England)

Prince Harry (prince of England)

Henry "Hank" Aaron (baseball player)

Henry "Hank" Azaria (actor)

Henry Fonda (actor)

Henry Ford (automobile innovator)

Henry Hudson (explorer)

Enrique Iglesias (singer)

Henry Kissinger (politician)

Henry David Thoreau (writer and
  philosopher)

Hank Williams (musician)

Holden

Meaning: Deep valley

Origin: English

Related names and spelling variations: *None*

Holden is an English surname that means "deep valley." Despite the popularity of J. D. Salinger's 1951 novel *The Catcher in the Rye* and its main character, Holden Caulfield, the name Holden didn't enter the U.S. charts until 1987, and has been increasing in popularity since then. Look for Holden to continue its climb. It fits into the same style of other rising names like Sawyer, Graham, and Walker. It's also a rare two-syllable name that doesn't have ready-made nicknames attached to it or many famous (or infamous) namesakes.

THIS NAME IN HISTORY

Holden Caulfield (character in J. D.
  Salinger's *The Catcher in the Rye*)

Hugo

Meaning: Heart, mind, spirit

Origin: German

Related names and spelling variations:
Hugh, Hubert

Hugo is the German form of the French name Hugh, which has an inspiring and optimistic definition—"heart, mind, spirit." Hugh was a popular given name in the Middle Ages. In the U.S., Hugh was initially much more popular, but recently Hugo has taken over. Hugo has that retro coolness about it that many parents find charming. Similarly styled names include Leo, Max, and Oscar. Perhaps Hugo is also due for a comeback?

THIS NAME IN HISTORY

Hugo Boss (fashion designer)

Hugh Dancy (actor)

Hugh Grant (actor)

Hugh Jackman (actor)

Hugh Laurie (actor)

Hugo "Hurley" Reyes (character on the
  TV show *Lost*)

The Invention of Hugo Cabret (novel by
  Brian Selznick)

Hunter

Meaning: Hunter

Origin: Old English

Related names and spelling variations: *None*

Hunter is another one of those names that is derived from an occupation. (Let's hope the name Stockbroker doesn't catch on.) In the Middle Ages, the name was typically used as a surname. The nobility class hunted boars from horseback; the lower castes snatched birds. Your little Hunter will stalk the noble fruit snack.

The name has had a choppy history on the charts. Most names have a fluid rise and fall between years, but Hunter started at #545 in 1880, dropped to #826 in 1881, rose to #623 in 1882, dropped to #841 the next year, and so on for the next several decades. It even dropped off the charts

1. Leif (Ericson)

2. Christopher (Columbus)

3. Vasco (da Gama)

4. Henry (Hudson)

5. Hernan (Cortez)

6. Ferdinand (Magellan)

7. Mungo (Park)

8. Isabella (Bird)

9. Valentina (Tereshkova)

10. Reinhold (Messner)

entirely in the mid-1930s. It was a continuous presence starting again in 1956 and has made a steady climb upward, reaching its peak in 2000 and slipping slowly since then. Hunter is part of the group of similarly styled names that are hot with parents today, including Sawyer, Cooper, and Wyatt.

THIS NAME IN HISTORY

Hunter Parrish (actor)
Hunter S. Thompson (journalist)
Tab Hunter (actor and singer)
Hunter (TV series)

Hi, My Name Is

Ii

Ian

Meaning: God is gracious

Origin: Scotland

Related names and spelling variations: *Iain, Ean, Ayaan*

There are approximately forty zillion international versions of the name John (okay, maybe a few dozen) and Ian is the Scottish variety. Popular with religious and traditional parents, John means "God is gracious." Ian is a great choice if you're looking for Scottish names or a clever way to honor a John in your family and yet remain a little unique. (We also like the rare "I" initial too.) Ian found its way to the U.S. charts for the first time in 1935. It's been in the top 100 since 1982 and has hovered between the 60s and 80s ever since.

THIS NAME IN HISTORY

Ian Anderson (musician)

Ian Astbury (singer)

Ian Fleming (author)

Ian Frazier (author)

Ian Kinsler (baseball player)

Ian Laperrière (hockey player)

Ian McEwan (author)

Sir Ian McKellan (actor)

Ian Ziering (actor)

Isaac

Meaning: To laugh

Origin: Hebrew

Related names and spelling variations: *Issac, Isaak, Ike*

In the Old Testament, Isaac was the poor tyke whose dad (Abraham) was going to sacrifice him as proof of his devotion, but was saved by an angel at the last minute. (Which leads one to wonder what Isaac's mom said when they got home that day. *Yeeaaah.* Not pleased.)

Isaac also has Hebrew origins and means "to laugh," which is a much more cheerful association, so let's stick to that one. Isaac also has great namesakes from many disciplines—there's Sir Isaac Newton the scientist, Isaac Mizrahi the fashion designer, and Isaac Asimov the science-fiction writer, to name a few. In the U.S., Isaac was a top 100 name for most of the late 1800s. It declined in popularity, but parents started liking it again in the 1970s. Today, it's very popular. Ike makes for a cool, retro nickname.

Isaac Asimov (scientist and author)

Isaac Bruce (football player)

Ike Davis (baseball player)

Dwight "Ike" Eisenhower (U.S. president)

Isaac Hanson (singer)

Isaac Hayes (singer)

Isaac Mizrahi (fashion designer)

Sir Isaac Newton (scientist)

Isaac Singer (founder of the Singer Sewing Machine Company)

Isaac Slade (singer)

Isaiah

Meaning: God is salvation

Origin: Hebrew

Related names and spelling variations: *Isiah, Izaiah, Izayah, Izaiah, Isaias, Isai*

Isaiah is another old-fashioned biblical name that's climbing the charts today. (Perhaps today's parents are a tad bit too optimistic about their little angels?) Either way, Isaiah is a Hebrew name that means "God is salvation" and was borne by one of the most notable biblical prophets. Despite the connection, Isaiah was not an overly popular given name until recently. Even though it's been on the U.S. charts since the 1880s, it didn't break into the top 100 for the first time until 1996. Other variations are popular with U.S. parents: Izaiah, Isaias, Isiah, Isai, and Izayah.

THIS NAME IN HISTORY

Isaiah Berlin (philosopher and historian)

Isiah Thomas (basketball player)

Isaiah Washington (actor)

Jj

Jack

Meaning: God is gracious

Origin: English

Related names and spelling variations: *Jak, Jackson, Jaxon, Jaxson, Jax, Jackie*

You'll find no shortage of children's books with your kid's name in them if you choose Jack. Think about Jack Sprat, Jack and the Beanstalk, and Little Jack Horner. Fun! Jack is a snappy nickname for John, which means "God is gracious." Even though it began as a nickname, it's become a full-fledged first name in its own right and quite popular at that. Jack has spent most of the years since the 1880s in the top 100 and has ranked in the top 50 since 2000.

The related name Jackson literally means "Jack's son." It broke into the top 100 for the first time in 1998 and has been quickly climbing since then. Now, it's slightly more popular than Jack. If you like the letter *X*, you might be drawn to one of these variations: Jaxon, Jaxson, Jax, and Jaxen.

THIS NAME IN HISTORY

Jack Black (actor)

Jackie Chan (actor)

Jack Johnson (musician)

Jack Kerouac (author)

Jack London (author)

Jack Nicholson (actor)

Jack Nicklaus (golfer)

Jackson Pollock (artist)

Captain Jack Sparrow (character in the *Pirates of the Caribbean* movies)

Michael Jackson

Jacob

Meaning: Supplanter, heel-grabber

Origin: Hebrew

Related names and spelling variations: *Jacoby, Jakob, Jakobe, Jake, Jaycob*

Jacob has been the #1 boy's name in the U.S. since 1999, and to get to the bottom of the name's origin you have to open up a whole mess of Old Testament. (It means "supplanter," or "heel grabber.") Jacob apparently had a bit of a competitive streak and was born holding his twin brother's heel. Later Jacob cons his twin into parting with his inheritance in exchange for a bowl of soup and tricks his blind father into blessing *him* instead of his twin.

But it's also just a really sweet name. You could call him Jakey. The name has been popular with parents for centuries, yet it still sounds fresh and young today. The most popular nickname for Jacob is Jake, which has become a popular given name in its own right.

THIS NAME IN HISTORY

Jacob Black (character in Stephenie Meyer's *Twilight* series)

Jakob Dylan (musician and son of Bob Dylan)

Jake Gyllenhaal (actor)

Jacob Marley (character in Charles Dickens's *A Christmas Carol*)

Jake Plummer (football player)

James

Meaning: Supplanter, heel-grabber

Origin: English

Related names: *Jim, Jameson, Jem, Jimmy, Séamas, Shamus, Jamie, Jacques, Giacomo, Diego, Iago, Hamish*

Even though they sound nothing alike, James is the English version of the name Jacob (which means "supplanter" or "heel-grabber"). No one probably called them "Jimmy," but there were two King Jameses in England, seven monarchs in Scotland, and two in Spain.

James also happens to be one of the most popular boy's names of all time, in the top 20 for the past century. James is also one of the few truly ageless names—when you hear it, you don't know whether the person referred to is six or sixty.

King James (several English and
  Scottish kings)

James Bond (fictional character
  created by Ian Fleming)

James Cameron (director)

Jim Carrey (comedian and actor)

James Dean (actor)

James Franco (actor)

James Madison (U.S. president)

Jim Morrison (musician)

James Taylor (singer)

Jared

Meaning: Descent

Origin: Hebrew

Related names and spelling variations: *Jarod, Jarred, Jarrod*

Jared is a Hebrew name that means "descent." Jared sounds like the quintessential 1960s or 1970s name, but it actually has ancient biblical roots. Jared is a figure from the Book of Genesis who reportedly lived for nearly a thousand years. In the U.S., Jared made the charts in 1881, but then dropped off and didn't become a regular fixture until 1950. It made a big jump in the 1960s and again in the 1970s, making it to the top 100.

THIS NAME IN HISTORY

Jared Allen (football player)

Jared Fogle (TV personality)

Jared Leto (actor)

Jared Padalecki (actor)

Jarrod Washburn (baseball player)

Jason

Meaning: Healer

Origin: Greek

Related names and spelling variations: *Jayson*

Jason is a Greek name that means "healer." Perhaps a good name to choose if you want him to be a doctor? Or if you're hoping to inspire an adventurer, you can look to the hero of Greek mythology, who went after the Golden Fleece battling Harpies and Sirens along the way.

Jason remains one of the most familiar and accessible of all the mythology names. In the U.S., it has been in the top 1,000 for all but one year since 1880. It entered the top 10 in 1971 and was the #2 name between 1974 and 1978, even inspiring baby name books like *Beyond Jennifer and Jason*. It's still quite popular with parents today.

THIS NAME IN HISTORY

Jason Aldean (singer)

Jason Bateman (actor)

Jason Kidd (basketball player)

Jason Lee (actor)

Jason Mraz (singer)

Jason Reitman (director)

Jason Segel (actor)

Jasper

Meaning: Horse rider; treasure keeper; imperial

Origin: Persian; Greek; German; Semitic

Related names and spelling variations: *None*

TOP TEN: NOBEL PEACE PRIZE WINNERS

1. Henry/Henri (Kissinger; Dunant; La Fontaine)
2. Albert (Lutuli; Schweitzer; Charles Albert Gobat)
3. Karl/Carl (Hjalmar Branting; von Ossietzky; Linus Carl Pauling)
4. Desmond (Tutu)
5. Elie/Élie (Wiesel; Ducommun)
6. Mohamed (ElBaradei)
7. George/Georges (Catlett Marshall; Pire)
8. Martin (Luther King Jr.)
9. Frédéric/Fredrik (Passy; Bajer; De Klerk)
10. Nelson (Mandela)

Jasper is a Persian name that has roots in the name Casper, which has a variety of meanings, including "horse rider," "treasure keeper," and "imperial," giving you several definitions to choose from when the in-laws ask, "What the heck does that mean?"

Jasper gained some popularity in the Middle Ages, but has never been overly common. In the U.S., it has been on the charts since 1880, when it ranked #139. It declined in popularity in the following years and hovered between the 600s and 700s for most of the 1960s through 1990s.

Then, a little vampire book (Stephenie Meyer's *Twilight*) hit the shelves in 2005 with the popular character Jasper Hale. Combine that with the fact that starlets Brad Paisley and Kimberly Williams Paisley named their son Jasper in 2009 and—kapow—Jasper became one of the year's top movers.

THIS NAME IN HISTORY

Jasper Johns (artist)

Jasper Hale (character in Stephenie Meyer's *Twilight* series)

Jasper Warren (son of Brad Paisley and Kimberly Williams Paisley)

Jay

Meaning: Bird

Origin: Latin

Related names and spelling variations: *Jai*

This short-but-sweet name isn't just for the birds. It's a stand-alone boy's name in its own right, as well as a nickname for many other *J* names like James, Jayden, and Jason. It has soared to some lofty heights; in the U.S., Jay was a top 200 name for most of the twentieth century, peaking in 1960. Perhaps the bird is flying the coop, however, as it's been dropping in popularity since the eighties.

THIS NAME IN HISTORY

Jay Leno (comedian)

Jai Rodriguez (TV personality)

Jay Sean (singer)

Jayden

Meaning: God has heard

Origin: Hebrew

Related names and spelling variations: *Jadin, Jadan, Jadon, Jaydon, Jaiden, Jaydin, Jaiden, Jaeden, Jaidyn, Jayden, Jadyn, Jaydan*

Parents love this pleasingly preppy name for boys or girls. Its raging success can be attributed to both Will Smith and Britney Spears choosing it for their babies, which is why many write this name off as a celebrity invention like Zuma or Pilot Inspektor. But Jayden has historical heft, having roots in the Hebrew name Jadon, which means "God has heard." He heard it—but can He spell it? Jayden currently has twelve spelling variants: Jadin, Jadan, Jadon, Jaydon, Jaiden, Jaydin, Jaiden, Jaeden, Jaidyn, Jayden, Jadyn, and Jaydan.

THIS NAME IN HISTORY

Jayden James Federline (son of Britney Spears and Kevin Federline)

Jayden Lund (actor)

Jaden Smith (actor, son of Will and Jada Pinkett Smith)

Jeffrey

Meaning: God's peace

Origin: English

Related names and spelling variations: *Geoffrey, Jeffery, Jeffree, Jeffry, Jeff, Geoff*

This dignified English name may be a derivative of the German name Gottfried, which means "God's peace." It's been a much-loved name for centuries, from the Middle Ages (Geoffrey Chaucer, author of the *Canterbury Tales*) to today (Jeffrey Bezos, founder of Amazon.com), and hit its high point in the 1960s in the U.S. Lately, it's suffered from declining numbers (thanks, Jeffrey Dahmer). The fancier, more anglicized Geoffrey spelling might be the contemporary twist this old classic needs.

THIS NAME IN HISTORY

Jeffrey Archer (author)

Jeffrey Bezos (founder of Amazon.com)

Jeff Bridges (actor)

Geoffrey Chaucer (author)

Geoffrey the Giraffe (Toys "R" Us mascot)

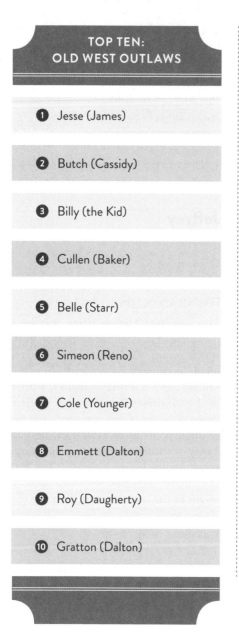

**TOP TEN:
OLD WEST OUTLAWS**

1. Jesse (James)
2. Butch (Cassidy)
3. Billy (the Kid)
4. Cullen (Baker)
5. Belle (Starr)
6. Simeon (Reno)
7. Cole (Younger)
8. Emmett (Dalton)
9. Roy (Daugherty)
10. Gratton (Dalton)

Jeff Goldblum (actor)
Jeffery Michael Gordon (NASCAR driver)
Jeff Probst (reality TV star)
Jeffrey Tambor (actor)
Jeffrey Toobin (journalist)

Jeremiah

Meaning: May God praise him

Origin: Hebrew

Related names and spelling variations:
Jeramiah, Jerimiah, Jerremiah

Jeremiah was a bullfrog? No, Jeremiah was a major prophet of the Old Testament who warned the people of Israel about disasters but was unheeded (hence the term "jeremiad"—a long, cautionary complaint). It derives from the Hebrew for "may God praise him." The name was popular among the Puritans in the 1500s, who were happy to name their children after a prophet of doom. In the U.S., Jeremiah has been a steady presence on the charts since the 1880s, but never overly popular. Jeremiah broke into the top 100 in 2001. Other spellings include Jeramiah and Jerimiah.

THIS NAME IN HISTORY

Jeremiah "Jerry" O'Connell (actor)

Jeremiah Tower (chef)

Joy to the World (aka "Jeremiah was a Bullfrog," song by Hoyt Axton and Three Dog Night)

Jeremy

Meaning: May God praise him

Origin: English

Related names and spelling variations:
Jeramee, Jeramey, Jeramie, Jereme, Jeremie, Jeromy, Jerry, Jem

Jeremy is an English form of the name Jeremiah, the aforementioned fire-and-brimstone prophet of the Old Testament. In the U.S., Jeremy first found its way onto the charts in 1942, leaping into the top 50 in 1971 and staying there until 1995. It's been in decline since then. One of the main characters in Harper Lee's *To Kill a Mockingbird* is named Jeremy, but he goes by Jem—a pretty cool nickname, though maybe a little close to Jame of *The Silence of the Lambs* infamy. The upside would be saying to your son, "Honey, you're such a Jem!"

THIS NAME IN HISTORY

Jeremy Affeldt (baseball player)

Jeremy Bentham (philosopher)

Jeremy "Jem" Finch (character in Harper Lee's *To Kill a Mockingbird*)

Jeremy Irons (actor)

Jeremy Northam (actor)

Jeremy Piven (actor)

Jeremy Renner (actor)

Jeremy Shockey (football player)

"Jeremy" (song by Pearl Jam)

Jerome

Meaning: Holy name

Origin: Greek

Related names and spelling variations:
Jerry, Geronimo

There's a pretty wide range of celebrities that could spur you to name your son Jerome. It has its roots in Greek, coming from the name Hieronymus (as in Hieronymus Bosch, the painter) and means "holy name." Bosch famously painted the sufferings of sinners in hell, but there's a contemporary source with a considerably more playful outlook. In *Seinfeld*, Elaine sometimes called Jerry Jerome, because Jerome is actually Jerry Seinfeld's given name. It's also the name of St. Jerome, who is credited with translating the Bible into Latin for the first time. Jerome has been on the U.S. charts since 1880, entering the top 100 in the late 1930s. It dropped a little after that, but remained in the top 200 until 1986. It's declined since then, making it a perfect pick if you like uncommon names.

THIS NAME IN HISTORY

Jerome Bettis (football player)

Jerome Brown (football player)

Jerome Harrison (football player)

Jerome K. Jerome (author)

Jerome Kern (composer)

Jerome "Jerry" Seinfeld (comedian)

TOP TEN: FAMOUS MALE IRISH WRITERS

1. James (Joyce)
2. Oscar (Wilde)
3. Jonathan (Swift)
4. William (Butler Yeats)
5. Samuel (Beckett)
6. George (Bernard Shaw)
7. Wystan (Hugh Auden)
8. Clive (Staples Lewis)
9. Brian (Friel)
10. John (Banville)

Jesse

Meaning: Gift

Origin: Hebrew

Related names and spelling variations: *Jessie*

If you're looking for a name to symbolize what a blessing your baby is in your life, then consider Jesse. Jesse is a Hebrew name that means "gift." Though it's also a biblical name, its more recent associations are likely to be with the African-American athlete who showed up Hitler in the Berlin Olympics (Jesse Owens) or with the outlaw Jesse James or the sometimes controversial politician Reverend Jesse Jackson. In the U.S., Jesse has been a steady favorite, but was actually at its most popular in the 1880s, peaking at #26 in 1882. It's spent much of the time since then in the top 100.

THIS NAME IN HISTORY

Rev. Jesse Jackson (politician and activist)

Jesse James (Wild West figure)

Jesse James (reality TV star)

Jesse Louis Lasky Sr. (founder of Paramount Pictures)

Jesse McCartney (singer)

Jesse Owens (track and field athlete)

Jesse Ventura (former Minnesota governor and professional wrestler)

"Jesse's Girl" (song by Rick Springfield)

Jett

Meaning: Jet

Origin: Latin

Related names and spelling variations: *Jet*

It's not a bird, but it is a plane, and jet is also a type of coal used in making jewelry and beads. Somehow we don't think either of those meanings are what's motivating parents to choose the name Jett lately. Face it: it just looks and sounds cool, and with Joan Jett the rocker, little girl or boy Jetts are born ready to pick up a guitar. Jett made its debut in 1999 at #794 and has been climbing the charts since.

THIS NAME IN HISTORY

Jett Jackson (character on the TV show *The Famous Jett Jackson*)

Jett Lucas (son of George Lucas)

Jet McCoy (realty TV star)

Jett Travolta (son of Kelly Preston and John Travolta)

Joan Jett (musician)

"Jet" (Wings song)

Jet (band)

Joaquin

Meaning: Given by God

Origin: Spanish

Related names and spelling variations: *Joachim*

The name Joachim is legendary—literally. Even though he's not named in the Bible, medieval legend has it that the Virgin Mary's father is named Joachim. (Mary's mom? Anne.) Joaquin is the Spanish version of the name Joachim, meaning "given by God." It made a brief appearance on the U.S. charts at the turn of the last century, but didn't become a permanent fixture until the 1940s. It has been increasing in popularity since then and has become more popular than ever before, with actor Joaquin Phoenix's notoriety helping give parents the idea.

THIS NAME IN HISTORY

Joaquín Andújar (baseball player)

Joaquin Miller (poet)

Joaquin Murrieta (Wild West figure)

Joaquin Phoenix (actor)

Joel

Meaning: Yahweh is God

Origin: Hebrew

Related names and spelling variations: *Joell, Yoel*

Though you might be tempted to name your son Joel Billy, your son would probably resent it. Despite the rock-and-roll associations, Joel is actually a biblical name with Hebrew origins meaning "Yahweh is God." It's been popular with religious parents for centuries, hitting its high points between the 1960s and 1980s. Since then it's floated around the low 100s, where it sits today. Joel is a good short name choice if you're looking to balance longer last names, but remember how easy it is for schoolyard bullies to rhyme one-syllable names.

THIS NAME IN HISTORY

Joel Coen (screenwriter and producer)

Joel Gray (actor)

Joel Lundqvist (hockey player)

Joel McHale (TV personality)

Joel Schumacher (screenwriter, director, and producer)

Billy Joel (singer)

John

Meaning: God is gracious

Origin: Hebrew

Related names and spelling variations: *Johan, Johnny, Juan, Gianni, Giovanni, Giovani, Giovanny, Jovanny, Jovaanni, Jean, Jovany, Geovanni, Jan*

You know a name is popular when it can be used *twice* as a nickname (John-John Kennedy Jr.). What can you say about the name John that hasn't been said before? It's a Hebrew name that means "God is gracious" and is one of the most popular names of all time. Since 1880, John has spent many years ranked #1 in the U.S. and has never dropped below #26. The name is so popular that many of the international variations have also made

the U.S. top 1,000, including: Evan, Juan, Ian, Sean, Giovanni, Ivan, Johan, and Gianni.

THIS NAME IN HISTORY

John the Baptist (biblical figure)

John Denver (musician)

John Donne (poet)

John Elway (football player)

John Lennon (singer)

John Locke (philosopher)

John F. Kennedy (U.S. president)

John F. Kennedy Jr. (aka John-John)

John Updike (author)

John Woo (director)

Gospel of John (one of the four Gospels in the Bible)

Jonah

Meaning: Dove

Origin: Hebrew

Related names and spelling variations: *Jonas*

Jonah is a biblical name with a fashionable (though still not entirely trendy) feel to it. It also means "dove," a traditional symbol of peace, love, and fidelity. (In the Bible, a dove brings Noah a sign that the Great Flood is over by carrying an olive branch to the ark in its mouth). Then there's the story of Jonah being swallowed by the fish—one of the most famous biblical stories (but possibly something your son would be teased about on the schoolyard). Jonah was a fairly steady presence on the U.S. charts in the late 1800s, but then fell off entirely until 1970. It's been slowly climbing, getting a boost in 1994, the year after *Sleepless in Seattle* came out—the adorable boy in the movie is named Jonah—and has kept on rising.

The name Jonas, meanwhile, lost quite a bit of ground between 2008 and 2009: 105 spots. That's quite a lot for one year—and especially surprising because of the popularity of the Jonas Brothers. Boy band backlash?

THIS NAME IN HISTORY

Jonah (biblical figure)

Jonah (character in *Sleepless in Seattle*)

Jonah Bayliss (baseball player)

Jonah Hill (actor)

J. Jonah Jameson (character in *Spider-Man* comics and movies)

Jonah Lehrer (author)

Jonah Winter (author)

Jonathan

Meaning: God's gift

Origin: Hebrew

Related names and spelling variations: *Johnathon, Jonathon, Johnathan, Jon*

Jonathan is a Hebrew name that means "God's gift," thus inspiring many overjoyed parents to pick it. More than one biblical figure has the name, also contributing to the name's popularity over the years as well. In the U.S., Jonathan has had a long run in the top 50, starting back in 1969, in part piggy-backing on the popularity of John, but having a

softer and more sophisticated sound to many parents' ears. (Do note, though, that Jonathan typically shortens to Jon instead of John, a fact many parents don't like.) Jonathan has been on a slight downward slide the last few years.

NAME FACTOID

Jonathan is made up of the same etymologic elements as the name Matthew, but in reverse order. That gives Jonathan and Matthew great potential as twins' names—the names have a meaningful connection, but aren't too overtly matched.

THIS NAME IN HISTORY

Johnathan Buck (baseball player)

Jon Gosselin (TV personality)

Jonathan Rhys Meyers (actor)

Jon Scieszka (author)

Jonathan Swift (author)

Jonathan Taylor Thomas (actor)

Jordan

Meaning: To flow down

Origin: Hebrew

Related names and spelling variations: *Jorden, Jordyn, Jordon*

Another name, like Joel, perhaps more famous for someone's last name than first (Air Jordan, anyone?). Jordan was the river where John the Baptist baptized Jesus, making it a popular pilgrimage site—and a popular baby name. Jordan has Hebrew origins and means "to flow down." For all but a few years since 1880, Jordan has been in the top 1,000 names for boys in

1. Friedrich (Nietzsche)

2. Wyatt (Earp)

3. Lech (Wałęsa)

4. Wilford (Brimley)

5. Chester (A. Arthur)

6. Baxter (Black)

7. Snazin (Smith)

8. Rudyard (Kipling)

9. Franz (Ferdinand, archduke of Austria)

10. Otto (von Bismarck)

the U.S. It reached the top 100 in the early 1980s and peaked at #26 in 1997. Also on the list are Jorden, Jordyn, and Jordon.

In the late 1970s, parents started using the name for their daughters. It even ranked in the top 100 from the end of the 1980s to 2007, but has started to drop. The Jordyn spelling has become the most popular for girls today, remaining in the girl's top 1,000. As it becomes a more popular girl's name, it's likely to lose popularity as a name for boys.

THIS NAME IN HISTORY

Jordan Farmar (basketball player)

Jordan Knight (singer)

Jordin Sparks (singer)

Michael Jordan (basketball player)

Jordan (Middle Eastern country)

River Jordan

Joseph

Meaning: God shall add

Origin: Hebrew

Related names and spelling variations: *Josef, Yosef, Joseph, Jose, Joe, Joey*

We say "your average Joe," but of course no two are the same. Joseph is a strong, classic name. It's from the Hebrew for "God shall add" and is generally thought to mean that God shall add another son— perhaps a good choice if you're hoping to have more? Its popularity may be due to the several Josephs in the Bible, including the Virgin Mary's husband and Joseph of

Arimathea, the person who took Jesus's body down from the cross after the crucifixion. The name became popular in the 1600s in England and, needless to say, Joseph is one of the most popular names in U.S. history. It has ranked in the top 15 for all but three years since 1880—each of those years it ranked #16. José, the Spanish version of the name, is also quite popular. Nicknames Joe and Joey have started showing up as independent names.

THIS NAME IN HISTORY

Joe Biden (U.S. vice president)

Joseph Conrad (author)

Joe DiMaggio (baseball player)

Joseph Heller (author)

Joseph Gordon-Levitt (actor)

Joe Jonas (singer)

Joey Lawrence (actor)

Joseph (several biblical figures)

Joseph and the Amazing Technicolor Dreamcoat (musical)

Joshua

Meaning: God is salvation

Origin: Hebrew

Related names and spelling variations: *Josue, Josh, Jesus*

Joshua, the given name of a host of young, studly actors these days, is a Hebrew name that means "God is salvation." The name has been around since the Bible—Joshua led the Israelites to the Promised Land after Moses's death. In the U.S., Joshua has been on the charts since 1880, but

was only moderately popular. It made big leaps in the 1960s and continued to rise, having been in the top 10 ever since. Joshua is part of the group of *J* names that parents today are so fond of, including Jacob, Joseph, Jayden, James, John, Justin, Jonathan, and Jordan.

NAME FACTOID

Among the hottest boys' names today, *J* shows up as the most common first letter—Jacob, Joshua, Jayden, Joseph, and James are all among the top choices.

THIS NAME IN HISTORY

Joshua Bell (violinist)

Josh Brolin (actor)

Josh Duhamel (actor)

Josh Groban (singer)

Josh Hartnett (actor)

Josh Holloway (actor)

Joshua Jackson (actor)

Joshua Rifkin (conductor)

Josiah

Meaning: God's fire, God heals

Origin: Hebrew

Related names and spelling variations: *Jos, Josias, Jasiah*

Josiah is a Hebrew name that means "God's fire" or "God heals"—lending the name both passion and compassion. Josiah was on the U.S. charts at the end of the 1800s, but then dropped off completely for all but a few years until 1975. It's been quickly moving up the charts since then and reached the top 100 in

2008, helped along by the 1999 debut of *The West Wing* and the presidential character Josiah Bartlet. Josiah is a fresher alternative to some of the more common *J* names like Jacob, Jayden, and John. Note, however, that one possible nickname, Josey, could lead to associations with the character or film *The Outlaw Josey Wales*.

THIS NAME IN HISTORY
Josiah Bartlet (character on the TV show *The West Wing*)
Josiah Wedgwood (potter)

Jude

Meaning: Praised

Origin: Greek

Related names and spelling variations: *Judah, Judd*

Jude is a nickname for the names Judah and Judas. It means "praised" and has become a full name in its own right. The name Judas belongs to the most notorious figure of the New Testament, Judas Iscariot, who betrayed Jesus (this obviously didn't make it popular among some religious groups). Jude started to shed that biblical baggage when it entered the U.S. charts in 1954. It spent most of the next few decades hovering between the 700s and 900s. Despite the Beatles song, it dropped off the charts again at the end of the 1980s and didn't reappear until 1996. The name is on the rise now and gaining popularity quickly. Jude has been one of the top movers on the U.S. charts recently, no doubt because of handsome and talented actor Jude Law.

Jude Deveraux (author)

Jude Law (actor)

"Hey Jude" (song by the Beatles)

Jude the Obscure (novel by Thomas Hardy)

Julian

Meaning: Youthful

Origin: Latin

Related names and spelling variations: *Julius, Julio, Julien*

Julian is Latin and comes from the name Julius, which means "youthful." Caesar was the most famous Julius ever (ironically, he was stabbed to death while still pretty youthful), and though he has the classic salad named after him, it's unlikely he's responsible for the mall-stand dessert classic the Orange Julius. Julian, the more common version today, has remained relatively popular since 1880, getting some help from John Lennon's son Julian having a few rock hits of his own. Julian landed in the top 100 for the first time in 2000 and has continued its way up the list, along with its root name Julius.

NAME FACTOID

The name Julian was used for both boys and girls before the sixteenth century. Since the 1500s it's been considered a boy's name, and girls are named the feminine versions Gillian, Jill, and Julia.

THIS NAME IN HISTORY

Julian Bream (musician)

Julian Casablancas (singer)

Julian Lennon (singer and son of John Lennon)

Julian Marley (singer and son of Bob Marley)

Julian McMahon (actor)

Julian Peterson (football player)

Julian Schwinger (Nobel Prize winner)

Justin

Meaning: Honorable, just

Origin: Latin

Related names and spelling variations: *Justus, Justyn, Justen*

This just in (couldn't resist)—Justin comes from the Latin name Justus, not surprisingly meaning "honorable" or "just." Justin has been a steady fixture on the top 1,000 since the late 1880s, but didn't hit the top 10 until 1987, where it stayed for four years. It's been slipping recently, though with the popularity of smooth-dancing pop star Justin Timberlake, it's likely to rise again. Justin would be a good pick if you're spelling purists—unlike other popular names that have spurred a variety of alternate spellings, the only spelling of this name in the 2009 top 1,000 is the traditional one.

THIS NAME IN HISTORY

Justin Hayward (musician)

Justin Lin (director)

Justin Long (actor)

Justin Miller (football player)

Justin Timberlake (singer)

Justin Tuck (football player)

Justin Wilson (chef and TV personality)

Kk

Keith

Meaning: Wood

Origin: Scottish

Related names and spelling variations: *None*

The name Keith has been around even longer than Keith Richards—and it's clearly aging much better. It started as a Scottish surname meaning "wood," but parents started using it as a first name in the 1800s. It's been quite popular ever since, first finding its way onto the U.S. charts in 1888. It continued to grow in popularity through the 1960s, reaching its peak in 1966 at #32, and declining after that. Keith is a good one-syllable choice if you like nickname-proof names (though note that it rhymes with "teeth," so be careful if your family has a history of dental abnormalities!). Keith is also a good choice if you like Scottish names but prefer not to use the trendier choices like Logan, Maxwell, or Brody.

THIS NAME IN HISTORY

Keith Carradine (actor)

Keith Haring (artist)

Keith Olbermann (news commentator)

Keith Richards (musician)

Keith Urban (musician)

Kellen

Meaning: Slender

Origin: Irish

Related names and spelling variations: *Kellan, Kellin, Kell*

Kellen is a cool-sounding Irish name that means "slender." It's a recent entry on the U.S. charts—despite fewer and fewer kids in America actually being slim—first appearing in 1981 at #617. It made small moves up and down the charts for a few years, but is getting more popular now. The current boost is likely helped by two things—the continued search for attractive, accessible Irish names and some good, old-fashioned star power in Kellan Lutz (of *Twilight* fame). But since the Kellen craze isn't in full swing yet, choosing it soon could put you slightly ahead of the name trend. But also be aware of the teasing limerick potential. *"I once knew a fellow named Kellen . . ."*

Kellen Hathaway (actor)

Kellan Lutz (actor)

Kellen Winslow (football player)

Kenneth

Meaning: Handsome

Origin: Gaelic

Related names and spelling variations:
Kennith, Kenny, Ken

Despite the not-exactly-George-Clooney looks of actor and director Kenneth Branagh, the name Kenneth means "handsome" in Gaelic. It was also the name of a king from the ninth century: Kenneth mac Alpin. Associations with handsomeness and royalty—that's quite a bit to recommend a name. In the U.S., Kenneth reached the top 100 in 1898 and stayed there until 2002. Not many names can claim the same enduring popularity. It's seen a small drop in recent years, but is still respectably popular. Affable nickname Kenny is a popular choice in its own right—though you wouldn't want your son to meet the various fates of cartoon Kenny of *South Park*!

THIS NAME IN HISTORY

Kenneth Dwane "Sox" Bowersox (astronaut)

Kenneth Branagh (actor)

Kenneth Cole (fashion designer)

Kenneth "Babyface" Edmonds (singer)

Kenneth Grahame (author)

Kenneth "Kenny" Loggins (singer)

Kenneth "Kenny" Rogers (singer)

Kenny of *South Park*

TOP TEN:
FAMOUS PAINTERS

1. Leonardo (da Vinci)
2. Michelangelo
3. Pablo (Picasso)
4. Salvador (Dalí)
5. Claude (Monet)
6. Frida (Kahlo)
7. Vincent (van Gogh)
8. Henri (Matisse)
9. René (Magritte)
10. Georgia (O'Keeffe)

Kevin

Meaning: Attractive

Origin: Gaelic

Related names and spelling variations: *Kev, Keven*

Does naming your child Kevin put you one degree closer to Kevin Bacon? Sadly, no, though Kevin does seem to be an especially common name among actors of the last generation. Perhaps it's no surprise, as Kevin is a Gaelic name that means "attractive"—more than appropriate for silver screen good looks. The name has been attractive on these shores as well, entering the top 1,000 list in 1921. It was moderately popular for the next couple decades and then reached the top 50 in the 1950s, where it has remained. Kevin is one of the rare popular names that has not inspired *too* many alternative spellings—Keven is the only other variation of Kevin that has appeared in the top 1,000 in recent years.

THIS NAME IN HISTORY

Kevin Bacon (actor)

Kevin Costner (actor)

Kevin Faulk (football player)

Kevin Garnett (basketball player)

Kevin Henkes (author and illustrator)

Kevin Kline (actor)

Kevin Nealon (actor)

Kevin Spacey (actor)

Kyle

Meaning: Narrows, straight

Origin: Gaelic

Related names and spelling variations: *None*

Kyle is a Gaelic name with geographic roots that means "narrows, straight" (no reference to sexual orientation, of course). Kyle made a brief appearance in the top 1,000 in 1881 and then dropped off for several years. It reached its height of popularity in the 1990s, when it spent most of the decade in the top 25. Kyle has that cool vibe that other names like Dylan and Logan share. It's probably the inspiration for newly popular names Kyler and Kylan.

THIS NAME IN HISTORY

Kyle Boller (football player)

Kyle Busch (NASCAR driver)

Kyle Chandler (actor)

Kyle Korver (basketball player)

Kyle MacLachlan (actor)

Kyle Massey (actor)

Kyle Petty (NASCAR driver)

Hi, My Name Is

LI

Lance

Meaning: Lance, spear

Origin: French

Related names and spelling variations: *Lando, Lancelot*

Lance is a French name that literally means "lance"—the giant spear that knights on horseback would use when dueling (which makes Lance Armstrong's name almost cartoonishly macho). It is also a shortened form of the romantic name Lancelot, which was also French, so it did not derive from lance a lot! Lance ranked in the U.S. top 1,000 for two years at the turn of the last century and didn't appear again until the mid-1930s. It was at its most popular in 1970, when it peaked at #76. The name has since fallen into the middle of the pack, despite Mr. Livestrong's popularity and his seven Tour de France titles. Lance is a perfect one-syllable pick if you want to avoid nicknames.

THIS NAME IN HISTORY

Lance Armstrong (cyclist)

Lance Bass (singer)

Lance Burton (magician)

Lando Calrissian (character in *Star Wars*)

Lance Gross (actor)

Landon

Meaning: Long hill

Origin: English

Related names and spelling variations: *Landon, Landin, Landyn, Landon, Landen, Landyn, Landin*

Landon is an English surname that means "long hill." The aristocratic-sounding name appeared in the top 1,000 a few times in the late 1800s and early 1900s but became a regular on the list starting in 1962, not long after Michael Landon began starring in the popular TV show *Bonanza*. Landon reached the top 100 in 2003 and has been climbing rapidly since then. There are several popular spellings of this name today, including Landen, Landyn, and Landin. Landon is part of the *-en/on/in* name trend along with other favorites Brandon, Jayden, Caden, and Braden. After Landon Donovan's performance at the 2010 World Cup in soccer, the name is likely to get another spike (oh, wait, that's volleyball . . .).

THIS NAME IN HISTORY

Landon Carter (actor)

Landon Cassill (NASCAR driver)

Landon Cohen (football player)

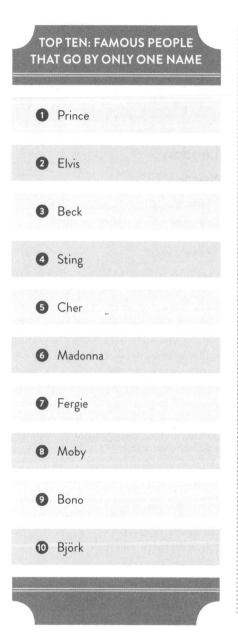

TOP TEN: FAMOUS PEOPLE THAT GO BY ONLY ONE NAME

1 Prince

2 Elvis

3 Beck

4 Sting

5 Cher

6 Madonna

7 Fergie

8 Moby

9 Bono

10 Björk

Landon Donovan (soccer player)
Landon Johnson (football player)
Landon Jones (author)
Landon Powell (baseball player)
Michael Landon (actor)

Lawrence

Meaning: From Laurentum; laurel

Origin: English

Related names and spelling variations: *Larry, Laurence, Laurie, Lars, Laurent, Lorenzo*

Lawrence is an English version of Laurence, a distinguished Latin name that means "from Laurentum." The name is also associated with laurel, an ancient symbol of victory and honor. As the story goes, Apollo fell in love with Daphne, who didn't return his affections. In an effort to protect her from Apollo, Daphne's father turned her into a laurel tree. After finding the tree, ever the romantic, Apollo wore a crown of laurel in remembrance. The crown of laurel became a symbol of victory, and has even given its name to the honors of poet laureate and Nobel laureate. All this gives the name Lawrence some very noble connections and a long history of popularity. Laurence was a popular name in the Middle Ages, but the Lawrence spelling has been more popular in recent U.S. history. Lawrence was a top 100 name from 1880 through the 1960s, and has been on the decline since then. Variations Lorenzo and Larry have become more popular recently.

In the Middle Ages, the name Laurence was used for boys and girls, as it still is in France.

THIS NAME IN HISTORY

Larry David (actor and producer)

Larry Fitzgerald (football player)

Larry King (TV personality)

Lorenzo Lamas (actor)

Lars Ulrich (musician)

Lawrence Welk (TV personality)

Theodore "Laurie" Laurence (character in Louisa May Alcott's *Little Women*)

Lawrence of Arabia (movie)

Lee

Meaning: Meadow

Origin: English

Related names and spelling variations: *Leigh*

Lee is an English name that means "meadow." It is short and simple and packed with personality. If you like names that don't come with a lot of bells and whistles, Lee is great, but it's also open to some serious schoolyard teasing and limericks. In the U.S., Lee was a top 100 name from 1880 through 1955. It remained in the top 200 through the 1980s (despite Lee Harvey Oswald), but has sharply declined since then. As a girl's name, the name is also spelled Leigh, but it hasn't made the girl's list since 1996.

THIS NAME IN HISTORY

Lee Daniels (actor)

Lee DeWyze (singer)

Lee Majors (actor)

Lee Marvin (actor)

Lee Harvey Oswald (J.F.K. assassin)

Lee Westwood (golfer)

Lee Jeans (denim brand)

Leon

Meaning: Lion

Origin: Latin

Related names and spelling variations: *Levon*

Leon is related to a family of Latin names that mean "lion" (we'll treat Leonard and Leonardo in the next entry, but, yes, Leo the lion was pretty much Lion the lion). The name has a retro feel to it that could be considered cool today, and, as name popularity usually goes through cycles, Leon's recent slump in popularity suggests it will soon be a candidate for a comeback. Leon has been on the U.S. charts since 1880 and was a top 100 pick for most of the time between then and the early 1940s.

NAME FACTOID

If you're astrology-minded parents, you might like the lion-related names for your little Leo born between July 23 and August 22.

1. Coco (Chanel)

2. Gianni (Versace)

3. Ralph (Lauren)

4. Georgio (Armani)

5. Valentino (Garavani)

6. Donna (Karan)

7. Karl (Lagerfeld)

8. Calvin (Klein)

9. Diane (von Fürstenberg)

10. Stella (McCartney)

THIS NAME IN HISTORY

Liván Hernández (baseball player)
Leon Panetta (politician and CIA director)
Leon Powe (basketball player)
Leon Trotsky (Russian political figure)
Leon Spinks (boxer)
Leon Washington (football player)
Kings of Leon (band)

Leonardo

Meaning: Brave lion

Origin: Italian; Spanish; Portuguese

Related names and spelling variations:
Leonard, Leo

Leonardo is the Italian, Spanish, and Portuguese version of the name Leonard and means "brave lion." There's hardly a cooler definition for a boy's name than that, and it only benefits by being the name both of one of the geniuses of the Italian Renaissance, Leonardo da Vinci, and one of today's most popular actors, Leonardo DiCaprio. DiCaprio, in fact, may be single-handedly responsible for bringing this name to modern parents' attention. Leonard was a favorite back in the early 1900s, but has been in a steady decline since then. Leonardo has taken the opposite path. It didn't make the charts for most of the early 1900s and then started to gain popularity.

NAME FACTOID

Not surprisingly, Leonardo DiCaprio's mom says that she was inspired by da Vinci when choosing her son's name.

Leonardo (character in Shakespeare's
   The Merchant of Venice)
Leonardo Bruni (historian)
Leonard Cohen (musician)
Leonardo da Vinci (artist)
Leonardo DiCaprio (actor)
Leonardo Fibonacci (mathematician)
Leonard Nimoy (actor)

Levi

Meaning: Associated, attached

Origin: Hebrew

Related names and spelling variations: *None*

"Are you wearing your Levi's?"—yes, your son would likely hear a lot of that at school (your other son Lee wouldn't have it quite so bad). As dominated as Levi is by the Levi Strauss denim company, Levi itself is a Hebrew name that means "associated" or "attached." Levi had been at its most popular in the U.S. in the 1880s, though it recently broke into the top 100 for the first time. Matthew McConaughey and Camila Alves used the name for their son in 2008, and that has certainly helped its popularity. The notoriety of Sarah Palin's would-be son-in-law Levi Johnston probably helped, too. Look for Levi to continue up the charts in the years to come. Choosing it today may put you ahead of the big boom (or right in the middle).

Levi Eshkol (former prime minister of Israel)
Levi Johnston (public figure)
Levi Leipheimer (cyclist)
Levi McConaughey (son of Matthew
   McConaughey and Camila Alves)
Levi Strauss (denim manufacturer)
Levi Stubbs (singer)

Liam

Meaning: Determined protector

Origin: Irish

Related names and spelling variations: *Lyam*

Liam is the Irish version of the name William and means "determined protector"—let's just hope his little sister doesn't think he's overdoing it! Liam made the U.S. charts for the first time in 1967, but then dropped off for a few years. It didn't start really gaining popularity until the mid-1990s, as part of the recent Irish name craze, and has been quickly climbing since. Liam would be a good fit for siblings Aidan and Keira. Oh, wait, Keira might not be so happy about it!

Liam Aiken (actor)
Liam Clancy (singer)
Liam Gallagher (singer)
Liam Lynch (director)
Liam McDermott (son of Tori Spelling
   and Dean McDermott)
Liam Neeson (actor)

Logan

Meaning: Little hollow, valley

Origin: Scottish

Related names and spelling variations: *None*

Logan is a Scottish surname that means "little hollow" or "valley." Logan is one of the new cool-kid names along with Max, Carter, and Jackson. Logan has jumped around a lot on the U.S. charts since the 1880s and has even fallen off of them for years at a time. It's come on strong since the 1990s, though. Logan has also been part of a new trend in unisex names, gaining popularity on the girls' chart. Other recent unisex converts are Ryan, Reese, and Morgan. All these names are likely to drop in popularity for boys as they rise on the girls' chart.

THIS NAME IN HISTORY

Logan (aka Wolverine, character in *X-Men*)

Logan French Kensing (baseball player)

Logan Mader (musician)

Logan Pause (soccer player)

Logan Ramsey (actor)

Logan's Run (film and novel by William F. Nolan and George Clayton Johnson)

Mount Logan (Canada's highest peak)

Louis

Meaning: Warrior

Origin: French, German

Related names and spelling variations: *Luiz, Luis, Lewis, Lou, Louie*

Louis is a French name with German roots (yes, that's possible), and it means "warrior." It's been a popular name of French royalty going back centuries—thus the fact that there was a Louis XIII, Louis XIV, and so on. In the U.S., Louis was a top 100 name between 1880 and 1959 but has been gradually falling down the charts since then. Today, the Spanish version, Luis, is much more popular than its French and German counterpart. That might not be true for long, though. Sandra Bullock named her son Louis in 2009, which could mean that the name is on the verge of a comeback.

NAME FACTOID

The Louis spelling is more popular in the U.S., but the Lewis spelling is more popular in England.

THIS NAME IN HISTORY

Lew Alcindor (basketball player—later Kareem Abdul-Jabbar)

Louis Armstrong (musician)

Louis Bardo Bullock (son of Sandra Bullock)

Lewis Black (comedian)

Louis C. K. (comedian)

Luis Castillo (baseball player)

Luis Armand Garcia (actor)

Luis Guzmán (actor)

Lou Diamond Philips (actor)

Louis Vuitton (fashion designer)

Jorge Luis Borges (author)

Meriwether Lewis (explorer)

Lucas

Meaning: Man from Lucania; light

Origin: Greek; Latin

Related names and spelling variations: *Lukas, Luke, Luciano, Luka, Lucian*

Use the force! Lucas and Luke are Latin versions of the Greek name Loukas. The name's meaning is found as both "man from Lucania" (Luciana is a region in Italy) and "light." The names have been popular for centuries due to the Gospel of Luke in the New Testament. However, Luke Skywalker from *Star Wars* was responsible for the boost both names saw after the first movie was released in 1977. Luke Perry may also have contributed to another boost in the 1990s, when he was on *Beverly Hills, 90210* (he had a similar effect on his character's name, Dylan). Lucas and Luke have been closely matched on the U.S. charts since the 1980s, with Luke having the slight edge for most of that time and Lucas only recently taking over the top spot.

THIS NAME IN HISTORY

Luca Brasi (character in *The Godfather*)

Luke Bryan (singer)

Lucas Grabeel (actor)

Luke Kelly (musician)

Luke Perry (actor)

Luke Skywalker (character in *Star Wars*)

Luke Wilson (actor)

George Lucas (screenwriter, director, and producer)

Cool Hand Luke (movie)

Gospel of Luke (one of the four Gospels in the Bible)

Mm

Malcolm

Meaning: St. Columba's servant

Origin: Gaelic

Related names and spelling variations: *None*

Malcolm is a powerful name, evoking both the civil rights activist Malcolm X and the best-selling *New Yorker* author Malcolm Gladwell (as well as, less powerfully, the TV show *Malcolm in the Middle*). It's a Gaelic name meaning "St. Columba's servant" (St. Columba was a patron saint of Ireland and Scotland), and many parents probably steered away due to Malcolm X's controversial life and legacy. But this well-known but uncommon name could use a boost in the rankings! Despite a constant presence on the U.S. charts since 1880, Malcolm has never ranked higher than #205, which it did back in 1928. It has fluctuated quite a bit over the years, but has been falling down the charts recently.

THIS NAME IN HISTORY

Malcolm Gladwell (author)

Malcolm McDowell (actor)

Malcolm Jamal Warner (actor)

Malcolm X (civil rights activist)

Malcolm in the Middle (TV show)

Marcus

Meaning: Warlike

Origin: Latin

Related names and spelling variations: *Marcos, Markus, Marc, Mark, Marco*

Marcus was originally a Roman name that may have come from the Roman god Mars, the god of war. (Beware of your little Marcus invading the neighbor's sandbox.) Rest assured, though—while notable figures from ancient Rome, such as the emperor Marcus Aurelius, bear the name, there's also the Gospel of Mark from the New Testament, proving that a "warlike" son need not grow up violent. In the U.S., Mark has been the more popular version of this name overall, maintaining a spot in the top 10 from 1955 through 1970. Both versions have been declining in popularity for several years now, but Marcus is slightly more popular today. Other widespread versions of the name are Marco, Marcos, Marc, and Markus. Marky Mark, now that Mark Wahlberg has gone back to using his real name, seems unlikely to catch on.

Marcus Antonius (ancient Roman statesman, known as Marc Antony in English)

Marcus Aurelius (ancient Roman emperor)

Mark Hamill (actor)

Mark Harmon (actor)

Marc Jacobs (fashion designer)

Mark Knopfler (musician)

Mark Mulder (baseball player)

Mark Ruffalo (actor)

Mark Twain (pseudonym of author Samuel Clemens)

Mark Wahlberg (actor)

Mark Zuckerberg (cofounder of Facebook)

Gospel of Mark (one of the four Gospels in the Bible)

Marshall

Meaning: Horse groomer; officer, marshal

Origin: French

Related names and spelling variations: *Marshal*

Marshall, where's the parade? Sadly, since 9/11 people are more likely to associate the word *marshal* with federal marshal than with the leader of the procession, and the name has lost popularity because of it. Perhaps if rapper Eminem (real name: Marshall Mathers) used his given name more often, Marshall could get a lift (like when the successful career of football player Marshall Faulk helped buoy the name in the 1990s). Marshall has been

TOP TEN: OSCAR-WINNING ACTORS

1. Jack (John) Nicholson (3)
2. Walter Brennan (3)
3. Tom Hanks (2)
4. Dustin Hoffman (2)
5. Gary Cooper (2)
6. Marlon Brando (2)
7. Sean Penn (2)
8. Spencer Tracy (2)
9. Daniel Day Lewis (2)
10. Fredric March (2)

consistently strong since 1880, and has spent all but four years ranked between the 100s and 300s. However, the name has been dropping recently. But fortunes swing: similarly styled names like August, Emmett, and Jasper have recently found themselves popular again after periods of disfavor.

THIS NAME IN HISTORY
Marshall Eriksen (character on the TV show *How I Met Your Mother*)
Marshall Faulk (football player)
Marshall Mathers (given name of rapper Eminem)
Marshalls (retail store)

Martin

Meaning: Warlike

Origin: Latin

Related names and spelling variations: *Marty, Mart, Martino*

We know what you're thinking. You name your kid this and you'll be raising someone destined to hear rhyming jokes about his name his entire childhood (he'd better avoid beans). But, similar to Mark and Marcus in being derived from Mars, the Roman god of war, the "warlike" Martin has been a consistent favorite in the United States since 1880. A top 100 name between 1880 and 1970, we have to believe that strong role models and celebrities—like civil rights activist Martin Luther King Jr. and film director Martin Scorsese—inspired parents to name their sons Martin in hopes of passing on the recognition and talent that comes along with it. And until Toby or Jayden can write a speech like "I Have a Dream," we think they've got a point.

THIS NAME IN HISTORY
Martin Lawrence (actor)
Martin Luther (Protestant theologian)
Martin Luther King, Jr. (civil rights activist)
Martin Scorsese (director)
Martin Sheen (actor)

Mason

Meaning: Stone worker

Origin: English

Related names and spelling variations: *None*

We're not saying your kid is going to be good with Legos or anything, but Mason is a good example of the old "use an occupation as a name" trick. It began as a last name in the Middle Ages and denoted a stone worker. Along with names like Carter, Cooper, and Hunter, it is also a great example of the blending of two major current name trends: occupational and surnames. Enjoying the boost that comes with trending, Mason has been on the U.S. charts since 1880, but has started to really gain ground since the 1990s, becoming more popular today than ever before.

THIS NAME IN HISTORY
Mason Jennings (musician)
Dave Mason (musician)

Jackie Mason (comedian)

James Mason (actor)

John L. Mason (inventor of Mason jars)

Sam Mason (celebrity chef)

Perry Mason (TV show and character)

Mason-Dixon Line (the U.S. boundary between the North and South)

Matthew

Meaning: Gift of God

Origin: Hebrew

Related names and spelling variations: *Mateo, Mathew, Matteo, Mathias, Matthias, Matias*

Matthew is one of the most recognizable names of all time, a top 10 name spanning three decades (1972–2008). In the New Testament, Matthew was one of the twelve apostles and wrote the first Gospel. And while this Hebrew name's origin lies in the religious meaning "gift of God," these days we're sure you can think of a few Matthews who fit the bill . . . McConaughey, Damon, Broderick. Don't want to give in to the trend? Another version of the name found in the Bible is Matthias, which would be a cool pick if you're looking for a similar, unique version of this popular name.

NAME FACTOID

The name Matteo has been one of the fastest rising boy's names recently. Look for it to continue to gain popularity.

THIS NAME IN HISTORY

Matthew Broderick (actor)

Matt Damon (actor)

Matt Groening (creator of *The Simpsons*)

Matt Lauer (television journalist)

Matt LeBlanc (actor)

Matthew McConaughey (actor)

Matthew Perry (actor)

Gospel of Matthew (one of the four Gospels in the Bible)

Max

Meaning: Greatest

Origin: Latin

Related names and spelling variations: *Maxim, Maximilian, Maximillian, Maximo, Maximus, Maxx*

Max, though a nickname for the longer "Max" names such as Maxim, Maximilian, and Maximus, is certainly not a humble name. It's from the Latin for "greatest" and will give you a valid reason to believe your son will be president, a nuclear physicist . . . or at least the first one on the block to potty train. And it seems parents are taking note: Max has been used as a first name in its own right for quite a while now, and it's one of the cool three-letter names parents are attracted to these days, including Leo, Eli, and Ian. In the U.S., Max has been growing in popularity since the 1980s, along with variations Maximus, Maximiliano, Maximilian, Maxim, and Maximo.

THIS NAME IN HISTORY

Max (character in Maurice Sendak's *Where the Wild Things Are*)

Max Baer (boxer)

Maksim Chmerkovskiy (dancer and TV personality)

Maxim de Winter (character in Daphne du Maurier's novel *Rebecca*)

Mad Max (movie)

Maxwell

Meaning: Mack's well or Mack's stream

Origin: Scottish

Related names and spelling variations: *Max*

Maxwell has a different origin than the other "Max" —it's a Scottish surname that literally means "Mack's well" or "Mack's stream." Though the lyrics of the Beatles' song "Maxwell's Silver Hammer" are a little disturbing ("Bang! Bang! Maxwell's silver hammer/Came down upon her head"), it's remained a popular name since the 1880s (there have been only four years that it didn't make the U.S. top 1,000). Maxwell reached its highest point in 1999 at #106 and has declined slightly since then. Maxwell is a great way to get to the cool nickname Max while still giving your son a name with options in adulthood.

THIS NAME IN HISTORY

Maxwell (singer)

Maxwell Anderson (playwright)

Maxwell Caulfield (actor)

Maxwell Smart (character on the TV show *Get Smart*)

John C. Maxwell (author)

Maxwell House (coffee manufacturer)

Micah

Meaning: Who is like God?

Origin: Hebrew

Related names and spelling variations: *Mycah*

Not to be confused with its homonym "mica," a mineral, Micah is a version of the wildly popular name Michael, which also means "Who is like God?" Micah is one of several ancient biblical names that have evolved into current hip choices for parents. In the U.S., Micah stepped into the top 1,000 for the first time in 1959 and later landed in the top 200 in 1998. Similar biblical picks that are newly minted cool names are Levi, Jonah, and Isaac. There is also a similar-sounding girl's name among Germanic nations: Maike.

THIS NAME IN HISTORY

Micah (biblical figure)

Micah Alberti (actor)

Micah Hinson (singer)

Micah Hoffpauir (baseball player)

Micah Owings (baseball player)

Micah Wright (author)

Michael

Meaning: Who is like God?

Origin: Hebrew

Related names and spelling variations: *Micheal, Mike, Mikey, Miguel, Mick, Michele, Mikhail, Mickey*

Michael is one of the most popular boys' names of all time. It is Hebrew and means "Who is like God?" (on the basketball court, perhaps Mr. Jordan?). Michael's biblical connection—he was one of the archangels—has certainly helped the name's popularity; it's been on the U.S. charts since 1880. It hit the top 10 in 1943, reached #1 in 1954, and remained the #1 name for boys in the U.S. for all but one year through 1998. Few names have been so popular for so long, and even fewer still sound current and fashionable after so many years of widespread use. Parents are also attracted to the ultra-friendly sounding nickname Mike. If you want a more unique nickname, consider Mick, which has been popular in Ireland.

THIS NAME IN HISTORY

Mikhail Baryshnikov (dancer)
Miguel de Cervantes (author)
Mike Ditka (football coach)
Michael J. Fox (actor)
Miguel Indurain (cyclist)
Michael Jackson (singer)
Michael Jordan (basketball player)
Michael Phelps (swimmer)
Mickey Rourke (actor)
Miguel Tejada (baseball player)
Maya and Miguel (PBS children's show)

Miles

Meaning: Soldier; mercy, grace

Origin: Latin; Slavic

Related names and spelling variations:
Myles, Milo

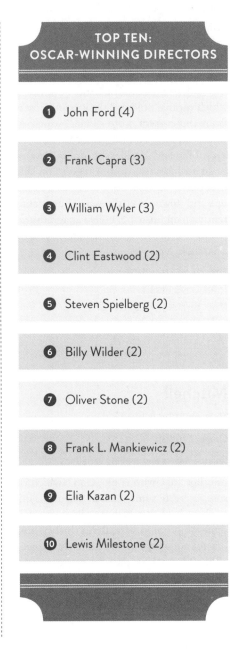

TOP TEN:
OSCAR-WINNING DIRECTORS

1 John Ford (4)

2 Frank Capra (3)

3 William Wyler (3)

4 Clint Eastwood (2)

5 Steven Spielberg (2)

6 Billy Wilder (2)

7 Oliver Stone (2)

8 Frank L. Mankiewicz (2)

9 Elia Kazan (2)

10 Lewis Milestone (2)

Miles is a bit of a mystery—a tough-yet-tender mystery, but a mystery none-theless. The name could come from Slavic roots meaning "mercy, grace." Its meaning could stem from the Latin word *miles*, which means "soldier." Or it could come from the current word "mile," which is what you'll be running once this kid is a toddler and decides he doesn't want to sit still for a second. A regular on the U.S. charts since 1880, Miles has had its ups and downs over the years, but is currently on an upswing. It also anagrams to "smile"—which is kind of cute if you're a Scrabble type.

THIS NAME IN HISTORY

Miles Davis (musician)

Miles Straume (character on the TV show *Lost*)

Milo Ventimiglia (actor)

Milo and Otis (movie)

Mitchell

Meaning: Who is like God?

Origin: English

Related names and spelling variations: *Mitch*

Another "one who is like God," which is sure to create some tension when Micah, Michael, and Mitchell are all up for the same job promotion in about thirty years. It's not a hugely popular name, but when all the Michaels in class have to use their last initial (Michael A. and Michael B.), your son will be happy that he's the only Mitchell in his school. Be wary of the nickname Mitch, however, as its rhymes make it an easy one to tease.

THIS NAME IN HISTORY

Mitch Albom (author)

Mitch Hedberg (comedian)

Mitch McConnell (politician)

Mitch Mitchell (musician)

Morgan

Meaning: Circling sea, bright

Origin: Welsh

Related names and spelling variations: *Morgin*

Morgan is traditionally a boy's name that comes from the Welsh name Morcant (in Celtic *cant* means "circle" or "completion"—maybe a good name if your next child will be the one to complete the family?). It's virtually nickname-free (Morg doesn't sound so good, right?), so keep that in mind. It's also undergone something of a gender realignment: it's been a moderately popular boy's name since 1880, but in the late 1970s, parents started using the name for their daughters. It made its way to the top 100 for girls in 1987—higher than it's ever been on the boys' chart—and the boys never really recovered, despite Morgan Freeman's impressive acting career. All the Morgans on eighties big-haired soap operas are probably responsible for that.

TOP TEN: PHILOSOPHERS

1. René (Descartes)
2. Immanuel (Kant)
3. Niccolò (Machiavelli)
4. Bertrand (Russell)
5. Karl (Marx, Popper)
6. Søren (Kierkegaard)
7. Simone (de Beauvoir)
8. Aristotle
9. Friedrich (Nietzsche, Engels)
10. Jean-Jacques (Rousseau)

THIS NAME IN HISTORY

Morgan Fairchild (actor)

Morgan le Fay (figure from the King Arthur legend)

Morgan Freeman (actor)

Morgan Grimes (character on the TV show *Chuck*)

Morgan de Toi (fashion design house)

J. P. Morgan (financial mogul)

Lee Morgan (musician)

Moses

Meaning: Child of God; drawn/saved from the water

Origin: Egyptian

Related names and spelling variations: *Moises, Mose, Moshe, Moishe*

You'd have to go back to the Bible to find a time when nearly everyone was naming their son Moses. Telling old Pharaoh off and splitting the Red Sea aside, the

TOP TEN: PHYSICISTS

1. Albert (Einstein)
2. Isaac (Newton)
3. Galileo (Galilei)
4. Nikola (Tesla)
5. Erwin (Schrödinger)
6. Gunnar (Nordström)
7. Wilhelm (Eduard Weber; Wien)
8. Osborne (Reynolds)
9. Leonard (Susskind)
10. Augustin-Jean (Fresnel)

name Moses is an underused biblical name whose most recent venture back into the mainstream world was courtesy of Gwyneth Paltrow and Chris Martin, whose son was born in 2006. But the name hasn't shot up the charts since then, so it doesn't seem as if the name benefitted that much from Moses Martin (though his big sister is named Apple, so who could blame parents for not trusting Gwyn's judgment?).

THIS NAME IN HISTORY

Moses (biblical figure)
Mose Allison (musician)
Moisés Alou (baseball player)
Moses Malone (basketball player)
Moses Martin (son of Gwyneth Paltrow and Chris Martin)

Hi, My Name Is

Nn

Nathan

Meaning: God has given

Origin: Hebrew

Related names and spelling variations:
Nathen, Nathaniel, Nathanael, Nathanial, Nate, Nat

Nathan is a Hebrew name that means "God has given"—a lovely meaning for a long-awaited child, perhaps? Nathan is a full name in its own right, but it's sometimes used as a nickname for Nathaniel. Both have identical roots and have been popular with parents. Amusingly, *nate* was a medieval English word for a buttock, but that usage has (thankfully) long since fallen out of currency. Nathaniel and Nathan have been duking it out on the U.S. charts since before the Civil War, with both found consistently in the top 100 for the past four decades.

THIS NAME IN HISTORY

Nathaniel "Nate" Archibald (character in Cecily von Ziegesar's *Gossip Girl* book series)

Nate Burleson (football player)

Nat King Cole (singer, born Nathaniel Adams Coles)

Nathan Hale (Revolutionary War figure)

Nathaniel Hawthorne (author)

Nathan Kress (actor)

Nathan Lane (actor and singer)

Nathan McCall (author)

Nate Robinson (basketball player)

Nathan's Famous (New York–based hot dog company)

Nate the Great (children's book series by Marjorie Sharmat)

Neil

Meaning: Cloud; passionate; champion

Origin: Gaelic

Related names and spelling variations:
Neal, Niall

Neil is a version of the Gaelic name Niall and may mean "cloud," "passionate," or "champion"—an appropriate first name for the first man on the moon (or a little boy dreaming of being an astronaut). The name was once found almost exclusively in Ireland and Scotland, but eventually spread to people in other places, including Canadian Neil Young, the Toronto, Ontario–born singer-songwriter, who certainly helped drive popularity of his first name in the 1970s, when Neil was most popular. Unfortunately, much like its namesake's music, Neil has been declining in popularity. Does Neil Patrick Harris have something to do with its slight uptick? Most likely. The Neil spelling has been more popular than the Neal spelling over the years—Neal hasn't made the charts since 2002.

THIS NAME IN HISTORY

Neil Armstrong (astronaut)

Neal Bledsoe (actor)

Neal Cassady (Beat Generation icon)

Neil Diamond (singer)

Neil Gaiman (author)

Neil Patrick Harris (actor)

Neil Lane (jeweler)

Neil Sedaka (singer)

Neil deGrasse Tyson (astrophysicist and TV personality)

Neil Young (singer)

Nicholas

Meaning: People's victor

Origin: Greek

Related names and spelling variations: *Nickolas, Nicolas, Nikolas, Nikoas, Nico, Niko, Nick, Nikolai, Cole*

Nicholas is from the Greek word for "people's victor," with "victor" coming from Nike, the Greek goddess of victory. Recent conquerors using the name Nicholas include Nick Frith, the teenage baseball player who beat brain cancer, Nicholas Jinadasa, the gold-medal-winning badminton champion, and Nicholas Buckland, who competed as a figure skater in the 2010 Winter Olympics. And St. Nicholas served as the popular inspiration for Santa Claus. The name has dropped from the top 10 baby names, but has remained pretty popular—which is particularly impressive since variations on the name, including Nicolas, Nikolas, and Nickolas, are also vying for parents' favor. The Nick Adams stories by Hemingway continue to lend the nickname Nick a masculine association that even Nick Drake's falsetto hasn't undone.

THIS NAME IN HISTORY

St. Nicholas (aka Santa Claus)

Nicolas Cage (actor)

Nick Cannon (actor)

Nick Drake (musician)

Nick Hornby (author)

Nick Jonas (musician)

Nicholas Sparks (author)

The Life and Adventures of Nicholas Nickelby (novel by Charles Dickens)

Noah

Meaning: To rest, to comfort

Origin: Hebrew

Related names and spelling variations: *None*

Noah is a Hebrew name that means "to rest, to comfort." Noah is also one of the most recognizable Bible names—Noah is famous for building the ark during the Great Flood and saving the animals two-by-two. The animal imagery has helped Noah's ark become a popular nursery theme for newborns. The name Noah has been used since the 1600s. In the U.S., the name has enjoyed mild success on the charts since 1880. Noah really took off in 1996 though when it hit the top 50 for the first time. Since then, and possibly thanks to the celebrity of *ER* star Noah Wyle, the name has continued to burn up the charts.

THIS NAME IN HISTORY

Noah (biblical figure)

Noah Adams (journalist)

Noah Baumbach (screenwriter and director)

Noah Gray-Cabey (actor)

Noah Lewis (musician)

Noah Webster (creator of America's first dictionary)

Noah Wyle (actor)

Noel

Meaning: Birthday, Christmas

Origin: French

Related names and spelling variations: *Noël*

Noel is a French name that means "birthday" and is strongly associated with Christmas and the celebration of Christ's birthday among Christians worldwide. *West Wing* fanatics will be the first to tell you that it's also the title of season two's Christmas episode. Parents are advised to avoid naming a child Noel if he already

TOP TEN: POPULAR FIREFIGHTER NAMES

❶ Charles

❷ Edward

❸ Gerard

❹ James

❺ Joseph

❻ Kevin

❼ Michael

❽ Timothy

❾ William

❿ Red

has a brother named Liam (do you really want to re-create the infamous sibling rivalry of the rock band Oasis?), and perhaps it's not such a good idea if your last name is Carroll. One famous Noel: Noël Coward (who may or may not have been fearful of Fifth Avenue holiday displays) would surely make a pithy and Oscar Wilde–worthy remark upon reading this entry.

THIS NAME IN HISTORY

Noël Coward (playwright and composer)
Noel Gallagher (musician)

Nolan

Meaning: Champion

Origin: Gaelic

Related names and spelling variations:
Nolen, Nollan, Nolyn

Steady-rollin' Nolan comes from the Gaelic surname for "champion." Perhaps because of another of its rhymes (more anatomical), Nolan has never really caught on in the U.S., although it's been increasing in popularity lately. The reason for this boost is unknown, although many will recall legendary baseball pitcher Nolan Ryan, highly revered during the name's resurgence in the 1980s for putting the fear of God—or at least fastballs—into his 100-mile-per-hour pitches. The only other recent Nolan in the news is film director Christopher Nolan, who crafted *The Dark Knight* and became an instant household name among action fans.

THIS NAME IN HISTORY

Nolan Gerard Funk (actor)
Nolan North (voice actor)
Nolan Ryan (baseball player)
Christopher Nolan (director)

Hi, My Name Is

Oo

Oliver

Meaning: Olive tree

Origin: Latin

Related names and spelling variations: *Olivier, Ollie*

Oliver may come from a Latin word meaning "olive tree," which has long been revered as a symbolic representation of virility and wisdom (due to its resistance to fire and drought) and, of course, as the olive branch of peace (not to mention a symbol of relief when a tired parent finally gets to have a martini). Aside from that, the word Oliver itself had not caught on as a name until fairly recently, in part because of the typically poorly received nickname Ollie (of puppets Kukla, Fran, and Ollie fame). Until now, its last entry on the top 100 was in 1903, but it's back on the rise recently. If you want your kid to be a bit ahead of the curve, Oliver might be a wise choice today.

THIS NAME IN HISTORY

Oliver Cromwell (English political figure)

Oliver North (author and political commentator)

Oliver Sacks (author and psychiatrist)

Oliver Stone (director)

Oliver Wendell Holmes Jr. (Supreme Court justice)

Oliver Twist (novel by Charles Dickens)

Oliver! (musical and movie)

Orion

Meaning: Son of fire

Origin: Greek

Related names and spelling variations: *Orien*

Orion is the name of the famed hunter in Greek mythology. The name means "son of fire"—most kids (and parents) would think that's pretty cool—and it's a rare case of a name referring more to the parents than the child. It disappeared from the charts for decades, especially during the years in which the powerful movie studio Orion Pictures went through a very public collapse, then reemerged on the outskirts of popularity in 1994, slipping in at #894. It's been tiptoeing toward the top 500 ever since. Orion is one of those hidden gems that parents haven't discovered yet. This would make a good choice if you want something unique, but not off the wall.

TOP TEN: PIRATES

1. John "Calico Jack" (Rackham)
2. William (Fly; "Captain" Kidd)
3. Edward ("Blackbeard" Teach; Low)
4. Howell (Davis)
5. Bartholomew ("Black Bart" Roberts; Sharp)
6. Anne (Bonny)
7. Mary (Read)
8. Edward ("Ned" Low)
9. Henry (Morgan; Every)
10. Stede (Bonnet)

THIS NAME IN HISTORY
Orion (Greek mythological figure)
Orion Noth (son of Chris Noth and Tara Wilson)
Orion (constellation)

Oscar

Meaning: Friend of the deer; divine spear

Origin: Irish; English

Related names and spelling variations: *Oskar, Osker*

Oscar is an Irish name that means "friend of the deer" and also has English roots, meaning "divine spear." (You can decide for yourself whether you think these definitions are contradictory or not.) Oscar has been around as a first name for centuries, and various famous Oscars have crossed a range of ethnic and cultural divides: English playwright Oscar Wilde, *Sesame Street* character Oscar the Grouch, and even heavyweight boxer Oscar De La Hoya are just a sampling. As for the most famous Oscar—the swashbuckling gentleman who graces the Academy Award—the story goes that he was named for the uncle of the Academy's executive secretary, which is so much less exciting than Bette Davis's claim that it was named after one of her many husbands.

Oscar has always been surprisingly popular in the U.S. The lowest it's ever been on the U.S. charts is #245 and the highest is #26, with its most popular stretch at the turn of the last century. Oscar is a great choice if you like vintage-sounding names that aren't too offbeat.

THIS NAME IN HISTORY

Oscar De La Hoya (boxer)

Oscar the Grouch (character on
Sesame Street)

Oscar Hammerstein (writer and producer
of musicals)

Oscar Peterson (musician)

Oscar Robertson (basketball player)

Oskar Schindler (credited with saving
hundreds of Jews in World War II)

Oscar Wilde (author)

Oscar (nickname of the Academy Award)

Owen

Meaning: Noble, well-born

Origin: Welsh

Related names and spelling variations:
Owain, Owin

Owen, considered to be the Welsh version of Eugene, likely means "noble, well-born." While Eugene has plunged in popularity over the past two centuries, Owen has steadily crept up the rankings. Its uptick has two possible sources: the baby boy born to a character from the 1990s nighttime drama *Party of Five* and A-list actor Owen Wilson, whose high-profile relationships, prominent nose, and whimsical films with Wes Anderson have inspired numerous hipster parents since his 1996 debut, *Bottle Rocket*.

THIS NAME IN HISTORY

Owen Davis (playwright)

Owen Nolan (hockey player)

Owen Schmitt (football player)

Owen Wilson (actor)

Clive Owen (actor)

Pp

Patrick

Meaning: Patrician, nobleman

Origin: Latin

Related names and spelling variations: *Patrik, Patryk, Pat, Patty, Padraic*

Patrick is, surprisingly, from Latin not Gaelic, and means "nobleman." Its popularity among the Irish (and Hollywood movies full of clichés about the Irish) can be attributed to Ireland's patron saint, St. Patrick, who converted so many Irish to Christianity in the fifth century that he changed the destiny of the nation. He's also responsible for St. Patrick's Day, but if your views of March 17 are on the negative side, don't let that deter you from this very popular traditional name. It was #30 for a few years in the 1960s, then began a steady decline. The popularity of *Grey's Anatomy* and its star, Patrick Dempsey, and the death of Patrick Swayze may have kept it from falling even farther. The nickname Pat is one of the most gender ambiguous names there is: just as likely to be short for Patricia as Patrick. And no, if you're having trouble remembering, the bunny in the famous children's book *Pat the Bunny* isn't named Pat—the title would then have needed a comma, as in *Pat, the Bunny*—it's just a suggestion (couldn't they have said "pet" to make it clearer?).

THIS NAME IN HISTORY

Patrick Dempsey (actor)

Patrick Duffy (actor)

Patrick Ewing (basketball player)

Pat Sajak (game show host)

Patrick Stewart (actor)

Patrick Swayze (actor)

St. Patrick (Catholic saint and namesake for holiday)

Paul

Meaning: Small

Origin: Latin

Related names and spelling variations: *Pablo, Paulo*

Paul comes from the Latin word for "small." St. Paul (or Saul, as that was his Roman name) of Tarsus, who is believed to have written much of the New Testament, is likely responsible for the name's consistent presence on the baby name charts. Paul was in America's top 100 for one hundred years in a row, although like many other previously common names, it is not as widespread as it once was. Most of the celebrities named Paul, such as McCartney and Simon, are not as much in the public eye, although fascination with Paul Cézanne and the rising popularity of Paul Rudd may have some small effect on keeping this name around.

THIS NAME IN HISTORY

Paul Bunyan (mythological lumberjack)

Paul Cézanne (painter)

Paul McCartney (singer)

Paul Newman (actor)

Pablo Picasso (artist)

Paul Revere (Revolutionary War figure)

Paul Rudd (actor)

Paul Simon (singer)

Peter

Meaning: Rock

Origin: Greek

Related names and spelling variations: *Pedro, Pierre, Pete, Piers, Pierce*

Peter has Greek roots and means "rock." St. Peter is considered the founding father of the Christian church and his name is symbolic of the movement. In the Bible, Jesus christens his apostle Simon as Peter, the "rock" upon which the church was to be built. Rocks have long been a symbol of stability and, in this case, the intended stability of the Christian church. That connection is undoubtedly what has made Peter such a popular name going all the way back to the Middle Ages. In the

U.S., Peter ranked in the top 100 between 1880 and 1996. It has been on the decline since then, but because of Peter Pan and Peter Rabbit, many new parents still identify the name with their childhoods, which should keep Peter at a respectable rank for many years to come.

THIS NAME IN HISTORY

Peter Bogdanovich (director)

Peter Gabriel (musician)

Peter the Great (ruler of the Russian Empire)

Peter Jackson (director)

Peter Krause (actor)

Pedro Martinez (baseball player)

Peter O'Toole (actor)

Peter Pan (character in J. M. Barrie's *Peter Pan*)

Peter Rabbit (character in Beatrix Potter's *Peter Rabbit*)

Pete Sampras (tennis player)

Pete Townshend (musician)

Phillip

Meaning: Horse lover

Origin: Greek

Related names and spelling variations: *Philip, Phil, Felipe*

Philip or Phillip is a Greek name that means "horse lover"—which you wouldn't think would make it that popular until you realize that equestrianism has been popular from ancient Greece to *Seabiscuit* and beyond. The trick with this name is

TOP TEN: FAMOUS ROCK DRUMMERS

1. Ringo Starr (The Beatles)
2. Ginger Bake (Cream); Fish (Marilyn Manson)
3. Neil Pert (Rush)
4. Lars Ulrich (Metallica)
5. Maureen Tucker (The Velvet Underground)
6. Mitch Mitchell (The Jimi Hendrix Experience)
7. Chester Thompson (Frank Zappa; Genesis)
8. Topper Headon (The Clash)
9. Carter Beauford (Dave Matthews Band)
10. Les Binks (Judas Priest)

deciding whether to spell it with one *l* or two. Both spellings of the name have remained popular since the late 1800s. In fact, Phillip and Philip would both be ranking higher, if only they were not two different words. Authors Philip Pullman and Philip Roth represent the old guard, when the one *l* was more popular, but fashion designer Phillip Lim and others have helped even the score for the two-*l* team.

THIS NAME IN HISTORY

Phil Collins (singer)

Phil Jackson (basketball player and coach)

Phillip Lim (fashion designer)

Phil Mickelson (golfer)

Philip Pullman (author)

Philip Roth (author)

Pierce

Meaning: Rock

Origin: English

Related names and spelling variations: *Pearce, Piers*

Pierce is an English version of the name Peter, which means "rock." Rocks are symbols of stability and longevity, which is a great sentiment to bestow upon your child. Pierce ranked in the U.S. top 1,000

Hi, My Name Is

between 1880 and the early 1900s, but then dropped off the charts until 1984. It made a huge leap in popularity in the mid-1990s, not long after Pierce Brosnan started playing super spy James Bond in the popular movie franchise. (Now that Daniel Craig has taken over playing Bond, he has the chance to improve the fortunes of *two* first names!) Pierce has continued to increase in popularity since then. It's still not too widespread, though, making it a good choice if you don't like trendy names.

THIS NAME IN HISTORY

Pierce Hawthorne (character on the
    TV show *Community*)
Pierce Brosnan (actor)
Franklin Pierce (U.S. president)
Piers Morgan (TV personality)

Preston

Meaning: Priest's town

Origin: English

Related names and spelling variations: *Pres*

The first time little Preston says a naughty word at the dinner table (that he heard from you) I'm sure "priest" won't be the first thing that comes to mind. But that's where his name comes from. Preston traces its roots back to an English surname that means "priest's town." It may have initially been used to identify someone who literally lived in or near a priest's town, not necessarily someone particularly holy-minded. Preston has been a steady presence on the U.S. charts, fluctuating between the 200s and 300s since the 1880s. Preston started to climb in the early 1990s and got a bump in 2006, the year after Britney Spears and Kevin Federline named their son Sean Preston.

THIS NAME IN HISTORY

Dr. Preston Burke (character on the
    TV show *Grey's Anatomy*)
Preston Foster (actor)
Preston Sturges (screenwriter, director,
    and producer)
Billy Preston (singer)
Robert Preston (actor)
Sean Preston Federline (son of Britney
    Spears and Kevin Federline)

Qq

Quentin

Meaning: Fifth

Origin: Latin

Related names and spelling variations: *Quenton, Quinten, Quintin*

Quentin is a Latin name derived from the name Quintus, which means "fifth." It's also one of the few viable Q names (the names Quade and Quimby—eh, not so much). Quentin made the U.S. charts for the first time in 1905. It has risen in popularity over the years, but never very high. The edgy director Quentin Tarantino is likely responsible for a small boost the name got in the mid-1990s, after he made a splash with his movie *Reservoir Dogs*. Other fashionable spellings include Quenton, Quintin, and Quinten. Quentin is also a great alternative to the trendier *-en/on/in* names Brandon, Jayden, Braden, and Caden.

THIS NAME IN HISTORY

Quentin Blake (illustrator)

Quentin Crisp (author)

Quentin Kopp (politician)

Quentin Richardson (basketball player)

Quentin Tarantino (director)

Quincy

Meaning: Fifth

Origin: Latin

Related names and spelling variations: *None*

Quincy is a Latin name and an English surname that means "fifth" and it is derived from the name Quintus. Perhaps the most famous historical Quincy is the sixth U.S. president, John Quincy Adams, while the most famous modern Quincy is musical powerhouse Quincy Jones. (One helped form the Monroe Doctrine; the other jammed with Michael Jackson. Both, equally cool.) Between 1880 and the 1950s, Quincy was off and on the U.S. charts. It became a regular in 1959 and grew in popularity into the 1970s, but is headed back down the charts today. Quincy is a retro name that could be ready for a shot at popularity. Quincy is also a good way to get to up-and-comer Quinn as a nickname.

THIS NAME IN HISTORY

Quincy Carter (football player)

Quincy Jones (musician)

Quincy, M.E. (TV show)

John Quincy Adams (U.S. president)

Hi, My Name Is

Quinn

Meaning: Leader; descendent of Conn

Origin: Irish

Related names and spelling variations: *Quin*

Give your kid the name Quinn and he might just end up the boss of circle time. Quinn, the most popular *Q* name, has Irish roots and means "leader" or "descendent of Conn." Quinn entered the U.S. charts for the first time in 1960, and has increased in popularity since then. Quinn is growing as a girl's name, too, becoming a steady presence on the girls' chart in 1995. The hot TV show *Glee* has a female character named Quinn, which may inspire even more parents to use the name for their daughters, leading to another name in the battleground between pink and blue.

THIS NAME IN HISTORY

Quinn Cummings (actor)

Quinn Fabray (character on the
 TV show *Glee*)

Quin Snyder (Basketball coach)

Joey Quinn (character on the
 TV show *Dexter*)

TOP TEN: G8 LEADERS

1. Barack (Obama)
2. Gordon (Brown)
3. Angela (Merkel)
4. Stephen (Harper)
5. Nicolas (Sarkozy)
6. Silvio (Berlusconi)
7. Taro (Aso)
8. Dmitry (Medvedev)
9. George (Bush: '08)
10. Yasuo (Fukuda: '08)

Rr

Randall

Meaning: Wolf's shield

Origin: English

Related names and spelling variations: *Rand, Randy, Randolph*

Randall is an English name that means "wolf's shield." (You know your superhero-obsessed first-grade boy is going to think that is *so* awesome.) The name was popular all the way back in the 1600s. In the U.S., Randall has made the top 1,000 almost every year since 1880. It was a top 100 name from 1948 through 1969, but it has been on a slide since then. Nickname Randy has fared a little better, remaining a top 100 name from 1948 through 1983.

THIS NAME IN HISTORY

Randall Cunningham (football player)

Randy Jackson (musician and TV personality)

Randy Johnson (baseball player)

Randy Quaid (actor)

Reece

Meaning: Passionate

Origin: Welsh

Related names and spelling variations: *Rhys, Reese, Rhett*

Reece is a variation of the Welsh name Rhys and means "passionate." Not a bad name to give to the fruits of your—*ahem*—ardent love. The name was popular in the Middle Ages and is still fashionable in the U.S. today. Both Reece and Reese have been popular spellings of the name. Reese has had an edge over Reece in the past, but recently Reece took the lead on the boys' chart. Reese Witherspoon has helped make this a popular name for girls. The Reese spelling entered the girl's list for the first time in 2000, and skyrocketed upward, making the name more common for Team Pink than Team Blue.

THIS NAME IN HISTORY

Reece Gaines (basketball player)

Reece Ritchie (actor)

Reese Witherspoon (actor)

Harry Reese (inventor of Reese's candy)

TOP TEN: GRAND SLAM SINGLES TITLES

1. Margaret Smith Court (31)
2. Steffi Graf (22)
3. Helen Wills Moody (19)
4. Martina Navratilova (18)
5. Chris Evert (18)
6. Roger Federer (16)
7. Pete Sampras (14)
8. Roy Emerson (12)
9. Björn Borg (11)
10. Rod Laver (11)

Reid

Meaning: Redhead

Origin: English

Related names and spelling variations: *Reed*

Reid is an English surname that means "redhead." No surprise, it was originally used as a nickname for someone with ginger hair. If you suspect a carrot-topped cutie is on the way, this might be a very sweet choice, but if your tyke is born blond, don't blame us. The Reed spelling entered the U.S. charts in 1881. Reid was off and on the charts between 1886 and 1917 before becoming a permanent presence. Since then, the spellings have closely tracked one another in popularity. Both spellings have been increasing in popularity, though Reid is slightly ahead.

THIS NAME IN HISTORY

Reed Hastings (founder of Netflix)
Reid Hoffman (founder of LinkedIn)
Harry Reid (U.S. senator)
Thomas Reid (Scottish philosopher)
Reed College (Oregon college)

Rex

Meaning: King

Origin: Latin

Related names and spelling variations: *None*

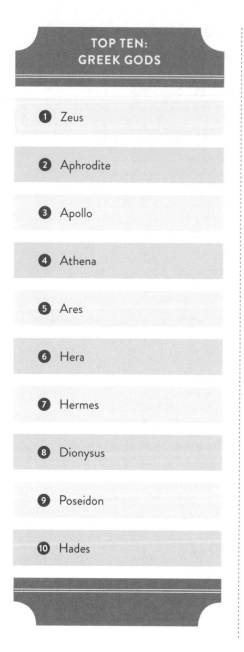

TOP TEN: GREEK GODS

1. Zeus
2. Aphrodite
3. Apollo
4. Athena
5. Ares
6. Hera
7. Hermes
8. Dionysus
9. Poseidon
10. Hades

Rex comes from the Latin and means "king," which might give your teenager a superiority complex. (But you just go ahead and remind him that you used to wipe his poo.)

It wasn't used as a first name until the 1800s. Prior to that it was a just a word that meant king—think Tyrannosaurus Rex and the Athenian tragedy *Oedipus Rex*. Rex has been on the U.S. charts since 1880. It reached its peak in 1951 at #171. It decreased in popularity afterward and even dropped off the charts for four years between 1999 and 2002. It entered again in 2003 and has slowly been on an upward path. Rex has the potential to become a big hit; think about the other three-letter names that are making a splash right now, such as Max, Leo, and Ian.

THIS NAME IN HISTORY

Rex Grossman (football player)

Rex Harrison (actor)

Rex Reed (writer)

Rex Ryan (football coach)

Rex Stout (author)

Rhett

Meaning: Advice; passionate

Origin: Dutch; Welsh

Related names and spelling variations: *Rhys*

Rhett has twin origins—from the Dutch meaning "advice" and as a form of the Welsh name Rhys, meaning "passionate." Who can hear the name Rhett and not think passion? The most famous Rhett is unquestionably Rhett Butler from

Margaret Mitchell's romantic novel *Gone with the Wind*. Surprisingly, Mr. Butler did not inspire parents to give a damn, however. The book and the movie came out in the 1930s, but Rhett didn't enter the U.S. charts until 1955. It has hovered between the 600s and 800s since then.

THIS NAME IN HISTORY
Rhett Akins (singer)
Rhett Bomar (football player)
Rhett Butler (character in Margaret Mitchell's *Gone with the Wind*)
Rhys Ifans (actor)

Richard

Meaning: Brave, hearty; power

Origin: German

Related names and spelling variations: *Ricardo, Ricky, Dick, Rick, Rich, Richie*

If Richard has a regal sound to it, there's a good reason. It was hugely popular in the twelfth century due to England's King Richard the Lionheart (he led one of the little military offensives called the Crusades). In the U.S., Richard was on the charts in 1880 and was a top 30 name for more than one hundred years, even spending quite a bit of time in the top 10. It started to decline in the 1970s and has very slowly fallen down the charts, though it hasn't gone far. One of the great things about Richard is the nickname potential. Dick isn't so popular anymore (for obvious reasons), but Rick, Ricky, and Richie are cute.

THIS NAME IN HISTORY
Richard Avedon (photographer)
Richard "Rick" Blaine (character played by Humphrey Bogart in *Casablanca*)
Richard Burton (actor)
Richard Gere (actor)
Ricky Gervais (comedian)
Ricky Martin (singer)
Ricardo Montalbán (actor)
Ricky Ricardo (character on the TV show *I Love Lucy*)
Richard Scarry (author)
Richard Simmons (exercise guru)
Richard Wagner (composer)
Little Richard (musician)

Riley

Meaning: Rye meadow; courageous

Origin: English; Irish

Related names and spelling variations: *Ryley, Reilly, Rylee, Ry*

Riley is a surname with English roots meaning "rye meadow" and Irish roots meaning "courageous." (Tell your little Riley that brave meaning when he's got to give up his binky.) Riley has a youthful, modern sound, but it's been on the U.S. charts for more than one hundred years. It was exclusively on the boy's list for most of that time and it was moderately popular. Recently, Riley has become a unisex name. It made the girl's list for the first time in 1990 and by 2002 it was more popular for girls than it was for boys.

Riley is more popular for boys than for girls in England, Ireland, and Scotland.

THIS NAME IN HISTORY

Riley Armstrong (hockey player)

Riley Chamberlin (silent film star)

Riley Cote (hockey player)

Pat Riley (basketball coach)

Robert

Meaning: Famous

Origin: German

Related names and spelling variations: *Roberto, Bobby, Rob, Robby, Rupert, Robin, Bob*

Robert sounds like such a humble name, right? The name actually comes from the German and means "bright" or "famous." Maybe that's the reason why there are so many well-known Roberts, Bobbys, and Robs. There have been numerous kings and saints with this name, and it was in the U.S. top 10 for all but two years for a stunning stretch from 1880 through 1989. If you're looking for less common names, you should consider these interesting versions: Rupert, Robin, and Roberto.

NAME FACTOID

In the Middle Ages, the nicknames Hob and Dob were popular for Robert. Perhaps a good opportunity for a unique, quirky nickname today?

THIS NAME IN HISTORY

Bob Barker (game show host)

Roberto Clemente (baseball player)

Robert DeNiro (actor)

Robert Frost (poet)

Rupert Grint (actor)

Robin Hood (legendary folk hero)

Robert F. "Bobby" Kennedy (politician)

Rob Mariano (reality TV star)

Bob Marley (musician)

Rupert Murdoch (media entrepreneur)

Robin Thicke (singer)

Roderick

Meaning: Famous ruler; red-brown

Origin: German; Welsh

Related names and spelling variations: *Rod, Roddy, Roderic, Rodrigo*

Even though your tot may only be the leader of the sandbox, the name Roderick might predict greater things for him. Roderick has German roots and means "famous ruler." (It also comes from the Welsh and means "red-brown.")

It was used in England between the twelfth and fifteenth centuries, but then didn't become popular again until the 1800s. The name has a romantic, dashing appeal—Jo March uses the Spanish version Rodrigo for a heroic character in one of her plays in Louisa May Alcott's *Little Women*, which debuted in the 1860s. Roderick has been on the U.S. charts for all but four years since 1880. It reached its peak in 1967 at #221, and has been declining since then. Roderick would be a great choice if you want a familiar but uncommon name, and Rod makes a totally manly sounding nickname.

Rod Laver (tennis player)

Roddy McDowall (actor)

Rod Serling (screenwriter)

Roderick Smith (football player)

Rod Stewart (singer)

Rodney

Meaning: Famous

Origin: English

Related names and spelling variations: *Rod*

Rodney is a name that can't get no respect. (Apologies to Mr. Dangerfield.) It sounds a little nerdy but its definition is stellar: Rodney comes from an English surname that may mean "famous."

Rodney has been around as a first name since the 1700s. In the U.S., it's been on the charts since 1880. It fluctuated in popularity quite a bit, but started to gain traction in the early 1900s. It entered the top 100 in the 1940s and peaked at #33 in 1965. It has been dropping steadily since then. Rodney feels like a 1960s- and 1970s-style name, which could make it a good pick if you're looking for something with retro cool.

THIS NAME IN HISTORY

Rodney Dangerfield (comedian and actor)

Rodney Stuckey (basketball player)

Rodney Yee (yoga instructor)

Rodney Strong (winemaker)

Roger

Meaning: Famous spear thrower

Origin: French; German

Related names and spelling variations: *Rodge, Rogelio, Rodger*

Roger is a French name with German roots that means "famous spear thrower." This name works if you happen to be an Olympic javelin thrower. Or perhaps this name is apropos since we can pretty much guarantee that your little boy will, at some point, use pretty much everything in your house as a weapon (his bread crust, his soup spoon).

Roger is also a classic choice with vintage roots—it was popular during the Middle Ages. Roger has been on the U.S. charts since 1880. It rose up the charts for the next several decades and entered the top 100 in the 1920s. It peaked at #22 in 1945 and has been on a downward slide since then. If javelin throwing isn't your sport, maybe you could be inspired by the talented tennis player Roger Federer.

THIS NAME IN HISTORY

Roger Ailes (media mogul)

Roger Clemens (baseball player)

Roger Craig (football player)

Roger Craig (baseball coach)

Roger Daltrey (singer)

Roger Ebert (film critic)

Roger Federer (tennis player)

Roger Maris (baseball player)

Roger Moore (actor)

TOP TEN: HEARTTHROBS IN JANE AUSTEN NOVELS

1. Fitzwilliam (Darcy)
2. George (Wickham; Knightley)
3. Edward (Ferrars)
4. Christopher (Brandon)
5. Frederick (Wentworth; Tilney)
6. John (Willoughby)
7. Edmund (Bertram)
8. Frank (Churchill)
9. Henry (Crawford; Tilney)
10. Reginald (De Courcy)

Roland

Meaning: Famous throughout the land

Origin: French; German

Related names and spelling variations: *Rollo, Orlando, Rolando*

Roland is a French name with German roots that means "famous throughout the land." (To keep this definition from going to your kid's head once he's grown, remind him of how often you used to wipe up his barf.)

The epic tale *The Song of Roland* (the oldest surviving major work of French literature) dates the name's use back at least as far as the 1100s. Roland has been on the U.S. charts since 1880. It peaked in the mid-1920s at #98. It stayed in the top 200 for a few decades, but has declined sharply recently. Actor Orlando Bloom may have single-handedly made the Italian version of the name cool. It hasn't had a big impact on the name's popularity yet, though.

THIS NAME IN HISTORY

Orlando Bloom (actor)

Roland Garros (aviator)

Roland Mouret (fashion designer)

The Song of Roland (epic poem)

Roman

Meaning: From Rome

Origin: Latin

Related names and spelling variations:
Romano

Roman comes from the Latin name Romanus and literally means "from Rome," making it a cute choice if you want to acknowledge Italian roots, an Italian honeymoon baby, or even just a love of Italy.

Roman has been in use since at least the tenth century. In the U.S. it entered the charts in 1882 at #821. It increased in popularity and has spent most of the years since then hovering between the 300s and 500s. It has been on an upward swing recently. Roman is also a good pick if you like names without built-in nicknames.

THIS NAME IN HISTORY

Roman Brady (character on *Days of Our Lives*)

Roman Polanski (director)

Ronald

Meaning: Ruler's advisor

Origin: Norse

Related names and spelling variations: *Ron, Ronnie, Ronny, Ronaldo*

Ronald is a Norse name that means "ruler's advisor." U.S. president Ronald Reagan was actually famous for having an astrological advisor, so maybe names do predict futures. Ronald has been popular dating back to the Middle Ages. In the U.S., Ronald entered the charts in 1883. It fluctuated quite a bit over the next several years, but then started to gain solid footing in the 1910s and rose up the charts. It entered the top 15 in 1933 and stayed there through 1954. It remained in the top 100 through 1990, possibly helped by the popularity of the aforementioned president. Ronald sounds a little old-fashioned these days, which is exactly what some parents may like about it.

NAME FACTOID

Ronald Reagan may have inspired the use of names Reagan and Regan, which have both gained some popularity over the last couple decades—mostly for girls.

THIS NAME IN HISTORY

Ron Artest (basketball player)

Ron Dellums (politician)

Ron Howard (actor and director)

Ronnie Lott (football player)

Ronald McDonald (mascot of McDonald's restaurants)

Ron Perlman (actor)

Ronald Reagan (U.S. president)

Cristiano Ronaldo (soccer player)

Rory

Meaning: Red ruler

Origin: Gaelic

Related names and spelling variations: *None*

Rory is one of many boys' names that mean "ruler" or "leader." (In this case, it comes from the Gaelic and means "red ruler.") There is something inherently funny about an infant who can't even hold his head up ruling anything, but it's a cute sentiment nonetheless.

The Irish form is Ruaidhrí and the Scottish form is Ruairidh. It's no surprise that the Rory spelling is the popular version in the U.S. today. As a boy's name, Rory made the U.S. charts for the first time in 1947, and has fluctuated quite a bit since then. Rory is on the path to becoming a unisex name, likely helped by the character Rory Gilmore on the hit TV show *Gilmore Girls*. It first appeared on the girls' chart in 2003 and is still hovering at the lower end of the top 1,000.

THIS NAME IN HISTORY

Rory Calhoun (actor)

Rory Cochrane (actor)

Rory Culkin (actor)

Rory Gilmore (character on the
TV show *Gilmore Girls*)

Rory Markas (sports announcer)

Rory McIlory (golfer)

Russell

Meaning: Little redhead

Origin: French

Related names and spelling variations:
Russ, Rusty, Rush

Russell is a French surname that means "little redhead," but you can pick it as a name for your boy even if you expect a little towheaded tyke or a brunet boy. Russell has been on the U.S. charts since 1880. It entered the top 100 in 1889 and stayed there for almost a century through 1982. It has declined in popularity quite a bit since then. Rusty and Rush are cute, unique nicknames that may draw you to the name.

NAME FACTOID

Some of the other names that mean "redhead" are Reid, Rogan, Rufus, Ginger, and Flannery.

THIS NAME IN HISTORY

Russell Brand (actor)

Russell Crowe (actor)

Russ Feingold (politician)

Rush Limbaugh (radio personality)

Russ Ortiz (baseball player)

Russell Simmons (mogul)

Bertrand Russell (philosopher)

Ryan

Meaning: Little king

Origin: Irish

Related names and spelling variations:
Ry, Rian

Ryan is an Irish name that means "little king." Of course, he'll rule over his stuffed animals to start, but just wait until he takes on kindergarten.

Ryan is one of the most popular Irish names today. Ryan made a brief appearance on the U.S. charts in 1906 and then disappeared for forty years until 1946. It made a slow, but steady, climb up the charts and reached the top 20 in 1976, where it has remained. Ryan has had some success as a unisex name. It entered the girls' chart for the first time in 1974. It was at its most popular in the early 1980s, but remains in the middle of the pack today.

THIS NAME IN HISTORY

Ryan Adams (musician)
Ryan Gosling (actor)
Ryan Howard (baseball player)
Ryan O'Neal (actor)
Ryan Phillippe (actor)
Ryan Reynolds (actor)
Ryan Seacrest (radio and TV personality)

TOP TEN:
HEARTTHROBS WITH ACCENTS

1 Jude (Law)

2 Clive (Owen)

3 Ewan (McGregor)

4 Daniel (Craig)

5 Heath (Ledger)

6 Gerard (Butler)

7 James (McAvoy)

8 Hugh (Jackman)

9 Robert (Pattinson)

10 Ed (Westwick)

Ss

Samuel

Meaning: God has heard

Origin: Hebrew

Related names and spelling variations: *Sam, Sammy*

Samuel is a Hebrew name that means "God has heard," as in "Yeah, lady, I hear ya—you want a son, right?" In the Old Testament, Hannah prays for a boy and—poof—she's buying blue. Good old Sammy wound up establishing the Hebrew monarchy, so perhaps it's also a good name if you like politics.

Samuel has a long history of popularity in the U.S. and has been a top 100 name since 1880. Back then it was #17, and some 130 years later it's still up near the top of the list, highlighting the trend toward old-fashioned names. One reason many parents like the name today is because of the cool and simple nickname, Sam.

THIS NAME IN HISTORY

Samuel Adams (founding father)

Samuel Beckett (author)

Samuel Clemens (author who wrote under the pen name Mark Twain)

Sammy Davis Jr. (entertainer)

Samuel L. Jackson (actor)

Samuel Morse (inventor)

Sammy Sosa (baseball player)

Sam Worthington (actor)

Yosemite Sam (cartoon character)

Saul

Meaning: Prayed for

Origin: Hebrew

Related names and spelling variations: *Shaul, Sol, Solly*

Saul is a Hebrew name that means "prayed for," perhaps a good name for a long-awaited child. Saul was also the name of a few prominent figures from the Old and New Testaments and the name has been especially popular with Jewish parents.

In the U.S., Saul was first on the charts in 1880 and for all but three years since then it has stayed there. Saul was at its most popular in 1997 at #270, and has dropped in popularity since then. Unlike other biblical names that have shed their strong biblical associations, Saul still feels very much like a name with religious history. If you're looking for an unmistakably religious name, Saul is a great choice.

1 Cassius (Clay) aka Muhammed Ali

6 Lennox (Lewis)

2 Mike (Tyson)

7 George (Foreman)

3 Evander (Holyfield)

8 Joe (Frazier)

4 Rocky (Marciano)

9 Riddick (Bowe)

5 Sonny (Liston)

10 Vitali (Klitschko)

THIS NAME IN HISTORY

King Saul (biblical figure)

Saul Bellow (author)

Saul Bass (designer)

Saul Williams (poet)

Sawyer

Meaning: Woodworker

Origin: English

Related names and spelling variations: *None*

Sawyer is an English occupational name that means "woodworker." (We can't imagine that modern occupational names, say, IT Specialist, have the same charm.)

The name Sawyer is a relatively new entry on the U.S. charts, making its first appearance in 1991. It ranked in the 400s to 500s until it made a huge jump in the mid-2000s. The popular and mysterious character Sawyer from the TV show *Lost* likely drove this leap. Sawyer will likely continue to gain ground, as parents who want to be ahead of name trends pick it. Sawyer is a great choice if you like names without ready-made nicknames.

THIS NAME IN HISTORY

James "Sawyer" Ford (character on the TV show *Lost*)

Diane Sawyer (journalist)

Tom Sawyer (character in Mark Twain's
   The Adventures of Tom Sawyer and
   The Adventures of Huckleberry Finn)
Sawyer Brown (musical group)

Scott

Meaning: Scot

Origin: English

Related names and spelling variations: *Scot,
Scotty, Scottie*

Scott is an English name that simply
means "Scot" (as in those kilt-wearing
dudes from Scotland). It's been used as a
way to describe someone from Scotland
for more than one thousand years.

Scott has been on the U.S. charts since
1880. It started to gain popularity in
1949 when it entered the top 100 for the
first time. It stayed there through 1995,
but has been on the decline recently. If
you're interested in honoring Scottish
roots, you may want to choose the name
Scott, like other parents have been doing
for centuries.

THIS NAME IN HISTORY

Scott Baio (actor)

Scott Bakula (actor)

Scott Disick (reality TV star)

Scott Hamilton (figure skater)

Scottie Pippen (basketball player)

Scott Wolf (actor)

Sean

Meaning: God is gracious

Origin: Irish

Related names and spelling variations:
Shawn, Shaun

Sean is the Irish version of the hugely
popular name John, which means "God
is gracious." Sean has long been popular
in Ireland and remains a top 10 name
still today.

In the U.S., Sean entered the charts in
1943 and it has consistently kicked the
collective butts of other spellings Shawn
and Shaun. Sean is a great no-nickname
option if you want the name you choose to
be the name you use.

THIS NAME IN HISTORY

Sean Astin (actor)

Sean Connery (actor)

Sean Hannity (news commentator)

Sean Hayes (actor)

Sean Lennon (musician, son of John
   Lennon and Yoko Ono)

Sean Marshall (baseball player)

Sean Penn (actor)

Sean Preston Federline (son of Britney
   Spears and Kevin Federline)

Shaun White (professional snowboarder)

Sebastian

Meaning: From Sebastï

Origin: Latin

Related names and spelling variations:
Sebastien, Bastian, Seb

Hi, My Name Is

The name Sebastian sounds as regal as classical music. That's probably because many people still associate the name with Johann Sebastian Bach (and the crab conductor from the Disney movie *The Little Mermaid*).

The name Sebastian goes back much farther than the composer or the crustacean—all the way to ancient Greece and Rome. The name has Latin roots meaning "from Sebastï"; Sebastï, a town in Asia Minor, has Greek roots meaning "respected." In the U.S., Sebastian did not become a regular on the charts until 1907. It dropped out of sight again in the 1950s, but has been increasing in popularity recently. Likely in thanks to that 1989 Disney crab, Sebastian went from #412 that year to #320 the following year.

The name made another major leap in 2000 when it hit the top 100 for the first time and has continued climbing since then. Unlike most longer names (like Alexander or Elizabeth), Sebastian does not have any well-recognized nicknames, so you're free to be as creative as you like.

THIS NAME IN HISTORY

Sebastian (character in Disney's
    The Little Mermaid)

Sebastian Cabot (actor)

Sebastian Cabot (explorer)

Sebastian the Ibis (mascot for the
    University of Miami)

Sebastian Janikowski (football player)

Sebastian Junger (author)

Sebastian Stan (actor)

Sebastian Telfair (basketball player)

Sebastian Vettel (race car driver)

Johann Sebastian Bach (composer)

Seth

Meaning: Placed, appointed

Origin: Hebrew

Related names and spelling variations: *None*

Seth is a Hebrew name that means "placed, appointed." In the Bible, Seth was one of the sons of that first couple, Adam and Eve. Seth is also another spelling of Set, the Egyptian god of the desert and of, uh, evil. Fortunately, the biblical association seems to have won out over the whole evil thing, as the name was popular with Puritans in England a few centuries ago.

In the U.S., Seth has been a regular on the charts since 1880, but didn't make big strides in popularity until the 1970s. It broke into the top 100 for the first time in 1980, but has slipped a little since then.

THIS NAME IN HISTORY

Seth Boyden (inventor)

Seth Eastman (painter)

Seth Green (actor)

Seth McClung (baseball player)

Seth McFarlane (creator of animated shows
    American Dad! and *Family Guy*)

Seth McKinney (football player)

Seth Meyers (actor)

Seth Rogen (actor)

TOP TEN: HEROES OF EPIC POEMS

1. Aeneas (*Aeneid*)
2. Achilles (*Iliad*)
3. Dante (*Inferno*)
4. Rama (*Ramayana*)
5. Odysseus (*Odyssey*)
6. Gilgamesh
7. Heinricherson (*Faust*)
8. Adam (*Paradise Lost*)
9. Beowulf
10. Arjuna (*Mahābhārata*)

Shane

Meaning: God is gracious

Origin: Irish

Related names and spelling variations: *None*

Proving how globe-trotting names can be, Shane is the Anglicized form of the name Sean, the Irish version of John, which comes from the Hebrew Johanan and means "God is gracious."

Using the name Shane would be a creative way for you to honor both Irish roots and a relative named John. Shane made its first appearance on the U.S. charts in the 1950s and reached the top 100 for the first time in 1969. It grew slightly more popular in the following years, but eventually dropped out of the top 100.

THIS NAME IN HISTORY

Shane Acker (director)

Shane Battier (basketball player)

Shane Doan (hockey player)

Shane Dorian (surfer)

Shane Haboucha (actor)

Shane Victorino (baseball player)

Shane (movie)

Silas

Meaning: Woods; to borrow

Origin: Greek; Latin; Aramaic

Related names and spelling variations: *Si*

Silas has Greek and Latin roots from the name Silvanus, meaning "woods," and Aramaic roots meaning "to borrow." One of the earliest references to the name Silas is in the New Testament, as St. Silas was an active guy in the first century. But if you're literary parents, you might be moved to pick Silas thanks to the famous George Eliot book *Silas Marner*.

Silas has been on the U.S. charts since 1880, when it ranked #140, its highest ranking ever. It declined in popularity over the next century and in the 1990s started to turn around. Silas has an old-fashioned charm and Si makes for a modern-sounding, cool nickname.

THIS NAME IN HISTORY

Silas Botwin (character on the TV
   show *Weeds*)

Silas Marner (book by George Eliot)

Simon

Meaning: To listen

Origin: Hebrew

Related names and spelling variations: *Simeon*

Simon is the anglicized version of the Hebrew name Simeon, meaning "to listen," something that we can absolutely guarantee your little Simon won't be doing all the time.

The name is used by a host of biblical figures, from Simon the Zealot to Simon the Leper, which may speak to the name's popularity in ancient times. Simon has been on the U.S. charts since 1880. It was at its most popular in the late 1880s, when it ranked #142 for a couple years. It declined in popularity through the 1960s, but then turned around, and has continued to climb. The name has had a somewhat nerdy rep in the last few decades, which actually makes it a prime candidate for transformation into a hip name today.

THIS NAME IN HISTORY

Simon Baker (actor)

Simon Cowell (TV personality)

Simon Rex (actor)

Solomon

Meaning: Peace

Origin: Hebrew

Related names and spelling variations: *Sol, Solly, Shlomo*

Solomon is derived from the Hebrew word *shalom*, which means "peace." It's a sweet sentiment, but experienced parents will laugh at you if you say you named your son Solomon because you just know he'll be a peaceful child.

Solomon was one of the Old Testament kings who had a rep for both good (founder of the first temple in Jerusalem; the wisdom thing) and not-so-great (seven hundred wives; idolatry).

TOP TEN: MOST DESTRUCTIVE HURRICANES

1. Katrina
2. Andrew
3. Wilma
4. Rita
5. Camille
6. Donna
7. Charley
8. Hugo
9. Celia
10. Eloise

The name Solomon ranked #198 on the U.S. charts in 1880, the only year it has ranked in the top 200. It declined in popularity into the 1960s, but has started to turn around. Sol or Solly make for cool, retro nicknames.

THIS NAME IN HISTORY
King Solomon (biblical figure)
Solomon Burke (singer)
Solomon Grundy (villain in *Superman* and *Batman* comic books; nursery rhyme character)
Solomon Islands (country)

Spencer

Meaning: Dispenser of supplies

Origin: English

Related names and spelling variations: *Spenser, Sponsor, Spence*

Spencer began as a surname and it indicated the person in a noble household who *dispensed* supplies or provisions. Get it? And it's fitting, given how much crap you'll be doling out all the time as new parents.

Spencer has been on the U.S. charts since 1880 and has been in the middle of the pack for most of that time. It made a big jump in 1992 when it hit the top 100 for the first time. Lady Diana's death (born Diana Spencer) in 1997 coincides with the name's highest ranking ever the following year at #84. Perhaps there's a connection. Perhaps there's not. Either

Hi, My Name Is

way the name has declined in popularity since then.

Spencer is a predecessor of the currently popular and similarly styled old-world occupational names like Mason, Carter, and Cooper. Spencer still has legs, though, and would be a great, less common alternative to those more popular choices.

THIS NAME IN HISTORY

Spencer Breslin (actor)

Spencer Fox (actor)

Spencer Hawes (basketball player)

Spencer Johnson (author)

Spencer Johnson (football player)

Spencer W. Kimball (former president of the Church of Jesus Christ of Latter Day Saints)

Spencer Pratt (reality TV star)

Spencer Tracy (actor)

Lady Diana Spencer (birth name of Diana, Princess of Wales)

Spenser: For Hire (TV show)

Stephen

Meaning: Crown

Origin: Greek

Related names and spelling variations: *Esteban, Steven, Steve, Stevie, Stephano, Stefan, Étienne*

Steven and Stephen both have Greek roots in the word *stephanos*, which means "crown." In the Stephen vs. Steven smackdown, even though Stephan was the original name, Steven with a *v* is now more popular.

There are Steven/Stephan versions all over the globe, from Stefan (Sweden) to Stefano (Italy) to Esteban (Spain). The *ph* version claims some notable Steves (scientist Hawking, horror writer King, three dozen various popes, rulers, and saints). But *v* Steven holds its own, too, with director Spielberg and martial arts master Seagal.

THIS NAME IN HISTORY

Stephen Colbert (political satirist)

Stephen Crane (author)

Stephen Jay Gould (evolutionary biologist)

Stephen Hawking (scientist)

Stephen King (author)

Steve Martin (actor and comedian)

Steven Seagal (actor and martial artist)

Stephen Sondheim (composer and lyricist)

Steven Spielberg (director)

Steven Tyler (singer)

Stevie Wonder (singer)

Tt

Tate

Meaning: Cheerful

Origin: Norse

Related names and spelling variations: *None*

Tate is a Norse name that means "cheerful," although we certainly can't guarantee your son will always have a happy disposition.

Tate entered the U.S. top 1,000 in 1971. It dropped off for all of the 1980s and made the charts again in 1990, claiming the next-to-last spot, #999. Tate climbed the charts through the mid-2000s, but has been on a downward slide the last few years.

Tate is one of those familiar, but never too common, names that many parents search for. Your little guy would probably be the only one with Tate on his kindergarten cubby.

THIS NAME IN HISTORY

Tate Donovan (actor)

Taylor

Meaning: Tailor

Origin: English

Related names and spelling variations: *Tay*

Taylor is one of those names in the midst of a girls vs. boys battle. Right now, Team Pink is on top. Go girls! Taylor has been on the boys' chart since 1880 and its use as a first name might have come in honor of U.S. president Zachary Taylor, the twelfth president, who died in 1850. Taylor for boys entered the top 100 in 1988, peaking at #51 in 1993. It's been on the decline since then.

Taylor for girls rose to the top 10 in 1993, where it stayed through 2000. It's dropped several spaces since then.

Two of the hottest young stars today share the name—Taylor Lautner (boy) and Taylor Swift (girl).

By the way, Taylor is an occupational name and means—you guessed it—"tailor."

Taylor Lautner (actor)

Taylor Mays (football player)

Taylor Momsen (actor)

Taylor Swift (singer)

Jonathan Taylor Thomas (actor)

Terrance

Meaning: Gracious, tender

Origin: Latin

Related names and spelling variations:
Terence, Terrence, Terry, Tyrese

Terrance comes from the Latin name Terentius, which may mean "gracious, tender"—one of the many names that you might give if you have, shall we say, optimistic, intentions. The first time your little Terry yanks the dog's tail, "tender" is not the first trait that comes to mind.

Terrance made the charts for the first time in 1932. It quickly grew in popularity, reaching #179 in 1979 and 1980. It has dropped in popularity since then. The traditional spelling of the name is Terence, but that doesn't appear on the U.S. charts anymore, while alternate spelling Terrence does.

THIS NAME IN HISTORY

Terry Bradshaw (sports analyst)

Terry Brooks (author)

Terence Trent D'Arby (musician)

Tyrese Gibson (rap artist and actor)

Terry Gilliam (actor)

Terrence Howard (actor)

Terry Pratchett (author)

TOP TEN: JAZZ MUSICIANS/SINGERS

1. Miles (Davis)
2. Duke (Ellington)
3. Benny (Goodman; Carter)
4. Billie (Holiday)
5. John (Coltrane; Patton)
6. Louis (Armstrong)
7. Ella (Fitzgerald)
8. Charlie/Charles (Parker; Mingus)
9. Ornette (Coleman)
10. Django (Reinhardt)

TOP TEN: INDIE FILM STARS

1. Jason (Schwartzman)
2. Ellen (Page)
3. Parker (Posey)
4. Zooey (Deschanel)
5. Emile (Hirsch)
6. Gael (García Bernal)
7. Chloë (Sevigny)
8. James (Franco)
9. Philip (Seymour Hoffman)
10. Maggie (Gyllenhaal)

Theodore

Meaning: God's gift

Origin: Greek

Related names and spelling variations: *Theo, Ted, Teddy*

Theodore is a Greek name that means "God's gift." You can be sure that a teenage Teddy will be using "God's gift . . . *to women*" as a pickup line one day a looong time from now. But it's also a charming meaning that could appeal to you if you have spiritual inclinations.

Theodore ranked in the U.S. top 100 from 1880 through 1944. Though it sounds old-fashioned, it's never been ranked below the top 314 names. Theodore is just the sort of vintage name that parents are reviving today, so it could be ready for a comeback. (Back in 1880 it was #70.) One of the best things about Theodore is that it has two very different, but equally cool, nicknames—Theo and Teddy.

THIS NAME IN HISTORY

Theodore Dreiser (author)

Theodor Geisel (given name of Dr. Seuss)

Theo Huxtable (character on *The Cosby Show*)

Ted Nugent (musician)

Theodore Roethke (poet)

Theodore "Teddy" Roosevelt (U.S. president)

Hi, My Name Is

Thomas

Meaning: Twin

Origin: Greek

Related names and spelling variations: *Tomas, Tom, Tommy, Thom*

One of the fun things about Thomas is that there is such a wide variety of namesakes that your little Tommy can look up to: from the biblical (the doubting Thomas apostle) to the whimsical (Thomas the Tank Engine), from the presidential (Jefferson) to the musical (The Who's rock opera *Tommy*), from literary (*Tom Sawyer*) to the libidinous (*Tom Jones*).

A Greek name that means "twin," Thomas is a classic boy's name that has appealed to parents for centuries. Thomas was in the top 50 names in the U.S. for a stunning 125-year stretch, from 1880 through 2005, and has fallen only slightly since then.

THIS NAME IN HISTORY

Tom Brady (football player)

Tom Cruise (actor)

Thomas Edison (inventor)

Tom Hanks (actor)

Thomas Hardy (author)

Tommy Hilfiger (fashion designer)

Thomas Hobbes (philosopher)

Thomas Jefferson (U.S. president)

Tom Jones (singer)

Tommy Lee Jones (actor)

Thomas Keller (chef)

Tom Petty (musician)

Tom Sawyer (character in Mark Twain's *The Adventures of Tom Sawyer*)

Thomas the Tank Engine (book by Rev. W. Awdry)

Thom Yorke (musician)

Tommy (rock musical by The Who)

Timothy

Meaning: Honoring God

Origin: Greek

Related names and spelling variations: *Tim, Timmy*

Timothy is a version of the Greek name Timotheos, which means "honoring God." You can remind your little Timmy of his holy obligation when he misbehaves.

The name is found in the New Testament, but wasn't widely used until the 1500s. In the U.S., Timothy was moderately popular between the 1880s and 1940s. It started to gain popularity and entered the top 30 in the 1950s, where it stayed for nearly forty years. Timothy's popularity has started to decline a little. Timothy is a classic name that manages not to be stuffy. Youthful Timmy makes a cute nickname for a little rug rat.

THIS NAME IN HISTORY

Tiny Tim (character in Charles Dickens's *A Christmas Carol*)

Tim Burton (director)

Tim Curry (actor)

Timothy Dalton (actor)

Timothy Geithner (U.S. secretary of the treasury)

Tim Lincecum (baseball player)

Tim McGraw (musician)

Tim O'Brien (author)

Tim Robbins (actor)

Titus

Meaning: Large; hero

Origin: Greek; Latin

Related names and spelling variations: *Tito*

Call your boy Titus and he's going to have some big things to live up to—the name may come from the Greek word for "large" and Latin for "hero." (We think he can do it. So does his daddy.)

When it comes to namesakes, however, the news is mixed. You've got the good—the Roman emperor who oversaw the completion of the Colosseum and comforted his people after the Mount Vesuvius eruption. Then there's Shakespeare's bloody play *Titus Andronicus* (you just don't want to know).

The name made only sporadic entries on the list of popular names from 1880 to the 1960s and has been in the 400s to 900s since then. Titus would be a great choice if you're looking for that uncommon, yet easy to pronounce, name.

THIS NAME IN HISTORY

Titus (Roman emperor)

Tito Jackson (singer)

Tito Puente (musician)

Titus Pullo (character on the TV show *Rome*)

Titus Andronicus (play by William Shakespeare)

Tobias

Meaning: God is good

Origin: Greek

Related names and spelling variations: *Toby, Tobin, Tobey*

Tobias is the Greek version of the Hebrew name Tobiah, meaning "God is good." This does not mean that your little Toby will always be good, but it can't hurt, no?

Irony aside, the definition has also obviously appealed to many religious parents. Tobias was on the U.S. charts in 1880, but only appeared again in a handful of years between then and 1967. Since then, the path hasn't been smooth, but Tobias has been on an upward trajectory.

Toby is an English version of Tobias and has been a popular name in its own right. It became a fixture in the top 1,000 in 1934. It took a predictable and smooth path up the charts, peaking in 1975 at #190. It has been dropping since then. It's surprising that Tobias and Toby haven't been more popular over the years as they are both uncommon yet approachable names.

THIS NAME IN HISTORY

Toby Flenderson (character on the TV show *The Office*)

Tobias Fünke (character on the TV show *Arrested Development*)

Toby Keith (singer)

Tobey Maguire (actor)

Toby Stephens (actor)

Tobias Wolff (author)

Todd

Meaning: Fox

Origin: English

Related names and spelling variations:
Tod, Toddy

Todd is an English name that means "fox." The name could appeal to wild animal lovers. Students of symbolism would appreciate the fox's rep for slyness and trickery (isn't every toddler boy "crazy like a . . ."?).

After a brief appearance on the U.S. charts in the 1880s, Todd dropped off until 1936. It quickly became popular and entered the top 100 in 1959, where it stayed through 1985. It has evened off quite a bit since then. Todd is a simple, unpretentious name that works well with a variety of last names—especially longer ones that are balanced by a shorter first name.

THIS NAME IN HISTORY

Todd Bridges (actor)

Todd Phillips (screenwriter and director)

Todd Rundgren (musician)

Todd Wellemeyer (baseball player)

Travis

Meaning: Crossroads, junction

Origin: French

Related names and spelling variations: *None*

Travis is one of the more enigmatic occupational names. It was a French name meaning "crossroads, junction," and was used as an occupational name for toll collectors.

There have been only four years since 1880 that Travis was not in the U.S. top 1,000 and the most recent year was all the way back in 1901. Travis was at its most popular from the 1970s through the 1990s, but has dropped in popularity since then. Despite the older history, Travis still has a modern ring.

THIS NAME IN HISTORY

Travis Barker (musician)

Travis Kvapil (race car driver)

Travis Pastrana (motocross rider)

Travis Tomko (pro wrestler)

Travis Tritt (singer)

Trenton

Meaning: Trent's town

Origin: English

Related names and spelling variations: *Trent*

How is it possible that the name of a poverty-stricken town in New Jersey wound up as one of the most popular names for boys in the U.S.?

Here's to hoping that the honor is due to patriotism. Trenton is an English name that means "Trent's town," and is the name of the capital of the Garden State. The city was settled in the late 1600s by a man named William Trent and it was the site of a crucial battle in the Revolutionary War where George Washington and his army defeated British troops.

As a boy's name, Trenton first made the U.S. charts in 1963 at #880. It has gradually gotten more popular since then. Though Trenton has a different origin than the name Trent (an English name that means "traveler, journey"), they obviously sound a lot alike. Trent has a longer history on the charts and was originally more popular, but has been taken over by Trenton.

City names turned first names are hot these days. Some other common ones are Brooklyn, Paris, London, and Memphis. (Detroit, another down-on-its-luck city, has not had a similar name-based renaissance.)

THIS NAME IN HISTORY

Trenton Doyle Hancock (artist)
Trenton Hassell (basketball player)
Trenton Knight (actor)
Trenton Rogers (actor)
Trenton Lee Stewart (author)

Trevor

Meaning: Big village; industrious

Origin: Welsh; Irish

Related names and spelling variations: *Trev*

Trevor has Welsh roots meaning "big village" and Irish roots meaning "industrious." Here's to hoping that the industrious part leads him to be the kind of kid who will clean his room.

Trevor sounds like a hip, modern name, but it made the U.S. top 1,000 for the first time back in 1956. The reason it sounds contemporary may be because it ranked in the top 100 from 1986 through 2003. It has dropped several slots since then. Trevor is still a cool-kid name and is a good style match for names like Ryan, Logan, and Reece.

THIS NAME IN HISTORY

Trevor Ariza (basketball player)
Trevor Hoffman (baseball player)
Trevor Howard (actor)
Trevor Nunn (director)
Trevor Pryce (football player)
Trevor St. John (actor)

Trey

Meaning: Three

Origin: Latin

Related names and spelling variations: *Tre*

Trey comes from the Latin word *tres*, which means "three" and is associated with playing cards and dice with that number of pips on them. Three is also a symbolic number—consider the Holy Trinity (the Father, Son, and Holy Spirit) and the phrase "third time's a charm." It could be a sly way to name your son "the third" without calling him, say, John III.

Trey entered the U.S. charts in 1964. It grew in popularity, peaking at #189 in 1999, and has been decreasing in popularity since then. Trey would be a good choice if you're looking for contemporary sounding names.

Hi, My Name Is

Tristan

Meaning: Unknown

Origin: Celtic

Related names and spelling variations: *Tristen, Triston, Tristin, Tristian, Trystan, Tristram*

One of the downers of the baby name set, Tristan's meaning cannot be confirmed, but many associate it with the Latin word *tristis*, which means "sad." On top of that, the Celtic legend of Tristan and Isolde is a heartbreaker. Tristan is sent to Ireland to fetch Isolde so she can marry a king. They fall in love instead, and Tristan goes off to fight the king, dies in battle, and she perishes of grief beside his body. (We did warn you.)

But the name does have charm, so much so that it first made the charts in 1971 at #861 and has been steadily working its way up since then. Some of its recent popularity is probably due to a 2006 movie *Tristan + Isolde* about the tragic duo.

Tristan has spurred a variety of spellings, including: Tristen, Triston, Tristin, Tristian, and Trystan.

THIS NAME IN HISTORY

Tristan Murail (composer)

Tristan Rogers (actor)

Tristan Tzara (poet)

Tristan Wilds (actor)

Tristan and Isolde (Celtic legend)

**TOP TEN:
KIDS' BOOK CHARACTERS**

❶ Harry (Potter)

❷ Eloise

❸ Madeline

❹ Olivia

❺ Sam (I Am)

❻ Arthur

❼ Peter (Rabbit)

❽ Amelia (Bedelia)

❾ George (Curious)

❿ James (and the Giant Peach)

Troy

Meaning: Soldier; curly hair

Origin: Irish; French

Related names and spelling variations: *None*

Troy may have Irish roots meaning "soldier" or French roots meaning "curly hair." Sure, one definition has nothing to do with the other, but that's the deal.

Troy is probably most famous for the Greek city of Troy—the site of the Trojan War and home of the legendary beauty Helen of Troy. As a first name, Troy has been in the U.S. top 1,000 since 1880. In the 1960s and 1970s it was in the top 100 names but has been sliding since then. Troy is a great one-syllable option if you prefer short names.

THIS NAME IN HISTORY

Troy Aikman (football player)

Troy Duffy (director)

Troy Glaus (baseball player)

Troy Polamalu (football player)

Tucker

Meaning: Fuller

Origin: English

Related names and spelling variations: *Tuck*

Tucker is an English occupational name with a long backstory. It means "fuller," and since there are no fullers listed on Monster.com, we'll explain. A fuller was someone who worked with garments and cloth, and "to full" was to tuck and gather along a seam to add fullness. So

Tucker might appeal to you if you're fashion mavens or if you appreciate complex etymology.

Tucker made the U.S. charts for the first time in 1978 at #974 and has been getting more popular since then. Conservative commentator Tucker Carlson may have helped give the name a boost.

THIS NAME IN HISTORY

Tucker Carlson (news commentator)

Tyler

Meaning: Tiler, tile maker

Origin: English

Related names and spelling variations: *Ty*

Tyler is one of many occupational names (see Mason and Parker). It refers, naturally, to a person who worked as a tiler or tile maker. The name Tyler didn't become a regular on the U.S. charts until 1946. It rose to the top 100 in 1981 and became a top 10 name in the 1990s, falling slightly since then. Tyler is short, sweet, and friendly and has cool nickname potential with Ty.

THIS NAME IN HISTORY

Ty Burrell (actor)

Tyler Florence (celebrity chef)

Tyler Hilton (actor)

Tyler Patrick Jones (actor)

Tyler Kennedy (hockey player)

Tyler Perry (actor and comedian)

John Tyler (U.S. president)

Steven Tyler (musician)

Hi, My Name Is

Tyrone

Meaning: Owen's land; young warrior

Origin: Irish; Latin

Related names and spelling variations: *Ty*

Tyrone has Irish roots meaning "Owen's land" and Latin roots meaning "young warrior." The "young warrior" thing will make sense when your little Tyrone goes to battle against the monsters under his bed.

Tyrone made the U.S. top 1,000 for the first time in 1937. It quickly gained popularity over the next decades, peaking at #132 in 1970, and has declined quite a bit since then. Tyrone sounds like the quintessential 1960s or 1970s name. If you're looking for a throwback to that period, you might be attracted to Tyrone; it's not old-fashioned, not contemporary, but somewhere in the middle.

THIS NAME IN HISTORY

Tyrone Power (actor)

Tyson

Meaning: Dye's son; firebrand

Origin: English

Related names and spelling variations: *Ty*

Tyson is English and has dual meanings. One is "Dye's son" (Dye is a nickname for the name Dionysia, the Latin form of Denise), a perfect choice if your name happens to be Dionysia.

Since that's not very likely, look to the other possible definition—"firebrand." Back in the olden days, apparently, Tison was a nickname given to someone hotheaded. We think this lets you off the hook for your tot's tantrums. *"What can I do? It's his name!"* Try it and let us know how it works out.

Tyson entered the U.S. charts in 1966. It peaked in 1984 at #239 and then started to decline over the next decade. Tyson turned around again in the late 1990s and has been gaining ground since.

THIS NAME IN HISTORY

Tyson Apostol (reality TV star)

Tyson Beckford (model and actor)

Tyson Chandler (basketball player)

Tyson Gillies (baseball player)

Tyson Ritter (singer)

Tyson Foods (poultry company)

Vv

Vance

Meaning: Marsh, bog

Origin: English

Related names and spelling variations: *Van*

If you're looking for a name that no other kids in kindergarten will share with your son, consider Vance. An English name that means "marsh, bog," Vance entered the U.S. charts in 1880 at #803. It spent most of the following decades in the top 500, peaking at #328 in 1969. It has dropped in popularity since then, even missing the charts entirely in 1998 and 2000, but recently snuck back on.

Van is a nickname for Vance (for Evan and Ivan, too) and it's just slightly more popular than Vance. Vance is similar in style to more popular names like Gavin, Mason, and Carter—so it's a good name if you want something a tad more unique but similar to these names.

THIS NAME IN HISTORY

Vance DeGeneres (actor)

Van Jones (environmental activist)

Van Morrison (musician)

Vivian Vance (actor)

Victor

Meaning: Victor

Origin: Latin

Related names and spelling variations: *Viktor, Vic*

It's no surprise what Victor means—it's a Latin name and literally means "victor." You will have to break it to him that this does not mean he will always win at Candy Land.

Victor has been a very steady favorite of parents, ranging between the #63 and #138 spots on the list of popular names in the U.S. Although Victor has always been popular, it's never reached the top 50. The name has been getting less common for the last several years.

THIS NAME IN HISTORY

Victor Borge (musician and comedian)

Victor Garber (actor)

Victor Hugo (author)

Victor Wooten (musician)

Victor Victoria (musical and movie)

Vincent

Meaning: To conquer

Origin: Latin

Related names and spelling variations:
Vincente, Vince, Vinnie

Vincent is the French form of the Latin name Vincens, meaning "to conquer." Vincent van Gogh conquered the art world, Vinny Testaverde tackled the gridiron. What will your little Vincent master?

Vincent has been a steady choice for U.S. parents since the 1880s, even spending a number of years in the top 100. Vincent peaked in 1966 at #58, and has been headed down the charts since the 1990s. Vincent is one of those names that's never been too popular or too unpopular, making it a very fine pick if you like that middle ground.

THIS NAME IN HISTORY

Vincent Canby (film critic)
Vin Diesel (actor)
Vincent D'Onofrio (actor)
Vince Gill (singer)
Vincent Lecavalier (hockey player)
Vince Lombardi (football coach)
Vincente Minnelli (director)
Vincent Price (actor)
Vinny Testaverde (football player)
Vincent van Gogh (artist)
Vince Vaughn (actor)

TOP TEN: LATE NIGHT TV HOSTS

1. Johnny (Carson)
2. David (Letterman)
3. Jay (Leno)
4. Ed (Sullivan; McMahon)
5. Conan (O'Brien)
6. Jimmy (Kimmel; Fallon)
7. Craig (Ferguson; Kilborn)
8. Merv (Griffin)
9. Bill (Maher)
10. Arsenio (Hall)

Ww

Wade

Meaning: River crossing

Origin: English

Related names and spelling variations: *None*

If you want a water-based name, Wade is a good choice. An English name, Wade means "river crossing." In Old English, it is also linked to the word *wadan*, which means "to go" and was a name given to a legendary sea monster.

Recently, the name has been more associated with cowboys than creatures (see Dallas Cowboys head coach Wade Phillips). In the U.S., Wade has been on the charts since 1880. It spent most of the time between then and the mid-1960s in the top 300 and then it started to increase in popularity. Wade peaked in 1966 at #183 and has been on the decline since then.

THIS NAME IN HISTORY

Wade Boggs (baseball player)

Wade Phillips (football coach)

Wade Robson (choreographer)

Walker

Meaning: Fuller

Origin: English

Related names and spelling variations: *None*

It takes a little time to get to the bottom of the name Walker. It's an English occupational name for a fuller (similar to the name Tucker). Fulling cloth involves treading it during the dying process, and *treading* is another word for walking. Hence Walker. Get it?

Walker was in the U.S. top 1,000 between 1880 and 1955. Then it dropped off the charts for a few decades before it became a regular fixture again in 1988. It gained popularity until 2005, but then dipped again. Walker is similar in style to other old-fashioned occupational names like Cooper, Tyler, and Hunter, but is much less common, making it a good choice if you want something a little more unique.

THIS NAME IN HISTORY

Walker Evans (NASCAR driver)

Walker Hancock (sculptor)

Walker Percy (author)

Walter

Meaning: Army leader

Origin: German

Related names and spelling variations:
Walt, Wally

Walter is a name with an unfortunate, and inaccurate, nerdy reputation. Far from implying a pocket-protector-wearing dork, Walter is a German name that means "army leader." All those tough-sounding Jacks and Maxes on the playground better watch out for Wally!

Walter was very popular in the Middle Ages, and while the name feels a little old-fashioned today, it does have a strong sound. In the U.S., Walter was a top 15 name from 1880 to the early 1920s. It stayed in the top 100 through 1972, but has been on the decline since then. Like other old-fashioned names, Walter has a kind of brainy charm that may make the name cool again.

THIS NAME IN HISTORY

Walt Lloyd (character on the TV show *Lost*)

Walter Cronkite (commentator)

Walt Disney (animator and filmmaker)

Wally Lamb (author)

Walter Matthau (actor)

Walt Whitman (poet)

TOP TEN: SPORTSCASTER NAMES

1. Marv (Albert)
2. John (Madden, McEnroe)
3. Vin (Scully)
4. Howard (Cosell)
5. Dick (Enberg, Vitale, Irvin Jr.)
6. Al (Michaels)
7. Brent (Musburger)
8. Joe (Buck)
9. Harry (Caray)
10. Chick (Hearn)

Warren

Meaning: Game warden

Origin: French

Related names and spelling variations: *Werner*

Warren is a name that could appeal to a wide variety of parents. It's an occupational name with French roots that means "game warden" and it also refers to a place to raise rabbits—making it a good choice if you're animal lovers. Then there's the wide variety of famous Warrens, from presidential (Harding) to sports-related (football player Warren Sapp).

Warren has been on the U.S. charts since 1880. It got a huge bump in the early 1920s, which coincides with the twenty-ninth U.S. president's tenure in the White House. Warren has been on a slow decline since then. The name did move up a few spots in recent years, though—perhaps because NFL star Warren Sapp charmed viewers with his fancy footwork on the TV show *Dancing with the Stars* in 2008.

THIS NAME IN HISTORY

Warren Beatty (actor)

Warren Buffett (investor)

Warren Harding (U.S. president)

Warren Sapp (football player)

Warren Zevon (musician)

William

Meaning: Determined protector

Origin: German

Related names and spelling variations: *Bill, Billy, Will, Wilhelm, Guillermo, Willie*

William—a German name that means "determined protector"—has a stunning record of popularity: it's been in the top 20 names in the U.S. since 1880. For all but thirty of those years, it's been in the top 10 names. Yes, there will likely be more than one William in your kid's class, but you'll always be able to find the keychain with his name on it at Disneyland.

There was a time in the ninth century (after the Norman Conquest, led by William the Conqueror) that the name William was even more popular than the perennially popular name John. When John took over in the Middle Ages, William remained the second most popular name for centuries. Despite its popularity, it has never snagged that coveted #1 spot in the U.S.

THIS NAME IN HISTORY

will.i.am (singer)

Bill Clinton (U.S. president)

Bill Cosby (comedian and actor)

Guillermo del Toro (director)

Will & Grace (TV show)

William "Buffalo Bill" Cody
(Wild West figure)

Will Ferrell (comedian and actor)

William H. Macy (actor)

Willie Mays (baseball player)

Willie Nelson (musician)

William Shakespeare (playwright)

William Shatner (actor)

Will Smith (actor and singer)

William Wordsworth (poet)

William Butler Yeats (poet)

Wyatt

Meaning: Strength in battle

Origin: English

Related names and spelling variations: *None*

Wyatt is an English name that means "strength in battle," a definition that matches the name's rugged appeal. It doesn't really matter that the only battle your little Wyatt will be fighting for many years is the one against the monsters under his bed.

The name is still widely associated with legendary lawman Wyatt Earp and the gunfight at the O.K. Corral. In the U.S., Wyatt was on the charts in 1880, but dropped off for a number of years between the 1920s and 1950s. In the following decades, Wyatt took a slow path up the charts, but started to rise quickly in the mid-1990s. Sheryl Crow named her son Wyatt in 2007, which may have given the already rising name an extra boost.

NAME FACTOID

Wyatt Earp fought alongside his brothers at the O.K. Corral. Their names were Morgan and Virgil. Wyatt and Morgan have recently become popular. Will Virgil be next? You decide.

THIS NAME IN HISTORY

Wyatt Crow (son of Sheryl Crow)

Wyatt Cenac (comedian and correspondent on *The Daily Show with Jon Stewart*)

Wyatt Earp (Wild West figure)

Xx

Xavier

Meaning: Bright; new house

Origin: Arabic; Basque

Related names and spelling variations: *Zavier, Xzavier, Javier*

Xavier may have Arabic roots meaning "bright" or Basque roots meaning "the new house." Xavier is also one of only a couple viable *X* names (the names Xiomar and Xidorn are just not as catchy).

The name became popular among Catholics because of St. Francis Xavier, the founder of the Jesuits. Today, the name has gone beyond its strong religious association and might even be better known among comic book fans, thanks to Professor Charles Xavier and his X-Men.

In the U.S., Xavier made the charts in 1890 and then disappeared until 1948. It made the list for a few decades (in the 400s to 800s) but then got a boost in the 1980s, dipping into the 200s. This may have been influenced by Xavier Roberts, who helped create the Cabbage Patch Kid craze.

Xavier is super popular these days, perhaps influenced by today's quirky parents, who like the cool *X* initial. The Spanish version of the name, Javier, is also becoming more common.

THIS NAME IN HISTORY

Xavier Adibi (football player)

Javier Bardem (actor)

Xavier Martínez (painter)

Xavier Roberts (co-creator of the Cabbage Patch Kids)

Xavier Nady (baseball player)

St. Francis Xavier (founder of the Jesuits)

Zz

Zachary

Meaning: God has remembered

Origin: Hebrew

Related names and spelling variations:
*Zachery, Zackary, Zackery, Zack, Zac, Zach,
Zechariah*

Zachary is a version of the Hebrew name Zechariah, meaning "God has remembered," which is a good thing because with a new baby around the house you'll be so sleep deprived you won't remember a freakin' thing.

The name debuted in the U.S. top 1,000 in 1946, slowly gained in popularity for a couple of decades before skyrocketing in the late 1970s, hitting #96 in 1976. The rare and cool *Z* initial probably helped that rise. Zachary was at its most popular in 1994 at #12. It has dropped a few spots since then.

With other old-fashioned biblical names coming back into style, maybe Zachary's root name, Zechariah, is also bracing for a boost.

THIS NAME IN HISTORY

Zach Braff (actor)

Zachery Ty Bryan (actor)

Zac Efron (actor)

Zach Galifianakis (comedian)

Zachary Levi (actor)

Zachary Quinto (actor)

Zecharia Sitchin (author)

Zachary Taylor (U.S. president)

Zach Thomas (football player)

GIRLS' NAMES

The popularity analysis is based on the Social Security data on first names from card applications for births. The data is first recorded for the year 1880.

Aa

Aaliyah

Meaning: High, lofty; sublime

Origin: Arabic

Related names and spelling variations: *Aaliya, Alea, Aleah, Aleea, Aleeyah, Alia, Aliah, Aliya, Aliyah, Aliye, Allia, Alliah*

When fifteen-year-old pop star Aaliyah's first album, *Age Ain't Nothing But a Number*, was released and climbed the charts in 1994, her first name hit the charts, too, reaching #202 in the same year. When she died in a plane crash in 2001, her name skyrocketed in popularity. This name just sings to parents!

Aaliyah is the female version of the Arabic male name Ali. Like Ali Baba in Scheherazade's 1,001 tales, fame and fortune may come to an Aaliyah by simply saying, "Open, sesame!" Or like Muhammad Ali, she could be a champion, besting even the greatest opponents.

THIS NAME IN HISTORY

Aaliyah (pop singer)

Abigail

Meaning: Father of joy

Origin: Hebrew

Related names and spelling variations: *Abbigail, Abagael, Abagail, Abbey, Abbie, Abbigayle, Abby, Abegail, Abigayle, Gail, Gale, Gayle, Abigale*

Today's parents think this name—popular as far back as the 1500s—is an old classic, but for most of the twentieth century, people just thought it was *old*. But the name became retro-cool in 2001 and has been in the top 10 ever since.

Abigail is a Hebrew name from the Bible that can be interpreted as "father of joy," but we're sure moms will love this one, too. And as a backup life plan, an Abby can always find a lucrative career as an advice columnist.

THIS NAME IN HISTORY

Abigail Adams (first lady)

Abigail Breslin (actor)

Abby Cadabby (*Sesame Street* character)

Abbie Cornish (actor)

Abby Kelley (abolitionist and women's rights activist)

Abigail Van Buren (original author of
"Dear Abby")
A Is for Abigail (children's book by
Lynne Cheney)

Addison

Meaning: Adam's son

Origin: English

Related names and spelling variations:
*Addeson, Addie, Addy, Addyson, Adison,
Adisson, Addisyn, Adyson, Adison*

This name had a gender change in recent
years. The name is actually unisex, but was
more popular for boys from 1880 to the
1930s. The mid-1990s saw its reappear-
ance, but this time as a girl's name. While
still unisex, your son might not appreciate sharing his name with so many girls.

And he'll know plenty of Addisons.
Thanks to Addison Montgomery, a
character on *Grey's Anatomy* and *Private
Practice*, the name's popularity took off in
2005 and 2006. Fans of both shows may
expect future Addisons to have great success in their career pursuits, but less luck
in their love lives.

THIS NAME IN HISTORY

Addison (character from *Saw II*)

Lt. Col. Addison Baker (Medal of Honor
awardee from World War II)

Dr. Addison Forbes Montgomery
(character from *Grey's Anatomy*
and *Private Practice*)

TOP TEN: AMERICAN FEMALE INVENTORS

1. Mary (Anderson; Walton)
2. Roxey (Ann Caplin)
3. Beulah (Louise Henry)
4. Ruth (Graves Wakefield; Handler)
5. Margaret (Knight)
6. Josephine (Cochrane)
7. Rachel (Fuller Brown)
8. Bette (Nesmith Graham)
9. Stephanie (Kwolek)
10. Barbara (Askins)

Addison Richards (actor)

Dr. Thomas Addison (physician for whom Addison's disease is named)

Adelaide

Meaning: Noble, kind

Origin: French; German

Related Names: *Adelaida, Adelade, Ada, Addy, Addie, Adelheid*

The name Adelaide enjoyed almost sixty years in the spotlight, but like zoot suits and the jitterbug, it lost its popularity in the 1940s. A French name with German roots that means "noble and kind," Adelaide has a singsongy sound and an old-fashioned, almost Victorian appeal.

Although it returned to the charts in 2005, Adelaide's still not trendy, making it a good pick for trendsetters and traditionalists alike. And Addie makes for a cute nickname.

THIS NAME IN HISTORY

Adelaide (character in the musical *Guys and Dolls*)

Adelaide (capital city of South Australia)

Adeline

Meaning: Noble

Origin: French

Related names: *Adele, Adelina, Adalyn*

The 2010s might be Adeline's decade. Although it dropped off the charts in 1954, it reappeared in 1999 and has been rising quickly ever since. Like old-fashioned Vivian, Violet, and Nora, Adeline is coming back into style.

Adeline, which first appeared in the 1500s, comes from the much older French name Adele. Although Adele is short and sweet, it hasn't been popular since 1969.

THIS NAME IN HISTORY

St. Adele (Catholic saint)

Adeline Genée (ballet dancer)

Adele Wechsler (fashion designer)

Adriana

Meaning: From the Adriatic Sea; black

Origin: Latin

Related names and spelling variations: *Adria, Adrian, Adrianna, Adrienne, Adrianne*

Adriana is the new Adrienne. Okay, it's not that new . . . Adriana has been in the U.S. top 1,000 since the 1960s. But while Adrienne, a favorite since the early 1900s, has been slipping in popularity over the last two decades, Adriana is more popular than ever, peaking in 2004 at #119, and alternative Adrianna isn't far behind.

Both names are female versions of the boy's name Adrian, meaning "from the Adriatic Sea" and "black." And like older brother Adrian—once the name of a great Roman emperor—these girls rule!

THIS NAME IN HISTORY

Adriana Caselotti (voice of Snow White in *Snow White and the Seven Dwarfs* in the 1937 Disney movie)

Adrianna Costa (entertainment reporter)

1. Felicity
2. Kirsten
3. Samantha
4. Molly
5. Addy
6. Josefina
7. Kit
8. Rebecca
9. Kaya
10. Julie

Adrianne Curry (model)
Adriana Lima (model)
Adrienne Rich (poet)
Adriana Trigiani (author)
Adriana Lecouvreur (Italian opera)

Ainsley

Meaning: One's own meadow

Origin: Scottish

Related names and spelling variations: *Ainslee, Ainsleigh, Aynsley*

Och aye! Ainsley, a classic last name in Scotland, hit the top 1,000 girls' names at #481 in 2001, and hasn't moved much since.

Ainsley isn't the only lastie to become a girl's firstie: Delaney, Paisley, and Peyton are recent last-name-firsters, too.

Ainsley means "one's own meadow." If you worry that the "grass will be greener" somewhere else, you might pick this in the hopes that your daughter will stay close to home or visit often.

THIS NAME IN HISTORY

Aynsley Dunbar (musician)
Ainsley Earhardt (TV journalist)
Ainsley Harriot (celebrity chef)
Ainsley Hayes (character on the TV show *The West Wing*)

Alana

Meaning: Handsome, harmonious; rock

Origin: Celtic

Related names and spelling variations: *Alanna, Alannah, Alanis, Alannis, Alani*

Alana, the feminine version of the Celtic name Alan, means "handsome, harmonious; rock," making it a great pick if you want a peaceful, steady daughter. But Alanis Morissette, whose name is an Alana spinoff, has enjoyed twenty years of fame by making music that's the opposite: gritty, confrontational, and emotionally charged. Isn't *that* ironic?

After entering the U.S. charts in 1944, Alana has been a steady presence (get it?) and is still gaining popularity.

THIS NAME IN HISTORY

Alana Blanchard (surfer)

Alana de la Garza (actor)

Alanis Morissette (singer)

Alannah Myles (singer)

Alana Stewart (actor)

Alexis, Alexandra

Meaning: Mankind's defender

Origin: Greek

Related names and spelling variations: *Alejandra, Aleksia, Alessandra, Alex, Alexa, Alexea, Alexia, Alexandria, Alexus, Lexi, Lexie, Lexy, Sandra*

Alexis and Alexandra are sure to be strong women. They're derived from Greek boy's names Alexius ("to defend, to help") and Alexander ("mankind's defender"), whose combined ranks include five Byzantine emperors and the Macedonian king Alexander the Great. Careful, parents: your little princess might think she's already a queen!

Alexis hit the charts in 1943 and peaked at #3 in 1999. Alexandra became a list regular in 1938 and hit the top 100 in 1984.

THIS NAME IN HISTORY

Alexia (Europop singer)

Alexia Barroso (stepdaughter of Matt Damon)

Princess Alexia (princess of the Netherlands)

Princess Alexia (princess of Greece and Denmark)

Alexia Admor (fashion designer)

Alessandra Ambrosio (model)

Alexis Bledel (actor)

Alexa Ray Joel (musician and daughter of Billy Joel)

Aleksia Landeau (actor)

Alexandra Paul (actor)

Alice

Meaning: Noble, kind

Origin: English; French

Related names and spelling variations: *Alys, Alis, Alisia, Alicia, Alisha*

Off with her head! Just kidding. Alice is a version of Adelaide, which means "noble and kind." But ever since Lewis Carroll sent his famous seven-year-old down a rabbit hole in 1865, the name has been all about adventure. The book sent the name on an adventure of its own: up to the top 15 for most years between 1880 and 1925, then slowly back down the list.

Neither a nineties actor (Silverstone) nor an R&B singer (Keys) could send Alice-variation Alicia back up the charts. The name hit the top 100 in 1972, but has been falling since.

THIS NAME IN HISTORY

Alicia Keys (musician)

Alicia Silverstone (actor)

Alice Walker (author)

Alice Waters (chef)

Alice's Adventures in Wonderland (novel by Lewis Carroll)

Alison

Meaning: Noble

Origin: French; Scottish

Related names and spelling variations: *Ali, Alisoun, Alisson, Allison, Alli, Allicen, Allie, Allisson, Ally, Allyson, Alyson, Alysoun, Alysson*

Alison, a nickname for Alice, has been used in Scotland for centuries. It wasn't until the twentieth century that England warmed up to this great name, but the word has spread—Alison entered the U.S.

TOP TEN: BRITISH PRINCESSES

1. Louise
2. Victoria
3. Elizabeth
4. Mary
5. Augusta
6. Alexandra
7. Caroline
8. Sophia
9. Charlotte
10. Anne

charts in 1934 and grew more popular for several decades. Soon some parents added another *l*. Allison first appeared in the U.S. top 1,000 in 1946 and made a big leap in 1958, right around the time that Robert Mitchum starred in Academy Award–nominated *Heaven Knows, Mr. Allison*. Allison outgrew Alison in the sixties, and is still the big sister today. For you sassy spellers, other siblings include Allie, Allyson, Alyson, Alisson, Allisson, and Ally.

THIS NAME IN HISTORY

Alyson Hannigan (actor)

Allison Iraheta (singer)

Allison Janney (actor)

Alison Krauss (bluegrass/country singer)

Ali Landry (actor)

Ali Larter (actor)

Allison MacKenzie (character in the novel, film, and soap opera *Peyton Place*)

Alison McGhee (author)

Alison Mosshart (musician)

Alison Sweeney (actor)

June Allyson (actor)

"Alison" (song by Elvis Costello)

Heaven Knows, Mr. Allison (movie)

Alyssa

Meaning: Noble

Origin: English

Related names and spelling variations:
Alissa, Alisse, Allissa, Allyssa, Alysa, Alyssia, Lissa, Lyssa

News flash, young parents-to-be: *Charmed* wasn't Alyssa Milano's first walk around the block. Neither was *Melrose Place*. Her breakout (no Proactiv pun intended) role as Samantha Micelli in *Who's the Boss?* made her first name break out, too. Alyssa, a version of Alicia that first hit the U.S. charts in the 1960s, soared in popularity in the mid-1980s . . . and has been there ever since.

THIS NAME IN HISTORY

Alyssa Milano (actor)

Alyssa Satin Capucilli (children's book author)

Alyssa Day (fantasy author)

Alisa Weilerstein (cellist)

Alyssum (flower)

Amanda

Meaning: Lovable

Origin: Latin

Related names and spelling variations:
Mandine, Mandy, Amandine

Just like Amanda Bynes's hit movie, this name is *What a Girl Wants*! But parents are starting to disagree: Amanda—a Latin name that means "lovable"—is slowly on its way out. The name rose to fame in the 1970s, maintained a spot in the U.S. top 10 between 1976 and 1995, and has been slipping ever since.

To be fair to this perennial classic, this isn't its first dance in and out of favor. The name came into usage in the 1600s, has been on the U.S. charts since 1880, and came in and out of favor once already before the seventies. So fear not, Amanda Bynes fans—just like the twenty-something retiree actor, this name is bound to make another comeback.

Amanda Bynes (actor)
Mandy Moore (singer and actor)
Amanda Peet (actor)
Amanda Seyfried (actor)
Oliver and Amanda (children's book series)
"Amanda" (song by Boston)
"Mandy" (song by Barry Manilow)

Amber

Meaning: Amber

Origin: Arabic

Related names and spelling variations: *None*

Amber has been popular since the Stone Age. Nope, not the name . . . the rock. Actually fossilized resin, it's most useful in jewelry and in warding off ghosts and demons.

Amber wasn't a first name until the 1800s, but it was on the U.S. charts for most of the time between 1880 and 1916. But unlike Beulah or Gladys, this gem of a name is no antique; it made a comeback in 1945, hit the top 100 in 1974, and stayed there for thirty years. Although the name has slipped a bit, if you're nature lovers, you'll still find Amber a much more socially accepted option than Skye, Rainbow, or Ocean.

THIS NAME IN HISTORY
Amber Tamblyn (actor)
Amber Valletta (model)
Forever Amber (novel by Kathleen Winsor)

Amelia

Meaning: Hardworking; rival

Origin: English

Related names and spelling variations:
Aemelia, Amalia, Amélie, Amelie, Amilia, Emelia, Millie, Milly

Amelia, a cross between Emily and Amalia, means "hardworking; rival." Today it's tied to the great aviatrix (there's a word you don't hear often!) Amelia Earhart, who went missing in-flight in 1937 and reappeared (or so Hilary Swank's performance suggests) in 2009's *Amelia*. Like Alice, Amelia is now synonymous with adventure.

You might pick Amelia for its nickname potential: Millie, Mia, and Lia are all cute options. After the 2001 movie that bears the name, more and more parents are flocking to French version Amélie instead. But classic Amelia remains a popular choice . . . and a great alternative to the ubiquitous Emily.

THIS NAME IN HISTORY
Amelia Earhart (aviatrix)
"Amelia" (song by Joni Mitchell)
Amelia (novel by Henry Fielding)
Amelia Bedelia (series of books by
   Peggy Parish)

Amelia's Notebook (series of books by Marissa Moss)

The Fabulous Destiny of Amélie Poulain (movie)

Amy

Meaning: Beloved

Origin: Latin; French

Related names and spelling variations: *Ami, Aimee, Amee, Aymee, Aimie, Aimy, Aimée, Amie, Amye, Amé, Aymi*

Parents, don't let Winehouse wreck this classic. Amy is an old name with Latin and French roots that means "beloved," and any girl with the name is sure to be a sweetie. It's been a favorite for years—it's been on the charts since 1880 and in the top 10 every year from 1969 through 1982, and it even peaked at #2 before starting to slide back down. Today Amy has fallen out of favor, but we expect it to be back before long. After all, Wino isn't Amy's only ambassador; with luck, your girl might be as pretty as Adams, as funny as Poehler, or as spunky as Sedaris.

THIS NAME IN HISTORY

Amy Adams (actor)

Amy Carter (daughter of former U.S. president Jimmy Carter)

Amy Grant (musician)

Amy Klobuchar (U.S. senator)

Aimee Mann (musician)

Amy March (character from Louisa May Alcott's *Little Women*)

Amy Poehler (actor)

Amy Sedaris (author)

Amy Tan (author)

Amy Winehouse (singer)

Anastasia

Meaning: Resurrection

Origin: Russian

Related names and spelling variations: *Any, Stacy, Stacey, Stasia*

Anastasia, a Russian name that means "resurrection," sounds too beautiful to be believed, more likely to be a perfume brand than a person. But the name, used as far back as the fourth century, is an old standard that's never quite seen its day in the sun. It was on the U.S. charts from 1880 to 1932, fell off for years, then became a permanent fixture again in 1963. It saw its peak at #264 in 1998, and has dropped slightly since then. Although its elegance might keep it from ever being a first pick, don't let it drive you away from the name; you can always chop it to Ana, Stacey, Stasia, or (. . . Asia?) whatever you want.

THIS NAME IN HISTORY

Anastasia Griffith (actor)

Anastasia Romanov (member of the imperial Russian Romanov family)

Anastasia (animated movie)

Andrea

Meaning: Manly

Origin: Greek

Related names and spelling variations: *Andria, Andi, Andra, Ondrea, Andy*

Brace yourselves, Mom and Dad: Andrea's an Italian version of the Greek name Andreas, which means "manly" . . . not a label you want to stick your daughter with at birth. But Andrea's manliness has never stopped parents from picking this beauty (though it might explain why dude-ish nickname Andy is so popular). Andrea appeared in the 1600s, has been on the U.S. charts most years since the late 1800s, and peaked at #23 in 1978.

THIS NAME IN HISTORY

Andrea Bowen (actor)

Andrea Jung (CEO of Avon)

Andrea McArdle (actor)

Andrea Mitchell (journalist)

SS *Andrea Doria* (cruise ship that sunk in 1956)

Angela

Meaning: Messenger of God

Origin: Latin; Italian

Related names and spelling variations: *Angelina, Angellina, Angie, Angelica, Angelique, Angel, Angeline, Angelis*

TOP TEN: BRITISH QUEENS

1. Elizabeth
2. Mary
3. Anne
4. Victoria
5. Jane
6. Caroline
7. Catherine
8. Adelaide
9. Alexandra
10. Boadicea

Both Latin Angela and her more elaborate sidekick Angelina are female versions of the name Angel, which means—yep, you guessed it—"messenger of God." Hey, who doesn't want an angelic little girl?

Angela has been used since the 1700s and was a U.S. top 10 for more than a decade between 1965 and 1979 before sliding back down the charts. Angelina's been in the top 1,000 since 1880, but only rose in popularity once action-hardened heroine Angelina Jolie hit theaters as Lara Croft in *Tomb Raider*. (Apparently her earlier role as "Acid Burn" in 1995's *Hackers* didn't seal the deal yet for American parents.)

THIS NAME IN HISTORY

Angela Bassett (actor)

Angelina Weld Grimké (journalist, playwright, and poet)

Angelina Jolie (actor)

Angela Kinsey (actor)

Angela Lansbury (actor)

Angela Merkel (German chancellor)

Angelina Ballerina (series of books by Katharine Holabird and Helen Craig)

"Angelina" (song by Harry Belafonte)

"Angela" (song by the Bee Gees)

"Farewell Angelina" (song by Bob Dylan)

Anna

Meaning: God has favored me

Origin: English

Related names and spelling variations: *Ann, Anne, Ana, Anya, Annie, Annika, Anika, Annette*

Hathaway hasn't managed to save her name from dropping down the U.S. list. Ann and Anne are the sorts of Christian classics, like Mary or Ruth (Eve and Ann/Anne-root Hannah are exceptions coming back into vogue), that have fallen out of favor today. And we understand why; in the Bible, St. Anne was Jesus's grandma. Who wants to give their daughter a grandma name?

Modern moms are more likely to link the name Anna to tennis bombshell Kournikova, magazine maven Wintour, or everyone's favorite orphan Annie. Although Ann and Anne are on their way out, their alternates are on the rise; popular versions include Anna, Annie, Annika, and Anika.

THIS NAME IN HISTORY

Princess Anne (English princess)

St. Anne (biblical figure, mother of the Virgin Mary)

Anne Frank (historical figure)

Anne Hathaway (actor)

Anna Kournikova (tennis player)

Anne Lamott (author)

Annie Lennox (musician)

Anna Paquin (actor)

Anna Wintour (editor-in-chief of *Vogue* magazine)

Annie (musical and movie)

Anne of Green Gables (novel by L. M. Montgomery)

Anna Karenina (novel by Leo Tolstoy)

"Anna Blue" (song by Cyndi Lauper)

Hi, My Name Is

TOP TEN: MORNING AND TALK SHOW HOSTS

1. Oprah (Winfrey)
2. Ellen (Degeneres)
3. Matt (Lauer)
4. Meredith (Vieira)
5. Al (Roker)
6. Regis (Philbin)
7. Kelly (Ripa)
8. George (Stephanopoulos)
9. Kathie Lee (Gifford)
10. Wendy (Williams)

Annabelle

Meaning: God has favored me; beautiful

Origin: English; French

Related names and spelling variations: *Annabella, Anabel, Annabel, Anabella, Anabelle*

Want to make sure your girl is a comeback kid? Just name her Annabelle. A mash-up of Anna ("God has favored me") and Belle ("beautiful"), Annabelle is two great names in one. But after decades in the popular crowd, it went out of favor after 1950, becoming geeky and uncool, and stayed there for the whole second half of the twentieth century. But don't count her out; Annabelle returned to her rightful place in the top 1,000 in 1995 and has been on the up-and-up ever since.

THIS NAME IN HISTORY

Annabella Sciorra (actor)

Annabelle Wallace (actor)

"Annabel Lee" (poem by Edgar Allan Poe)

April

Meaning: To open; the month of April

Origin: Latin

Related names and spelling variations: *Abrielle, Avril*

April, a Latin word that means "to open," is the first full month of spring. Like the month, the name promises great things to come. But don't be surprised if baby April is a bit stormy, maybe even cold—if you want a bright sunny baby, May might be a better pick—but rest assured she'll grow out of it.

April made its first appearance in the U.S. top 1,000 in 1939, got big in the sixties, and peaked in 1979 at #23, surrounded by other nature names like Crystal, Dawn, and Heather. It fell quickly once the nature thing ran its course, but we still think April's a keeper.

THIS NAME IN HISTORY
April Bowlby (actor)
Avril Lavigne (singer)

Arianna

Meaning: Most holy

Origin: Italian

Related names and spelling variations: *Ariana, Aryanna, Aryana, Ariadne, Ariane, Arianne*

Arianna is the Italian version of Ariadne, Greek mythology's bride of the wine-guzzling god Dionysus. Careful, parents—that girl loved to party!

Today, Arianna's spotlight is stolen by the founder of the Huffington Post, Arianna Huffington. The name hit the top 1,000 in 1982 and has rocketed, probably thanks to Huffington, up the charts. Alternate Ariana isn't far behind. But consider Ariadne—intriguing and rare, this gem has never made the top 1,000.

THIS NAME IN HISTORY
Ariadne (Greek mythological figure)
Princess Ariane (princess of the Netherlands)
Arianna Huffington (journalist)
Ariana Richards (actor)
Ariana Afghan Airlines (national airline of Afghanistan)

Ariel

Meaning: Lion of God

Origin: Hebrew

Related names and spelling variations: *Arielle, Ariela, Ariele, Ariell, Ariella, Ariellia, Rielle*

Ariel is a Hebrew name that means "lion of God," but today the name makes parents think of mermaids. When The Little Mermaid came out in 1989, the name was at #210. The next year, it had jumped to #94. Today the mermaid bubble has popped, but Ariel is still a great pick if you not-so-secretly want your little girl to be a mermaid (or to remind people of one).

THIS NAME IN HISTORY
Ariel (character in The Little Mermaid)
Ariel (character in Shakespeare's The Tempest)

Ariel (character in Shakespeare's
    A Midsummer Night's Dream)
Ariel Durant (author)
Ariel Meredith (model)
Ariel Sharon (prime minister of Israel)

Ashley

Meaning: Ash tree clearing

Origin: English

Related names and spelling variations: *Ash,
Ashlee, Ashly, Ashli, Ashlie, Ashleigh, Ashlea*

Remember when Ashley Olsen was still that adorable little girl on *Full House*? Parents couldn't forget her for years—although Ashley had already been a top 10 name for four years when the show started in 1987, she kept the name on the list until a decade after the show ended in 1995. In her current career as a fashion designer, she just can't seem to muster the name recognition she could as a toddler; but Ashley still remains a popular choice.

Ashley is technically a unisex name—*Gone with the Wind* Scarlett's heartthrob was named Ashley Wilkes, and the name was #282 on the boy's charts in 1980—but we just can't recommend naming a son such a popular girl's name.

THIS NAME IN HISTORY

Ashley Bryan (children's book author)
Ashley Judd (actor)
Ashley Olsen (actor)

Ashley Paris (basketball player)
Ashlee Simpson (singer and actor)
Ashley Tisdale (actor)
Ashley Wilkes (character in Margaret
    Mitchell's *Gone with the Wind*)
Ashley Wolff (children's book illustrator)

Aubrey

Meaning: Elf king

Origin: French

Related names and spelling variations:
Aubree, Aubrie

Here's a secret: Aubrey's a French name that means "elf king." Keep it to yourself, though . . . your girl won't appreciate the elf association *or* the title (she prefers "queen," if you please).

So why "king"? Aubrey has spent most of its life as a boy's name, popular in the Middle Ages and appearing on the boys' list until 2002. Aubrey the girl appeared as if by elf magic and swept her brother into history.

THIS NAME IN HISTORY

Aubrey Beardsley (illustrator and author)
Aubrey Davis (author)
Aubrey Epps (baseball player)
Aubrey Drake Graham (musician known
    as Drake)
Aubrey Huff (baseball player)
Aubrey O'Day (singer)
"Aubrey" (song by Bread)
Aubrey Organics (line of skin care products)

Audrey

Meaning: Noble; strength

Origin: English

Related names and spelling variations: *Audree, Audrie, Audrina, Audry, Audra*

Audrey Hepburn may have been star of the moment in her heyday, but her name was already twenty years out of style. Audrey was in the top 100 in the twenties and thirties (giving it vintage charm today!), then fell out of favor for the rest of the century. A decade after Hepburn passed away in 1993, Audrey's back in favor; it returned to the top 100 in 2003. Audrey retains its classic vibe—despite its newfound popularity—and is a great pick if you can't stand nicknames.

THIS NAME IN HISTORY

Audrey (character in Shakespeare's *As You Like It*)

Audrey Hepburn (actor)

Audra McDonald (singer and actor)

Audrey Meadows (actor)

Audrina Patridge (reality TV star)

Audrey Penn (author)

Audrey Tautou (actor)

Audrey Wells (director)

Audrey (magazine)

Aurora

Meaning: Dawn

Origin: Latin

Related names and spelling variations: *Aurore*

Think your daughter glimmers like a ribbon of light in the sky? We know you do. Consider the name Aurora, a nature name that isn't too obvious and an old standard that's never quite "in."

Aurora has been on the U.S. charts nearly every year since 1880, but has never broken the top 200. Just like a shimmering sky-ripple, it flew to #360 in 1923, faded out for years, then slowly swooped back up the charts. No matter how popular it gets, Aurora is sure to sound unique.

THIS NAME IN HISTORY

Aurora (character in Disney's *Sleeping Beauty*)

Aurora Borealis (northern lights)

Autumn

Meaning: Autumn season

Origin: Latin

Related names and spelling variations: *None*

Summer, Winter, and Spring all have been top 1,000 names, but Autumn is the hands-down winner of the seasonal names. Maybe parents love the colors of fall foliage and that warm feeling they get on a crisp October day. But we think it just sounds the prettiest (after all, Fall has never been a popular name).

Autumn made the top 1,000 in the late 1960s and reached the top 100 in 1997.

THIS NAME IN HISTORY

Autumn Reeser (actor)

Autumn de Wilde (photographer)

Autumn (Vivaldi concerto)

Hi, My Name Is

The Autumns (indie rock band)

"To Autumn" (poem by John Keats)

Ava

Meaning: Birdlike

Origin: Latin

Related names and spelling variations: *Avah*

Ava is a Latin name that means "birdlike." We prefer to think of Ava not as gangly, big-beaked, and covered in feathers, but as elegant, slender, sleek, and perhaps soaring.

Ava has sure soared in recent years. On the U.S. charts—but in the middle of the pack—since 1880, the name took off during the last fifteen years—it ranked #737 in 1995, #180 in 2000, and #9 in 2005, remaining in the top 10 after that.

THIS NAME IN HISTORY

Ava (medieval poet)

Ava Barber (singer)

Ava Benton (character on *All My Children*)

Ava Cowan (fitness celebrity)

Ava Gardner (actor)

Avery

Meaning: Elf counselor

Origin: French

Related names and spelling variations: *Averi, Averie*

Avery, French for "elf counselor," might be riding high on super-popular Ava's coattails. Similar-sounding Ava has taken off in the past fifteen years, and Avery has followed close behind.

Avery is a unisex name that's historically been most popular for boys. It hit the U.S. girls' charts for the first time in 1989, at about the same time that Ava became a trend, and hasn't stopped climbing since. Not only are unisex names getting wildly popular for girls (and getting ruined for boys as a result), Avery is also originally a last name—another huge naming trend of the moment.

THIS NAME IN HISTORY

Avery Arable (character in *Charlotte's Web* by E. B. White)

Avery Fisher (audio specialist)

Tex Avery (cartoonist)

Bb

Bailey

Meaning: Bailiff; berry clearing; castle wall

Origin: English

Related names and spelling variations:
Bailee, Baylee, Bailee, Baylee, Bayleigh, Baileigh, Bailee

Bailey is an old English word with three distinct meanings—an English nickname for a bailiff, a berry clearing (this comes from the words "beg leah," or berry wood), and a castle wall. But for the younger generation, the name Bailey was put on the map by troubled teenager Bailey Salinger in *Party of Five*. Of course, we know you don't want your girl's life to be as conflicted as Bailey's . . . but, of course, she won't grow up as an orphan (knock on wood).

Bailey—another unisex name—had to fight itself to survive. Bailey hit the boy's charts back in the 1800s and got popular in the 1990s—*Party of Five*'s heyday—rising from #768 in 1994 to #277 the next year. Bailey the girl rose quickly at around the same time, hitting the charts in 1983 and reaching #60 by 1998. Like most trendy unisex names, Bailey couldn't stay popular for *both* genders. One had to go . . . so

Bailey the boy fell quickly out of favor, while Bailey the girl kept its status.

THIS NAME IN HISTORY

Bailey Hanks (actor)

Bailee Madison (actor)

Bailey Quarters (character on the TV show *WKRP in Cincinnati*)

Bailey Salinger (character on the TV show *Party of Five*)

Bill Bailey (baseball player)

Beetle Bailey (comic strip)

Dr. (Miranda) Bailey (character on the TV show *Grey's Anatomy*)

George Bailey (character in the movie *It's a Wonderful Life*)

Baileys Irish Cream (alcoholic beverage)

Bella

Meaning: Beautiful

Origin: Italian

Related names and spelling variations:
Bell, Belle

Bella is Italian for "beautiful," but it also sounds a bit dark and foreign . . . almost like a vampire queen. Okay, it only got that association recently; Bella is the main

TOP TEN: ADVICE COLUMNISTS

1. Abby (Dear Abby)
2. Ann (Landers)
3. Carolyn (Hax)
4. Marjorie (Proops)
5. Claire (Rayner)
6. Dan (Savage)
7. Helen (Bottel)
8. Marie (Manning)
9. Phillip (Hodson)
10. Susan (Quilliam)

character in Stephenie Meyer's *Twilight* series. The first book, *Twilight*, came out in 2005 and is already a blockbuster movie. So are its three sequels. Not since *Harry Potter* has a book series captivated this large of an audience.

And that audience, it seems, has named every single one of its daughters after its new heroine. Bella, which reappeared on the U.S. top 1,000 in 2000 after almost seventy years off the list, has made a supernatural climb through the list. Bella's also a frequent nickname for Isabella (the *Twilight* character's full firstie), which is a top pick for U.S. baby girls today.

THIS NAME IN HISTORY

Belle (character in Disney's *Beauty and the Beast*)

Bella Cruise (daughter of Nicole Kidman and Tom Cruise)

Bella Freud (fashion designer)

Bella Swan (character in the *Twilight* series by Stephenie Meyer)

Bella Thorne (actor)

Bella Donna (album by Stevie Nicks)

Belle Époque (period of European history)

"Bella Notte" (song from Disney's *Lady and the Tramp*)

Bella Sara (children's game)

Belle and Sebastian (musical group)

Bethany

Meaning: House of figs

Origin: Hebrew

Related names and spelling variations:
Beth, Bethenny

Bethany is a Hebrew name that means "house of figs." *Real Housewives of New York City* star Bethenny Frankel has given this name a new panache. A self-assured entrepreneur and no-nonsense New Yorker, Frankel may inspire you to pick her name if you hope to see the same qualities in your little girl.

On the U.S. charts since 1949, Bethany was in the top 100 between 1983 and 1988, but has since dropped. If you're looking for an Elizabeth without the Lizzie, Bethany is a modern-sounding alternative.

THIS NAME IN HISTORY

Bethany Dempsey (model)

Bethenny Frankel (reality TV star)

Bethany Joy Galeotti (actor)

Bethany Hamilton (surfer)

Bethanie Mattek-Sands (tennis player)

Bianca

Meaning: White

Origin: Italian

Related names and spelling variations:
Blanche, Blanca

Bianca, an Italian name that means "white," sounds alluringly foreign to American parents. The name has also gained a sense of adventure from Miss Bianca, a character that today's parents might remember from the *Rescuers* movies.

Bianca has been in the 100s and 200s since 1986, but has never become super-popular, making it a great pick if you're looking for a name that's both familiar and unusual.

THIS NAME IN HISTORY

Bianca (characters in Shakespeare's
   Othello and *The Taming of the Shrew*)

Bianca Solderini (character in
   Anne Rice's *Vampire Chronicles* books)

Miss Bianca (character in *The Rescuers*
   movies)

Bianca de la Garza (news anchor)

Bianca Jagger (actor)

Bianca Kajlich (actor)

Bianca Lawson (actor)

Bianca Ryan (singer)

Brenda

Meaning: Sword blade

Origin: Old Norse

Related names and spelling variations: *Bren*

Brenda has Norse roots, but was long popular in Ireland and Scotland. It means "sword blade" and is an old familiar standby. And like most old familiar standbys, it's fallen out of favor over the last decade. Brenda first made the charts in 1925 and was a top 20 between 1948 and 1964. Too classic to disappear entirely, this name will see its time at the top again . . . but probably not for another decade or more.

THIS NAME IN HISTORY

Brenda Joyce (author)

Brenda Lee (singer)

Brenda Song (actor)

Brenda Walsh (character on the TV show *Beverly Hills, 90210*)

Brianna

Meaning: High, noble

Origin: Celtic

Related names and spelling variations: *Briana, Bree, Breanna, Bryanna, Brina*

Back in the 1500s, someone must have wanted to name their daughter Brian . . . but that wouldn't have been socially acceptable. So Brianna was born and has been growing in popularity ever since.

Brianna, like its root Brian, means "high" and "noble." Slightly less conventional than other older names, Brianna and its alternative spellings are fashionable today.

THIS NAME IN HISTORY

Brianna Brown (actor)

Breanna Conrad (reality TV star)

Briana Evigan (actor and dancer)

1. Carson (Daly)
2. Hilarie (Burton)
3. Jesse (Camp)
4. Daisy (Fuentes)
5. Damien (Fahey)

6. Ananda (Lewis)
7. "Downtown" Julie Brown
8. Kennedy
9. Matt (Pinfield)
10. Ed (Lover)

Brianna Keilar (journalist)
Briana Scurry (soccer player)
Briána (species of fish)
Jamaica and Brianna (series of children's books by Juanita Havill and Anne Sibley O'Brien)

Bridget

Meaning: Exalted one

Origin: Gaelic

Related names and spelling variations: *Brigette, Brigitte, Brigitta, Gita, Bridie, Britta, Birgit, Biddy*

Brigitte Bardot was a superstar . . . but since she retired in 1973 her name has all but disappeared from the charts. This seems wrong somehow. Brigitte is the French form of Bridget, which comes from the Gaelic name Brighid (a real attention-grabber name)—a goddess in Celtic mythology—whose name may mean "exalted one." Bridget's been on the U.S. charts since 1880, peaked at #112 in 1973 (the year Brigitte Bardot retired, maybe there's a connection?), and has been sliding back down the list ever since. Nicknames Bridie and Biddy make it an interesting pick, as do its international variations: Britta (Swedish) and Brigitta (German).

THIS NAME IN HISTORY

Britta Perry (character on the TV show *Community*)

Brigitte Bardot (actor)

Bridget Fonda (actor)

Bridget Moynahan (actor)

Brigitte Nielsen (actor)

Bridgette Wilson-Sampras (actor)

Bridget Jones's Diary (book and movie by Helen Fielding)

Brittany

Meaning: From Brittany

Origin: Celtic

Related names and spelling variations: *Brit, Britney*

Brittany is a region in northwestern France infamous for its rain. But locals know that it's filled with hilly green countryside and steeped in heavy Celtic roots (and it only rains *some* of the time). The name Brittany, which simply means "from Brittany," evokes the same sense of beauty and heritage as the region the name is based on.

Brittany hit the U.S. charts in 1971, rocketed up the list to the top 10 in 1986, and stayed there until 1995. The Britney spelling entered the charts in 1980 and rose quickly over the next few years. When Britney Spears came along, the spelling got another boost in popularity. Her recent tabloid scandals may be responsible for the name's drop back down the list. In the battle of Brittany vs. Britney, the former wins, hands down.

THIS NAME IN HISTORY

Brittany Daniel (actor)

Brittany Murphy (actor)

Brittany Snow (actor)

Britney Spears (singer)

Brooke

Meaning: Stream, brook

Origin: English

Related names and spelling variations: *Brook*

Brooke means exactly what you think it does: "brook" or "stream." The different spelling throws nature-name haters off the scent, making Brooke the ultimate nod-to-nature-yet-normal name.

Brooke rose in popularity in the 1970s and has been fueled by a steady "stream" of famous Brookes, from Shields in the seventies and eighties to Hogan today.

THIS NAME IN HISTORY

Brooke Adams (actor)

Brooke Anderson (news anchor)

Brooke Astor (philanthropist and socialite)

Brooke Bennett (Olympic swimmer)

Brooke Burke (TV personality)

Brooke Hogan (reality TV star, daughter of Hulk Hogan)

Brooke Mueller (actor)

Brooke Shields (actor)

Brooke White (singer)

Brooklyn

Meaning: Unknown

Origin: Dutch

Related names and spelling variations:
Brooklynn, Brooklynne

Brooklyn, known best as a New York City borough, is Dutch in origin. Baby Brooklyns and modern Brooklynites alike might want to take a trip over to the Netherlands to visit the namesake village Breukelen.

The name Brooklyn follows the current trend of naming children after locations (London, Paris, and Asia are trending, too). Although David and Victoria Beckham named their son Brooklyn in 1999, the name hasn't caught on for boys. It's made a dash to popularity for baby girls, with the Brooklyn spelling edging out Brooklynn.

THIS NAME IN HISTORY

Brook Lynn Ashton (character on *General Hospital*)

Brooklyn Beckham (son of David and Victoria Beckham)

Brooklyn Decker (model)

Brooklynn Proulx (actor)

Brooklyn (New York City borough)

Cc

Camila

Meaning: Young ceremonial attendant

Origin: Latin

Related names and spelling variations:
Camille, Camilla, Kamila, Kamilla, Kamille

When Prince Charles got caught cheating with Camilla Parker Bowles, her name—though suddenly in the public eye—didn't exactly shoot up the charts. Years later, when divorced Prince Charles started to see Parker Bowles again, American parents must have found a soft spot for the other woman. Camilla took huge strides up the charts in the early 2000s, while alternate Camila—a newcomer on the list in 1997—rose even higher. Camila has its roots in ancient Rome and Roman mythology, making it a good pick for parents who like a helping of history along with their names. The French version of the name, Camille, is also a pretty choice. Look for the Camilla spelling to increase as parents start looking for more ways to get to newly stylish nickname Millie.

THIS NAME IN HISTORY

Camila Alves (TV personality and model)
Camilla Belle (actor)
Camilla Parker Bowles (Duchess of Cornwall and the second wife to Prince Charles)
Camilla Cavendish (British journalist)
Kamala Harris (politician)
The Lady of the Camellias (novel and play by Alexandre Dumas)

Carly

Meaning: Free man; farmer

Origin: German

Related names and spelling variations: *Karlee, Carley, Carlie, Carlee, Karlie, Karly, Karli, Karley, Carleigh, Karleigh, Carli*

Carly, the female version of the German name Carl, means "free man" or "farmer." Carly Simon, the most famous example, fits her firstie perfectly; strong-willed and outspoken but tender and emotional, Simon (though not a farmer) is nothing if not free. Look for some of her characteristics in your own baby Carly.

1. Madison
2. Savannah
3. Sydney
4. Austin
5. Charlotte
6. Cheyenne
7. Jackson
8. Paris
9. Adelaide
10. Bristol

Carly hit the top 1,000 in 1973 (about the same time that Simon's career took off) and became a fast favorite, peaking at #122 in 1995.

THIS NAME IN HISTORY
Carly Fiorina (politician)
Carly Patterson (gymnast)
Carly Phillips (author)
Carly Pope (actor)
Carly Simon (singer)
Carly Smithson (singer)

Carmen

Meaning: Song

Origin: Latin

Related names and spelling variations: *Carmine*

Carmen, from a Latin word that means "song," has been on the U.S. charts since 1881 and is most associated with the opera by the same name. But as young parents know, Carmen Sandiego lent the name a dash of mystery, intrigue, roguishness, and cunning in *Where in the World Is Carmen Sandiego?* (And ever since the game show aired, we can't get its theme song out of our heads.)

Carmen peaked in 1968 at #142 and has been slowly slipping down the charts ever since.

THIS NAME IN HISTORY
Carmen Electra (actor)
Carmen Miranda (singer)

Carmen (opera by Bizet)
Where in the World is Carmen Sandiego?
   (computer game, game show, and song)

Caroline

Meaning: Free man; farmer

Origin: French

Related names and spelling variations: *Carolyne, Karolyne, Karoline, Carolina, Carolyn*

Caroline and Carly are close cousins. Caroline stems from the French Charles, while Carly stems from German Carl, but both mean "free man." Caroline Kennedy, JFK's daughter, lends her strong mind and successful career to the name; parents might find some of her strength in their own "Sweet Caroline."

Popular among the wealthy since the 1600s, Caroline was in the top 100 in the 1880s, then dropped out of popularity. It's come back to the top 100 only recently. Try Carolina for a change.

THIS NAME IN HISTORY

Princess Caroline (Princess of Hanover, daughter of Grace Kelly and Prince Rainier III)

Carolina Herrera (fashion designer)

Caroline Kennedy (daughter of President John F. Kennedy and Jacqueline Bouvier Kennedy)

Caroline Rhea (actor and comedian)

"Sweet Caroline" (song by Neil Diamond)

Cassandra

Meaning: Prophetess

Origin: Greek

Related names and spelling variations: *Cass, Cassie, Kassandra*

In Greek mythology, Cassandra has the power to tell the future, but she's cursed so that nobody will believe her predictions. Hopefully your baby Cassandra will have only unusual foresight (nobody ever believes people with unusual foresight, either) and strong common sense.

The name Cassandra was used in the Middle Ages and has been in the U.S. top 1,000 since 1942. It ranked in the top 100 between 1982 and 2000, but has dropped since then. Chic Cassie is also popular today. If you're a mythology fan looking for a less conventional name, try Persephone, Artemis, or Athena.

THIS NAME IN HISTORY

Cassandra (Greek mythological figure)

Cassandra Wilson (jazz musician)

Cassidy

Meaning: Curly-haired

Origin: Irish

Related names and spelling variations: *Kassidy*

Cassidy comes from the Irish last name O'Caiside. The Cassidy last name belonged to both a fictitious cowboy (Hopalong) and a real outlaw (Butch),

TOP TEN: NATURE NAMES

1. Aurora
2. Linden
3. Wren
4. Magnolia
5. Nova
6. Blaze
7. Poppy
8. Ash
9. Rowan
10. Autumn

gaining a sense of adventure and danger from both. Cassidy first hit the list as a first name in 1981 and shot up in popularity when Kathie Lee Gifford gave the name to her daughter in 1993.

THIS NAME IN HISTORY
Cassidy Freeman (actor)
Cassidy Gifford (daughter of Kathie Lee and Frank Gifford)
Kassidy Osborn (singer)
Butch Cassidy (Western outlaw)
David Cassidy (actor and singer)
Hopalong Cassidy (fictional cowboy)

Cecilia

Meaning: Blind

Origin: Latin

Related names and spelling variations: *Cecelia, Celia, Cissy, Sisley, Sheila, Cecily, Cicely*

Paul Simon and Art Garfunkel sang a surprisingly upbeat lament about Cecilia, a young love who'd strayed from the song's narrator. But we're sure your baby girl will be steady and loyal in any relationship—Cecilia and love, after all, are both "blind."

Cecilia has been popular for more than a century, perhaps because it's never become *too* popular. It's been on the U.S. charts since 1880, but hasn't wandered much from its sweet spot in the 200s to 400s.

Cecilia Bartoli (opera singer)
Cecilia Cassini (fashion designer)
Celia Cruz (singer)
Cicely Tyson (actor)
Cecily von Ziegesar (author)

Celeste

Meaning: Celestial, heavenly

Origin: Latin

Related names and spelling variations: *Celine, Céline, Céleste, Celestine*

Celeste translates to the word it most sounds like: *celestial*, which means "heavenly." If you think your girl is a gift from the heavens, look no further—this is her name.

Celeste has been on the charts since 1880 and has been only mildly popular. It peaked at #204 in 2004 and has fallen since then. For a more "olde worlde" flavor, try Celestine.

THIS NAME IN HISTORY
Celeste Bradley (author)
Celine Dion (singer)
Celeste Holm (actor)

Charlotte

Meaning: Free man

Origin: French

Related names and spelling variations:
Charlie, Charlee, Charlize, Lottie

For the younger crowd, this name reeks of that come-and-gone pop-punk band Good Charlotte. Ignore that and remember the steady and loyal spider from *Charlotte's Web*. We imagine your daughter will inherit some of her finer qualities. And a small taste for pop-punk. We warned you.

Around since the 1600s, Charlotte was a top 100 name for many years at the turn of the last century and into the 1950s. After a lull in its popularity, it's gained new ground in the past years.

THIS NAME IN HISTORY
Charlotte Brontë (author)
Charlotte Church (singer)
Charlize Theron (actor)
Charlotte York (character on the
    TV show *Sex and the City*)
Charlotte's Web (children's book by
    E. B. White)
Good Charlotte (pop-punk band)

Chelsea

Meaning: Chalk landing

Origin: English

Related names and spelling variations: *Chelsia*

Although Chelsea technically means "chalk landing," it probably originates from the Chelsea district of London. Associate it with the Chelsea neighborhood in New York City if you don't know London. And if you don't know either, well, "chalk landing" is as good a definition as any.

Chelsea entered the top 1,000 in 1969, quickly became a top 50 name, and stayed there from 1985 to 1995.

THIS NAME IN HISTORY

Chelsea Clinton (daughter of Hillary and Bill Clinton)

Chelsea Handler (actor and comedian)

Cheyenne

Meaning: Hard to understand

Origin: Native American

Related names and spelling variations: *Shyanne, Cheyanne*

The meaning of Cheyenne is hard to understand. No, really, that's its meaning. Read the first sentence again. The name Cheyenne comes from the Native American Cheyenne Nation. After appearing in the top 1,000 in 1980, it stayed in the top 100 between 1994 and 2000.

THIS NAME IN HISTORY

Cheyenne Jackson (actor)

Cheyenne McCray (author)

Cheyenne, Wyoming

Chloe

Meaning: Green shoot

Origin: Greek

Related names and spelling variations: *Chloë, Chloé, Cloey, Khloe, Khloey, Khloe, Kloe*

Chloe, a name from Greek mythology, means "green shoot"—likely a reference to the name's association with Demeter, the Greek goddess of fertility. You might choose the name if you need a spark of color in your own life. Current Chloes include actor Chloë Sevigny and sister-to-Kim, Khloé Kardashian.

Even though Chloe sounds like a timeless classic, it almost went extinct in the twentieth century. The name was hardly used from the early 1900s through the 1940s and was practically unheard of until 1981. Then the name had a green shoot of its own—after a quick rise, it hit the top 40 in 2000 and broke into the top 10 in 2008.

THIS NAME IN HISTORY

Chloe Agnew (singer)

Chloe Dao (reality TV star)

Khloé Kardashian (TV personality)

Chloë Moretz (actor)

Chloë Sevigny (actor)

Daphnis and Chloe (ancient Greek romance by Longus)

Chloé (fashion house)

Christina

Meaning: Christian

Origin: Latin

Related names and spelling variations: *Christy, Christie, Kristina, Tina, Kristy, Kristie, Christa, Kerstin, Christine, Cristina, Krista, Kristin*

Christina is the feminine version of Latin Christian, which means exactly what it says. For Christian parents, this name is an obvious favorite—lead your daughter into your chosen faith by her own name. Non-Christian parents can choose this name for its simple beauty.

Christina has been on the U.S. charts since 1880 and was a top 50 name from 1968 to 1995, rising as high as #12. Like most other then-popular names, it's been on the decline ever since.

THIS NAME IN HISTORY

Christina Aguilera (singer)
Krista Allen (actor)
Christina Applegate (actor)
Christie Brinkley (model)
Kristin Davis (actor)
Christine Feehan (author)
Christina Hendricks (actor)
Christina Milian (singer)
Christina Ricci (actor)
Christine Taylor (actor)
Christy Turlington (model)
Kristi Yamaguchi (figure skater)

Claire

Meaning: Clear, bright; famous

Origin: French

Related names: *Clare, Clara, Clarabelle, Clarissa, Clarice*

TOP TEN: ALL-TIME BEST-SELLING AUTHORS

1. William (Shakespeare)
2. Agatha (Christie)
3. Barbara (Cartland)
4. Georges (Simenon)
5. Danielle (Steel)
6. J. K. (Rowling)
7. Leo (Tolstoy)
8. Jackie (Collins)
9. Dean (Koontz)
10. Stephen (King)

Claire, the French version of Latin Clara, means "clear, bright, famous." Clara was the more popular name for nearly a century, ranking in the top 15 between 1880 and 1899 and outranking its French sibling until the 1970s. While both versions are currently on the rise, Claire is keeping its lead on more-classic Clara.

THIS NAME IN HISTORY

Clara (character in Tchaikovsky's
    The Nutcracker)
Clara Barton (founder of the American
    Red Cross)
Clara Bow (silent film star)
Claire Danes (actor)
Claire Forlani (actor)
Clair Huxtable (character on the TV
    show *The Cosby Show*)
Claire Martin (singer)
Claire McCaskill (U.S. senator)
Claire Trevor (film noir star)
Claire's (chain of accessory stores)

Claudia

Meaning: Lame

Origin: Latin

Related names and spelling variations: *Claudette, Claudine, Gladys*

Claudia seems to get big every thirty years. While it's been on the U.S. charts since 1880, it's had two big bursts of popularity. The name made waves in the 1940s, then submerged again, only to reappear in the 1970s. Parents, this name is due for a comeback.

The feminine form of Latin Claudius, Claudia means "lame" . . . but don't let that stop you. Classic, feminine, and vintage, this name is anything but its definition.

THIS NAME IN HISTORY

Claudia Black (actor)
Claudette Colbert (actor)
Gladys Knight (singer)
Claudia Schiffer (model)
Claudine Wong (newscaster)

Cora

Meaning: Maiden

Origin: Greek

Related names and spelling variations: *Coralie, Coraline, Coretta, Corabel*

After Neil Gaiman's children's book and book-based movie by the same name made it big, Coraline—and its root name, Cora—are set to make a comeback.

Cora was a top 100 name from 1880 to 1912, then fell out of favor throughout the 1900s, which lends the name a vintage quality. This classic is already coming back into favor—watch for Coralie, Coretta, Corabel, and especially Coraline to follow suit.

Coretta Scott King (civil rights activist)

Coraline (book by Neil Gaiman)

Courtney

Meaning: From Courtenay; short nose

Origin: English; French

Related names and spelling variations: *Court, Kourtney, Courtenay*

From *Friends* star Courteney Cox to struggling singer Courtney Love (and with a bit of Kourtney Kardashian in between), Courtneys are everywhere. And no wonder—the name was in the top 100 between 1976 and 2002. But due in no small part to its long popularity, the name's on its way down.

Courtney means "from Courtenay" or "short nose" and was once a unisex name. After finally falling off the boys' charts in 2001, it's now almost exclusively for girls.

THIS NAME IN HISTORY

Courteney Cox (actor)

Kourtney Kardashian (reality TV star)

Courtney Love (singer)

Courtney Thorne-Smith (actor)

Crystal

Meaning: Ice

Origin: Greek

Related names and spelling variations: *Krystal, Christelle, Cristal*

Think your baby girl's a gem, but not ready for the more unique Emerald, Jade, or Amethyst? Look no further than ever-popular Crystal.

Crystal comes from a Greek word that means "ice," but we all know it as the rock, a symbol of virtue that's said to have healing powers. Crystal entered the U.S. charts in 1884 and enjoyed a long reign in the top 50 from 1973 to 1992, peaking at #9 in 1982. It's slipped since its heyday, but with such a precious meaning attached to such a pretty name, it won't fall far.

THIS NAME IN HISTORY

Crystal Bowersox (singer)

Crystal Gayle (singer)

Crystal Renn (model)

Cynthia

Meaning: Moon

Origin: Greek

Related names and spelling variations: *Cindy, Cyndi*

For sky-gazers who love a full moon but just can't name their girl Luna, consider Cynthia. A Greek name that means "moon," Cynthia is an old favorite with plenty of nickname potential.

Cynthia has been on the charts since 1880 and spent most of the fifties and sixties in the top 20, hitting #7 in 1957. Today, Cynthia is on its way out, while former nickname Cindy has become a full-fledged first name itself. In the top 1,000 since 1938, Cindy is enjoying a slow climb—possibly propelled by Crawford, Margolis, and Lauper—up the charts.

THIS NAME IN HISTORY

Cindy Brady (character on the TV show
   The Brady Bunch)

Cindy Crawford (model)

Cyndi Lauper (singer)

Cindy Margolis (model and actor)

Cindy McCain (wife of Senator
   John McCain)

Cynthia Nixon (actor)

Cynthia Rowley (fashion designer)

Dd

Daisy

Meaning: Day's eye

Origin: English

Related names and spelling variations: *None*

Grab your old cutoff shorts, moms—we all know where Daisy's fame comes from today. Daisy might be getting a recent surge in respectability from the likes of Fuentes and Martinez, but the name still recalls the bombshell from *Dukes of Hazzard*.

Daisy should actually carry some vintage charm. It hit its highest ranking at #48 in the 1880s, then began a slow decline throughout the twentieth century. Even those namesake short-short "Daisy Dukes" couldn't stop the name's slow downward fall. But after a 120-year slide, this old favorite is on its way up. Maybe in the future, you'll be able to think of a Daisy other than Duke.

THIS NAME IN HISTORY

Daisy Buchanan née Fay (character in F. Scott Fitzgerald's *The Great Gatsby*)

Daisy Duke (character on the TV show and movie *Dukes of Hazzard*)

Daisy Fuentes (TV personality)

Daisy Martínez (celebrity chef)

Daisy Miller (novella by Henry James)

Dana

Meaning: From Denmark; God is my judge

Origin: Irish; Hebrew

Related names and spelling variations: *Danette, Danna*

Here's a sad story from the unisex names file: Dana—an Irish name that means "from Denmark" and the girl's version of the Hebrew name Daniel, meaning "God is my judge"—was predominantly a boy's name until it hit the top 100 on the girls' charts in the '60s. Since unisex names aren't usually popular on both charts for long, it's no surprise that Dana dropped right off the boys' charts in 1997. Now here's the sad bit: after almost two decades as a top 100 name for girls, Dana the girl fell quickly in the early nineties. What a waste of a good name!

THIS NAME IN HISTORY

Dana Carvey (actor)

Dana Delany (actor)

Dana Jacobson (sportscaster)

Dana Perino (former White House press secretary)

1 Heather (Mills)

2 Anna Nicole (Smith)

3 Kevin (Federline)

4 Marion (Davies)

5 Ivana (Trump)

6 Jerry (Hall)

7 Rachel (Hunter)

8 Peggy (Hopkins Joyce)

9 Darva (Conger)

10 Robin (Givens)

Danielle

Meaning: God is my judge

Origin: Hebrew; French

Related names and spelling variations:
Daniela, Daniella, Dannie

Watch your step, Danielle—your sister Daniela has it in for you. Both names are female versions of Daniel, which means "God is my judge." Danielle has long been the more popular name, hitting the U.S. charts in 1938 and ranking in the top 100 between 1971 and 2004. But Daniela, a newcomer to the charts in 1971, just eked past big sister Danielle in 2007, and is still just a nose higher than Danielle.

THIS NAME IN HISTORY

Daniela Bianchi (actor)

Danielle Brisebois (actor)

Danielle Darrieux (actor)

Danielle Fishel (actor)

Daniela Mercury (singer)

Daniela Peštová (model)

Danielle Steel (author)

Daphne

Meaning: Laurel

Origin: Greek

Related names and spelling variations:
Daphna

Hats off to Daphne! Daphne is a Greek name that means "laurel." In Greek mythology, Daphne escaped amorous Apollo by turning herself into a laurel

Hi, My Name Is

plant, a trick you don't see too often these days. People have been handed laurels, both literally and figuratively, as a symbol of honor ever since.

Daphne has been on the U.S. girls' list since 1889, but peaked at only #266 in 1962. It declined afterward, but has recently started rising again.

THIS NAME IN HISTORY

Daphne Blake (character in *Scooby-Doo*)
Daphne du Maurier (author)
Daphne Zuniga (actor)

Delilah

Meaning: Leader

Origin: Arabic

Related names and spelling variations: *Lila, Lilah*

"Hey there, Delilah!" Go ahead and get used to it, Mom and Dad—everyone's going to be saying it to your baby girl for years to come. Part of what made the Plain White T's hit song so popular, besides its tearjerking message, was the name Delilah itself; although it sounds classic and pretty, it's never quite been popular.

Delilah, an Arabic name that means "leader," was the woman who double-crossed Samson in the Bible. This might have turned Christian parents away from the name, and it's seen long stretches of unpopularity. But the Plain White T's gave Delilah its place in the sun—when the song came out in 2007, the name shot up the charts, and has continued to climb.

THIS NAME IN HISTORY

Delilah (biblical figure)
"Hey There Delilah" (song by the
Plain White T's)

Denise

Meaning: Follower of Dionysius

Origin: Greek

Related names and spelling variations:
Denny, Dinisia

A Greek name that means "follower of Dionysius," Denise is all about good times with great wine. Denise Richards—ex-wife of actor Charlie Sheen and ex-girlfriend of John Stamos and Bon Jovi guitarist Richie Sambora—fits her name like it was made for her. But despite its raucous trappings, Denise just sounds old today. It hit the top 100 in the 1950s, peaked at #23 in '55 and '56, and has been on the decline ever since. If you're looking for another good-time name without the retro baggage, try Portuguese version Dinisia.

THIS NAME IN HISTORY

Denise Austin (fitness expert)
Denise Crosby (actor)
Denise Richards (actor)

Desirée

Meaning: Desired

Origin: French

Related names and spelling variations:
Desiree, Desirae

Desirée, a French name that means "desired," sounds like it's tied firmly to romance. But a few centuries ago, it was more of a Christian virtue name, like Charity or Faith. Today Desirée is all about love . . . with perhaps a splash of physical attraction.

Desirée hit the U.S. charts in 1954, rose quickly and spent one year (1983) in the top 100, but has declined quickly since the early 2000s. Parents, if the accent throws you off, just drop it!

THIS NAME IN HISTORY

Des'ree (singer)

Desirée Ficker (triathlete)

Desirée Goyette (singer)

Desirée Rogers (former White House social secretary)

Destiny

Meaning: Destiny, fate

Origin: English

Related names and spelling variations:
Destinee, Destiney

Just like Faith, Hope, Harmony, Heaven, and Genesis, Destiny is a name that tries to bless its holder with good fortune from birth. Just be ready to hear a lot of Darth Vader impressions: "It is your *destiny!*"

Destiny, an English name with the same meaning as the word, has been on the U.S. charts since 1975. It rose quickly, hit the top 100 in 1994, and continued to climb.

THIS NAME IN HISTORY

Destiny Hope Cyrus (given name of Miley Cyrus)

Destinee Monroe (singer)

Destiney Sue Walker (reality TV star)

Destiny's Child (musical group)

Diana

Meaning: Heavenly, divine

Origin: Latin

Related names and spelling variations:
Dianna, Dianne, Diane, Dian, Dyan, Deanna, Di

Diana was Wonder Woman's real name, but the world found a real Wonder Woman in the early eighties. On July 29, 1981, Diana Spencer married Prince Charles and became Princess Diana. Her name was most popular in the forties and fifties, but got a boost when it became *royal.* It slipped slightly but rose again when Diana was killed in a tragic crash in 1997.

THIS NAME IN HISTORY

Dyan Cannon (actor)

Dianne Feinstein (U.S. senator)

Dian Fossey (zoologist)

Diana Krall (singer)

Diane Lane (actor)

Diana Prince (Wonder Woman's alter ego)

Diana Rigg (actor)

Diana Ross (singer)

Diane Sawyer (news anchor)

Princess Diana Spencer (princess of Wales)

Diane von Fürstenberg (fashion designer)

Ee

Eden

Meaning: Place of pleasure

Origin: Hebrew; English

Related names and spelling variations: *Edan*

Baby girls are endless sources of pleasure and joy (although raising them can seem quite the opposite), so what better name than Eden? A Hebrew word that means "place of pleasure," Eden is best known as the garden where the Old Testament's original couple, Adam and Eve, were created, tempted, and exiled.

The name Eden first hit the girls' chart in 1986 and has been quickly gaining ground since 2000. It may be on its way to the top 100, though it's not there yet. Parents who name their daughters Eden today are ahead of a trend!

NAME FACTOID

Eden entered the boys' chart for the first time in 2008, at #902.

THIS NAME IN HISTORY

Eden Capwell (character on the soap opera *Santa Barbara*)

Eden Espinosa (actor)

Eden Harel (TV personality)

Eden Mahoney (daughter of Marcia Cross and Tom Mahoney)

Eden Riegel (actor)

Eden Sher (actor)

Barbara Eden (actor)

East of Eden (novel by John Steinbeck)

Garden of Eden

Eleanor

Meaning: Sunbeam

Origin: French

Related names and spelling variations: *Elinor, Ellie, Leonore, Nell, Nelly, Lenore*

If you look hard enough, you can always find a more acceptable replacement for that sixties-era hippie name you're thinking of. Moonglow can become Luna or Cynthia, Star can become Esther, and Sunbeam can become Eleanor, a French version of the name Helen that means exactly that. It has vintage appeal, too—on the charts since 1880, Eleanor was a top 100 name from the late 1890s through 1942, hitting #25 in 1920, then falling back out of favor for decades. Just like a sunrise, it's been coming back since the 1990s. Parents, jump aboard this trend before it gets too popular!

Eleanor of Aquitaine (queen of France and
England)

Elinor Dashwood (character in Jane
Austen's *Sense and Sensibility*)

Eleanor Parker (actor)

Eleanor Powell (actor)

Eleanor Roosevelt (first lady)

"Eleanor Rigby" (song by the Beatles)

Elizabeth

Meaning: God is my oath

Origin: Hebrew

Related names and spelling variations:
*Elisabeth, Elissa, Eliza, Lizbeth, Lisbet, Lizeth,
Aliza, Liz, Lizzie, Beth, Betsy, Betsey*

Elizabeth, a Hebrew name that means
"God is my oath," is almost terrifyingly
popular. A royal name with a long history, Elizabeth hasn't fallen below #26 on
the U.S. girls' charts in the 130 years that
these records have been kept.

Part of the appeal of Elizabeth is that it
has so many nicknames—Liz, Beth, Eliza,
Betty, Betsy, Tetsie, Elsie, Lizbeth, Bessie,
Libby, and Buffy, to name a few—that you
don't have to settle on one. Elizabeth is a
great pick if you want a name that has it
all . . . or just can't decide what to name
your daughter.

THIS NAME IN HISTORY

Queen Elizabeth (queen of England)

Elizabeth Bennett (title character in Jane
Austen's *Pride and Prejudice*)

Eliza Dushku (actor)

Elizabeth "Betty" Ford (first lady)

Elizabeth Gilbert (author)

Elisabeth Hasselbeck (TV personality)

Betsey Johnson (fashion designer)

Lizzie McGuire (title character of TV show)

Liza Minnelli (singer and actor)

Lisbeth Salander (character in Stieg
Larsson's *Millennium Trilogy*)

Elisabeth Shue (actor)

Elizabeth Cady Stanton (suffragette)

Elizabeth Taylor (actor)

Ella

Meaning: Fairy maiden; complete

Origin: English; German

Related names and spelling variations: *Elle*

Ella is an English name that means "fairy
maiden" and a German one that means
"complete." It's also a great nickname
for Isabella, Gabriella, Stella, or any
other name that ends in *-ella* . . . but it's
also wildly popular in its own right. This
might be due to *Ella Enchanted*, a novel
by Gail Carson Levine, but we think it's
just because people can't stop singing
Rihanna's 2007 hit "Umbrella." Ella . . .
ella . . . ella . . .

Before its recent dance with fame, Ella
was a top 15 name in the 1880s. Then it
slowly dropped, falling out of the top
100 in the late 1920s and leaving the
list entirely in the 1980s before climbing
back up.

THIS NAME IN HISTORY

Ella Josephine Baker (civil rights activist)

Ella Fitzgerald (singer)

1. Paris (Hilton)
2. Peaches (Geldof)
3. Amanda (Hearst)
4. Anna (Anisimova)
5. Athina (Onassis Roussel)
6. Lydia (Hearst-Shaw)
7. Liesel (Pritzker)
8. Ivanka (Trump)
9. Allegra (Versace)
10. Nicole/Nicky (Richie; Hilton)

Elle McPherson (model)

Ella Enchanted (novel by Gail Carson Levine)

Emerson

Meaning: Emery's son

Origin: German

Related names and spelling variations: *Emery*

Emerson, a German name that means "Emery's son," is a unisex name that's semi-popular on both the boys' and girls' charts. Careful, parents—this can't last. As with Dana, Aubrey, Avery, and Bailey, society will soon choose if Emerson is a boy's first or a girl's, and in nearly every case, the boy's name bows gracefully out of favor. So baby girl Emerson is probably a safe bet.

Emerson was a steady fixture on the boy's chart between 1880 and 1968, then started drifting in and out. It's been back in vogue since 1998, but Emerson the girl's name, which first became popular in 2002, has quickly surpassed the boy's name. See? Society's choice is already being made!

THIS NAME IN HISTORY

Emerson Rose Tenney (daughter of Teri Hatcher and Jon Tenney)

Emerson Drive (musical group)

Ralph Waldo Emerson (author)

Emily

Meaning: Rival

Origin: Latin

Related names and spelling variations: *Emilee, Emmalie, Emely, Emilie, Emmalee*

Emily is a name to be reckoned with. From a Latin word meaning "rival," Emily bested its competition and reigned supreme at #1 from 1996 to 2007 (a long haul for the #1 slot). Emily was finally dethroned in 2008 by her own archrival (and similar-sounding sister), Emma. But with so many appealing Emilies representing the name—from Dickenson to Deschanel, with some "Auntie Em!" thrown in for good measure—this fave isn't going anywhere.

THIS NAME IN HISTORY

Auntie Em (character in L. Frank Baum's
The Wonderful Wizard of Oz)

Emily Blunt (actor)

Emily Brontë (author)

Emilie de Ravin (actor)

Emily Deschanel (actor)

Emily Dickinson (poet)

Emily Hughes (figure skater)

Emily Post (author and etiquette expert)

Emma

Meaning: Healer of the universe

Origin: German

Related names and spelling variations:
Ema, Emmy, Emme

Emma, be glad your name has evolved from its forerunners, Emintrude and Irmgard. Oh, we think both names are classic, but we don't remember anyone asking Irmgard to the prom.

Emma's a Germanic name that roughly means "healer of the universe." That's a lot for your baby daughter to live up to, parents, but we're sure she'll be a professional at cheering you up on gloomy days. The name had a heyday in the early 1900s, dropped way down for decades, then started a quick ascent in the late seventies. When Ross and Rachel gave the name to their daughter in a 2002 episode of *Friends*, the name jumped from #13 (2001) to #4 (2002), and it took the #1 spot from sister Emily in 2008. *Twilight*-fueled Isabella knocked poor Emma down after just one year, but Emma's still a hot pick among parents.

THIS NAME IN HISTORY

Emme (model)

Emma Bovary (character in Gustave
Flaubert's *Madame Bovary*)

Emma Geller-Green (Rachel and
Ross's baby on *Friends*)

Emma Lazarus (poet)

Emma Roberts (actor)

Emmy Rossum (actor)

Emma Thompson (actor)

Emma Watson (actor)

Emma Woodhouse (title character of
Jane Austen's *Emma*)

Hi, My Name Is

Erica

Meaning: Constant ruler

Origin: Norse

Related names and spelling variations: *Erika, Ericka, Erykah*

Erica is the feminine form of the name Eric, which means "constant ruler." Erica was originally used as a first name in the late 1700s. Erica made the U.S. charts for the first time in 1945. It quickly increased in popularity and was a top 100 name between 1972 and 1998, peaking at #31 for a few years at the end of the 1980s. *All My Children*'s iconic character Erica Kane may have helped give the name this boost. It has been on the decline recently, but Erica remains a strong name with a solid meaning that should appeal to you if you like classic, traditional names.

THIS NAME IN HISTORY

Erykah Badu (singer)
Erika Christensen (actor)
Erica Hill (commentator)
Erica Jong (author)
Erica Kane (character on the soap opera *All My Children*)

Erin

Meaning: Ireland

Origin: Irish

Related names and spelling variations: *Eire, Erinne, Aerin, Airin*

TOP TEN: FEMALE
CELEBS WHO DIED TOO SOON

1. Marilyn (Monroe)

2. Karen (Carpenter)

3. Aaliyah

4. Diana (Princess of Wales)

5. Janis (Joplin)

6. Gia (Carangi)

7. Brittany (Murphy)

8. Selena

9. Jayne (Mansfield)

10. Sharon (Tate)

"Oh, hey, *Erin Go Bragh*!" Yep, Erins get that a lot. The phrase translates best to "Ireland forever," and Erin itself is an old romantic nickname for Ireland. The name's an obvious choice if you want to honor Irish roots, but its appeal extends beyond Irish pride. Erin hit the top 100 in 1971 and stayed there until 2004 (partly fueled by *Erin Brockovich*'s box office success), dropping a bit since. If you want to get Irish eyes smiling, you might consider Keira or Cassidy—Erin got a bit too big for its britches.

THIS NAME IN HISTORY

Erin Andrews (sportscaster)

Erin Brockovich (consumer advocate)

Esther

Meaning: Star; myrtle

Origin: Persian; Hebrew

Related names and spelling variations: *Essie, Esta, Hester, Hedy, Hettie, Hetty, Estée, Ester*

Esther is both a Persian name that means "star" and a Hebrew name that means "myrtle," making this beauty a double whammy for committed nature name lovers. For religious parents Esther is also one of only two books in the Bible named after a woman (Ruth is the other).

Old-school Esther was a top 100 name between 1882 and 1935, then declined in popularity until 1970, and has been holding steady since. Consider modern twists like Esta or Estée!

THIS NAME IN HISTORY

Esther (biblical figure)

Esther Hicks (author)

Estée Lauder (cosmetics entrepreneur)

Esther Rolle (actor)

Esther Williams (actor)

Hester Prynne (character in Nathaniel Hawthorne's *The Scarlet Letter*)

Eva

Meaning: Living

Origin: Hebrew

Related names and spelling variations: *Eve, Evie*

The letter *V* is so hot right now. Ava, Avery, Evelyn, and even Genevieve have the letter to thank—at least in part—for their rising success. Add Eva to this list. A letter away from Ava, Eva hit #99 in 2009, on the top 100 for the first time since the 1930s. Shorter and simpler Eve has missed the trend. Most recognizable as the Bible's first lady, Eve has been moderately popular since the 1880s but seems unable to break past the middle of the list.

Both Eva and Eve are Hebrew names that mean "living." If you're looking for something a bit longer, you might consider Evelyn or Evangeline.

Eva and Eve have Hebrew roots and mean "living." That's a great meaning to bestow on a newborn. Eva has been on an upswing over the last decade—recently

Hi, My Name Is

entering the top 100 for the first time—probably helped by the ultra-popular Ava.

Eve is, of course, famous as one half of the biblical duo Adam and Eve. Despite this strong biblical connection, or maybe even because of it, Eve has been only a moderately popular name in the U.S. since the 1880s. It even dropped off the charts entirely for over a decade between 1985 and 1997. Eve is back now, but still in the middle of the pack. Eve would be a great choice if you want a familiar, but unique, name. It also has that chic *V* parents enjoy in Ava and Avery.

THIS NAME IN HISTORY

Eve (biblical figure)

Eva Gabor (actor)

Eva Green (actor)

Eva Longoria (actor)

Eva LaRue (actor)

Eva Mendez (actor)

Eva Marie Saint (actor)

Eva Perón (first lady of Argentina)

Evangeline

Meaning: Good tidings; gospel

Origin: Greek; Latin

Related names and spelling variations: *Evangelica, Evangelina, Evangelista*

Fairly common from 1881 to 1966, Evangeline dropped off the charts entirely for several decades So it's a good thing that Evangeline Lilly's parents were way ahead of the trend—the *Lost* star's unique name jumped back on the charts during the hit show's six-year run. Disney's 2009 feature *The Princess and the Frog* featured another Evangeline, giving the venerable oldie another much-needed boost.

A Greek name that means "good tidings" and a Latin one that means "gospel," Evangeline has unmistakably Christian roots (think "evangelist"). But with America's current fling with *V* (the letter, not the show), Evangeline's ready for—and finding—a larger audience.

THIS NAME IN HISTORY

Evangeline (character in Disney's
    The Princess and the Frog)

Evangeline Lilly (actor)

Linda Evangelista (model)

"Evangeline, A Tale of Acadie" (poem by
    Henry Wadsworth Longfellow)

Evelyn

Meaning: Desired, wished for

Origin: English

Related names and spelling variations: *Evelin, Evalynn, Evalynne, Evelynne*

Evelyn's an impossibly pretty name with an equally attractive pedigree. The name is preceded by other great name picks like English Aveline, Germanic Avelina, English Evlin, Irish Eibhlinn, and the word *avis* ("bird"). It also has a rich history—Evelyn peaked in 1915 at #10, then fell down the charts for nearly a century. It just hit the top 100 again in 2002—on the wings of Ava, Avery, and Eva, perhaps—and has been climbing since. Not only is this name super-vintage, it's got America's Most Wanted Letter: *V*. Besides, what kid doesn't want to be desired?

Ff

Faith

Meaning: Faith

Origin: Latin

Related names and spelling variations: *Faithe*

Of all the virtue names, Faith is the pick of the litter (she definitely has her sister Charity beat!). What does Faith have that the others don't? We can't say for sure, but it's short, sweet, and pretty. Two celebrity singers—Hill and Evans—don't hurt, either.

Faith, as you might guess, was especially popular with Puritan parents back in the 1600s. It's been in the top 1,000 for most years since 1880, but only got really popular in the late 1990s (about when Faith Hill's career began to pick up steam). Faith peaked at #48 in 2002 and has been sliding slowly back down since.

THIS NAME IN HISTORY

Faith Evans (singer)

Faith Ford (actor)

Faith Hill (singer)

Felicity

Meaning: Fortunate, lucky

Origin: Latin

Related names and spelling variations: *Flicka, Felice, Felicienne*

When *Felicity* debuted in 1998, America was reminded that the name, at once fun-loving and Latin-based classical, was even an option. Although Felicity never saw the light of day on the U.S. girls' chart until 1998, it was #390 in 1999. But just as hit TV shows come and go, this name is on its way out, slipping ever since that #390 peak. Nickname lovers will adore Felicity's offbeat option, Flicka.

THIS NAME IN HISTORY

Felicity Huffman (actor)

Felicity (TV show)

My Friend Flicka (novel by Mary O'Hara)

Fiona

Meaning: Fair, white

Origin: Celtic

Related names and spelling variations: *Fee*

TOP TEN: OSCAR-WINNING ACTRESSES

1. Katharine Hepburn (4)
2. Ingrid Bergman (3)
3. Elizabeth Taylor (2)
4. Sally Field (2)
5. Jane Fonda (2)
6. Jodie Foster (2)
7. Hilary Swank (2)
8. Glenda Jackson (2)
9. Meryl Streep (2)
10. Bette Davis (2)

Fiona is a recent addition as a girl's name option. Okay, that's misleading—the name's been around since the 1700s—but it never hit the U.S. charts until 1990. When fiercely tender Fiona Apple released her debut album in 1996, the name got a solid kick-start up the charts, and it soared higher when the 2001 movie *Shrek* introduced strong-willed and spirited Princess Fiona.

Fiona is a Celtic name that means "fair, white," but the name turned green after *Shrek* introduced Princess Fiona, a fair maiden who turns into an ogre at night, and it's stayed green ever since.

THIS NAME IN HISTORY

Fiona Apple (singer)
Princess Fiona (character in the *Shrek* movies)

Gg

Gabriella

Meaning: God has given me strength; man of God

Origin: Hebrew

Related names and spelling variations:
Gabriela, Gabrielle, Gabby, Gaby

Gabrielle's getting the *-ella* treatment, dropping its super-feminine *-elle* ending and becoming pretty, popular Gabriella. The nineties were Gabrielle's decade. On the charts since 1957, it flew in popularity at the end of the century, hitting the top 100 in 1990 and peaking at #46 in 1999. Gabriella didn't even hit the charts for the first time until 1974, but it's shooting up the list, passing Gabrielle on her way down in 2006. So why the switch? Vanessa Hudgens might be the answer—her character Gabriella Montez from *High School Musical* may have pushed the name to its current heights, but the movie, released in 2006, can't explain the name's original boost. We think the boost is linked to the current popularity of the boy's version, Gabriel.

THIS NAME IN HISTORY

Gabrielle Carteris (actor)

Gabrielle Bonheur "Coco" Chanel
    (fashion designer)

Gaby Hoffman (actor)

Gabrielle Reece (volleyball player)

Gabriella Rocha (shoe designer)

Gabriela Sabatini (tennis player)

Gabrielle Union (actor)

Genevieve

Meaning: White phantom; woman of the people; blessed, fair

Origin: Welsh; Celtic; French

Related names and spelling variations:
Genevra, Geneva, Gena, Genie, Ginny, Genoveva, Geneviève

Genevieve is our modern-day Guinevere, the heartthrob of Sir Lancelot. If nobody but a knight will be good enough for your baby girl, consider Genevieve!

Okay, kidding. Genevieve has a little something for everyone. It's Celtic for "woman of the people" and Welsh for "blessed, fair." Mystical, powerful, *and* pretty? Jump on board, parents. You won't be the first; after falling out of the heights of popularity from the early 1900s (when it was in the top 100) through the 1960s, Genevieve is leisurely making her way back up the charts.

Genevieve Cortese (actor)
Genevieve Gorder (TV personality)
Genevieve Jones (designer)
Genevieve Morton (model)

Georgia

Meaning: Farmer

Origin: Greek

Related names and spelling variations:
Georgina, Georgette, Giorgia, Jorja

Good news, parents: no matter where you live, Georgia is guaranteed to be a bona fide southern belle! Sharing the name with the southern state has given Georgia all of its trappings: a sunny smile, a bright disposition, and the prettiness of a peach!

Georgia was a top 100 name for all but one year from 1880 to 1911, then dropped like a peach from a tree in the 1950s, but is gaining ground again.

THIS NAME IN HISTORY
Georgina Chapman (fashion designer)
Jorja Fox (actor)
Georgia O'Keeffe (artist)

Gianna

Meaning: God is gracious

Origin: Italian

Related names and spelling variations: *Giana, Gia, Jianna*

Gianna might sound like a foreign princess, but it's just a foreign commoner—the Italian version of Jane. So go join the other Janes, Gianna, right behind Juanita . . . and ditch that prettier-than-thou attitude.

Like Jane, Gianna means "God is gracious," making it a great pick for Christian parents, but Gianna in particular has appeal enough for anyone. Simple yet foreign, this one's a keeper. Gianna only hit the U.S. charts in 1989 (#888), and has already climbed into the top 100. Want to show off your Italian roots or taste for the classical? Give this exotic Jane a try.

THIS NAME IN HISTORY
Gianna Maria-Onore Bryant (daughter of Vanessa and Kobe Bryant)
Gianna Angelopoulos-Daskalaki (Greek politician)

Giselle

Meaning: To pledge

Origin: French

Related names and spelling variations: *Gisele, Gizelle, Gizele, Gisselle, Gisela*

Giselle may sound like *haute Francais*—like Jacques or Guy—but it's become totally accessible for an American audience in the last twenty years. Giselle made its debut (more French!) on the list in 1983 and has been on the rise ever since, thanks to both supermodel Gisele Bündchen (a

Hi, My Name Is

1. Trista Sutter (*The Bachelorette*)
2. Fantasia Barrino (*American Idol*)
3. Omarosa Manigault-Stallworth (*The Apprentice*)
4. Heidi Pratt (*The Hills*)
5. Tiffany "New York" Polland (*Flavor of Love*)
6. Tila "Tila Tequila" Nguyen (*A Shot at Love with Tila Tequila*)
7. Adrianne Curry (*America's Next Top Model*)
8. Kimora Lee Simmons (*Kimora: Life in the Fab Lane*)
9. Brooke Hogan (*Hogan Knows Best*)
10. Aubrey O'Day (*Making the Band*)

Brazilian-born model with German parents who bears a French name . . . strange, *n'est-ce pas?*) and Princess Giselle from Disney's *Enchanted*.

THIS NAME IN HISTORY

Giselle (queen of Bavaria from 1001 to 1038)

Princess Giselle (character in the Disney movie *Enchanted*)

Gisele Bündchen (model)

Giselle Fernández (journalist)

Giselle Potter (children's book illusrator)

Giselle (ballet)

Grace

Meaning: Grace

Origin: Latin

Related names and spelling variations: *Gracie*

Grace, like Faith or Hope, is a super-popular virtue name that means exactly what it says. It was in the spotlight at the turn of the twentieth century, then fell from—well, from grace—for most of the century. Something switched in the late seventies, though, and it's been gaining ground ever since.

Princess Grace (actor, princess of Monaco)

Gracie Allen (actor and comedian)

Grace Jones (actor and model)

Gracie Katherine McGraw (daughter
of Faith Hill and Tim McGraw)

Grace Paley (author)

Grace Slick (singer)

Gracie Mansion (official mayoral residence
for New York City, named for Archibald
Gracie)

Will and Grace (TV show)

Gretchen

Meaning: Pearl

Origin: German

Related names and spelling variations:
Greta, Gretel

Believe it or not, Greta and Gretchen are German version of the name Margaret, which means "eats vegetables only on Fridays." Nah, we're kidding . . . it means "pearl," a much better trait to give to your newborn daughter. Both Greta and Gretchen were on the charts back in the 1880s, but they've gone their separate ways since. Gretchen peaked in the seventies, hitting a high of #191 in 1973, but has dropped since, almost to the point of missing the list entirely. After falling off the charts completely from 1983 to 1998, Greta's back, and she's claiming some of her sister's former fame. Both names have a distinct and unique sound (that's absolutely nothing like Margaret), and if you adore that distinctive *gr* sound, you're sure to love either name.

THIS NAME IN HISTORY

Greta Garbo (actor)

Gretchen Mol (actor)

Gretchen Rossi (reality TV star)

Greta Van Susteren (news commentator)

Gretchen Wilson (singer)

Hansel and Gretel (German folk tale)

Hh

Hailey

Meaning: Hay clearing

Origin: English

Related names and spelling variations:
Hailee, Hailie, Haley, Haylee, Hayley, Haylie, Haleigh

The first Hailey that comes to our mind is Eminem's oft-referenced daughter Hailie Scott, followed closely by child star Haley Joel Osment . . . but we don't actually think either brought the name to its current place on the charts (okay, maybe Osment). Hailey is an English surname that means "hay clearing" and the name with perhaps the most spelling variations on the boys' or girls' charts (and in the English language?). "Hay-Lees" come in all orthographical shapes and forms, including Hailey, Haley, Haylee, Hayley, Hailee, Haleigh, and Haylie. Like a dresser from IKEA, this cute name comes with great parts, but only vague directions on how to build it . . . so feel free to make it yours.

THIS NAME IN HISTORY

Haylie Duff (actor)

Haylie Ecker (violinist)

Hayley Mills (actor)

Hailey Anne Nelson (actor)

Alex Haley (author)

Leisha Hailey (actor)

Halley's Comet

Hannah

Meaning: God has favored me

Origin: Hebrew

Related names and spelling variations:
Hana, Hanna

When *Hannah Montana* aired, Hannah was on every little girl's tongue . . . but the name actually dropped somewhat during the show's run. (We bet parents just got tired of Miley.) Hannah, a Hebrew name that means "God has favored me" given to a woman who appears in the Bible, was popular around the turn of the 1900s, then declined in use through the sixties. It had a big surge in popularity in the late 1980s and a top 10 run between 1995 and 2007, but a year after *Hannah Montana* aired in 2006, the name started to fall, although not very far. And now that this show's headed off air, we can't help but wonder what's in store for this name's future. Try shortened Hana for a spelling alternative.

Hannah Gruen (character in Carolyn
    Keene's *Nancy Drew* series)

Hannah Arendt (German philosopher)

Hanna Sheehy-Skeffington (founder of
    the Irish Women's Franchise League)

Hannah Storm (news anchor)

Hannah Swensen (character in Joanne
    Fluke's *Murder She Baked* series)

Hannah Teter (snowboarder)

Hannah Van Buren (first lady)

Hanna-Barbera (animation studio)

Hannah and Her Sisters (Woody Allen movie)

Hannah Montana (TV show)

Harmony

Meaning: Harmony

Origin: Greek

Related names and spelling variations:
Harmonie

Harmony isn't a name—it's a state of
being. It's *also* a name that refers to that
state of being. So someone named
Harmony is sure to exist in harmony
with . . . well, herself, at least. And that's
something. Harmony made it onto the
U.S. charts in 1975, fell off again in 1985,
and wasn't seen again until the late
nineties (it wasn't a decade of harmony,
you could say!), though it's been rising
quickly ever since. If you want a music
name with no nicknames—sorry, Melody,
but Mel can be a turnoff—try Harmony.

THIS NAME IN HISTORY

Harmony Korine (director)

Hazel

Meaning: Hazel tree

Origin: English

Related names and spelling variations: *Hazelle*

Just like Sage, Hazel is both a plant name
and a color name. (Sage is also a virtue
name that means "wisdom," but do you
really have to have it all?) Hazel was in the
top 100 between 1886 and 1936 and hit
#18 in 1897. Then it dropped all the way
down the charts and fell off them from
the mid-1970s to the mid-1990s. Thanks
in part to Julia Roberts's baby daughter,
Hazel is back again. Hazel is vintage but
totally fresh today.

THIS NAME IN HISTORY

Hazel Mae (sportscaster)

Hazel Moder (daughter of Julia Roberts
    and Daniel Moder)

Heidi

Meaning: Noble, kind

Origin: German

Related names and spelling variations:
Adelheid

Heidi is a nickname for Adelheid, the
German version of Adelaide, but it's
surpassed them both. And we get why—
Adelaide's a bit dated, and Adelheid's just
a bit . . . much. A consistent presence on
the charts since 1942, Heidi held a spot in
the top 100 from 1966 to 1983 before slipping down in the ranks. This name shouts

Hi, My Name Is

"seventies," giving it a retro feel, and what little girl wouldn't want to share a name with Heidi Klum?

Heidi Klum (model and TV personality)
Heidi Montag (reality TV star)
Heidi (book by Johanna Spyri)

Helen

Meaning: Sunbeam

Origin: Greek

Related names and spelling variations: *Helena, Helene, Ilene, Elena, Ilona, Jelena, Aileen, Elena, Ileana, Ellin, Ellen, Alina, Elaine, Eleanor, Ilka*

Helen's a nature name in disguise. It comes from a Greek name that may mean "sunbeam." Lots of parents are skipping nature-names-once-removed like Helen today and heading straight for Aurora, Lily, and Rose. But Helen's still a great pick if you want a classic, vintage name, but also want to pay homage to that big, bright lightbulb in the sky. Helen's been popular ever since Helen of Troy. It ranked in the top 100 from 1880 to 1958 and was in the top 10 between 1891 and 1935. It's been on the decline since, but this name never quite seems to go out of style. Also check out variations like Helene (or Hélène), Ellen, Elaine, Ilene, Aileen, Alina, and Eleanor.

THIS NAME IN HISTORY
Helena Bonham Carter (actor)
Helena Christensen (model)
Helen Hunt (actor)
Helen Keller (author)
Helen Mirren (actor)
Helena Grace Rutherford (daughter of Kelly Rutherford)
Helen of Troy (Greek mythological figure)

Holly

Meaning: Holly

Origin: English

Related names and spelling variations: *Hollie*

Holly reminds you of Christmas for a reason—it's a plant name that comes from the holly tree, used for Christmas decoration more in carols (ever really seen a bough of holly?) than in the modern world. It first entered the U.S. charts in 1936, gained popularity quickly thanks to Truman Capote's character Holly Golightly in *Breakfast at Tiffany's*, then held its place in the top 100 from 1969 to 1990. Holly has been slipping a bit lately, maybe thanks to *The Girls Next Door*'s Holly Madison, but it's still winning places in many parents' hearts. Don't wait until December to give this one to your daughter; it's cute, friendly, and not just for Christmas babies (unlike Noelle).

THIS NAME IN HISTORY
Holly Marie Combs (actor)
Holly Golightly (character in Truman Capote's *Breakfast at Tiffany's*)
Holly Hunter (actor)
Holly Robinson Peete (actor)

1. Chloé (by Chloé)

2. Ralph (by Ralph Lauren)

3. Oscar (by Oscar de la Renta)

4. Marc (Jacobs by Marc Jacobs)

5. Stella (by Stella McCartney)

6. Jessica (McClintock by Jessica McClintock)

7. Adrienne (Vittadini by Adrienne Vittadini)

8. Grace (Amazing Grace by Philosophy)

9. Shalimar (by Guerlain)

10. Angel (by Thierry Mugler)

Hope

Meaning: Hope

Origin: English

Related names and spelling variations:
Esperanza

With the number of diapers you're about to change, you'll swear this girl's springs are eternal. Give her the name Hope, so she'll have a bit of dignity, at least. One of the most popular virtue names, Hope has been in the top 1,000 for all but one year since 1880, peaking at #144 in 1999.

THIS NAME IN HISTORY

Hope Williams Brady (character on *Days of Our Lives*)

Hope Davis (actor)

Hope Dworaczyk (model)

Esperanza Spalding (musician)

Emery Hope Sehorn (daughter of Angie Harmon and Jason Sehorn)

Ii

Iris

Meaning: Iris; rainbow

Origin: Greek

Related names and spelling variations: *Irisa*

Get this: not only is Iris a part of your eyeball and a beautiful flower, it's a Greek word that means "rainbow." Nature fans, rejoice—you just found a nature name times three! Iris peaked in 1929 at #196, fell a lot after that, but has had an upswing in the last decade. Some other flower names for your flower children include Daisy, Violet, and Rose. Some other eyeball names, we guess, would be Cornea, Pupil (this one also means "student"!), and Optic Nerve. Please don't name your daughter Optic Nerve.

THIS NAME IN HISTORY

Iris Chang (author)

Iris DeMent (singer)

Iris Johansen (author)

Iris Murdoch (author)

Isabella

Meaning: God is my oath

Origin: Italian

Related names and spelling variations: *Isabelle, Isobelle Izabelle, Izabele, Bella, Bell, Belle*

Isabella's yet another play on Elizabeth, which means "God is my oath." But this particular Elizabeth—and there are plenty of them—has shot up the charts in the last decade, becoming the most popular girl's name in 2009. There's only one reason for this: the release of *Twilight* as a book and movie series, featuring Isabella "Bella" Swan (Bella's a great nickname, by the way, but it's one that's going to be terribly popular for decades to come . . . or burn out from its own ubiquity). Although Isabella still sounds old-fashioned, it's one of the vintage names that's really making the scene today.

THIS NAME IN HISTORY

Queen Isabella (queen of Spain)

Isabelle Adjani (actor)

Isabel Allende (author)

Isabella Leong (actor)

Isabella Leonarda (composer)

Isabella Rossellini (actor)

Isabella "Bella" Swan (character in the
   Twilight series by Stephenie Meyer)

Isobel "Izzie" Stevens (character on
   the TV show Grey's Anatomy)

Isabel Toledo (fashion designer)

Ivy

Meaning: Ivy

Origin: English

Related names and spelling variations: *Ivie*

Ivy's a great plant name that hasn't been too common in recent years. Its most famous bearer this century is none other than Poison Ivy, a villainess from the *Batman* comic series. And why not? She's committed to the environment and she's breathtakingly beautiful . . . she was even played by Uma Thurman in 1997's *Batman and Robin*. Ivy peaked at #258 in 1882, fell far down the list, but just started gaining again recently. A stylish and underused botanical name, Ivy will appeal to some nature-name parents. You can also consider Marigold, Poppy, or Zinnia.

THIS NAME IN HISTORY

Ivie Anderson (singer)

Ivy Compton-Burnett (author)

Poison Ivy (villainess from the DC Comics
   Batman series)

Jj

Jacqueline

Meaning: Supplanter, heel-grabber

Origin: French

Related names and spelling variations: *Jackie, Jacqui, Jacquelyn, Jaqueline, Jaclyn*

Jacqueline is the feminine form of French Jacques, which comes from the name James . . . but this gal has so much more pizzazz! With nicknames Jackie and Jacqui, it's got short and cute covered, and Jacqueline itself is regal and classic, but modern, too. Jacqueline hit the list for the first time in 1898, then spent only one year between 1928 and 2003 outside the top 100. It got two big boosts: one from First Lady Jacqueline Kennedy in the sixties, then another from *Charlie's Angels* star Jaclyn Smith in the eighties. It's fallen a few spots recently, but don't worry, Jacqui fans—this one's not going anywhere.

THIS NAME IN HISTORY

Jacqueline Bisset (actor)

Jackie Collins (author)

Jacqueline Bouvier Kennedy Onassis (first lady)

Jaclyn Smith (actor)

Jada

Meaning: Jade; he knew

Origin: Spanish; Hebrew

Related names and spelling variations: *Giada, Jayda, Jaeda, Jade, Jaida*

Jada may seem like a simple spelling variation of the name Jade, but it's so much more—it's actually the Spanish version of the mineral (giving it that foreign flair) and a Hebrew name that means "he knew." So let it serve as a constant reminder to your daughter—Daddy knows what you're up to! Jada didn't make the list until the late 1960s, then finally broke into the top 200 names in the mid-1990s. When Jada Pinkett Smith became a star in her own right, the name had another big surge.

THIS NAME IN HISTORY

Jade Raymond (video game producer)

Jada Rowland (children's book illustrator and actor)

Jada Pinkett Smith (actor)

Jada (musical group)

Jada Toys (maker of collectible car models)

Jane

Meaning: God is gracious

Origin: English

Related names and spelling variations:
*Janelle, Janet, Janey, Janice, Jayne, Jean, Joan,
Ivana, Johanna, Jana, Janina, Jeanne, Sheena,
Sinéad, Gianna, Giovanna, Juanita*

Jane? "That's not my name!" This name
has seen a slight uptick in the past few
years, and we think the Ting Tings' too-
catchy song—denying that its narrator is
named Jane—had something to do with
it. Honestly, Jane's been so popular over
the years that we would've guessed that
that was her name, too. If you still haven't
figured out what her name is—and we
haven't, either—here are some Jane-based
possibilities: Janelle, Janet, Janey, Jayne,
Jean, Joan, Ivana, Johanna, Jana, Janina,
Jeanne, Sheena, Gianna, Giovanna, or
Juanita. If you go through the whole list
of names that came from Jane, *one* of them
ought to be that girl's name.

THIS NAME IN HISTORY

Jane Austen (author)

Jane Fonda (actor)

Jane Goodall (anthropologist)

Jane Krakowski (actor)

Jane Lynch (actor)

Jane Seymour (actor)

Jane Eyre (book by Charlotte Brontë)

Janelle

Meaning: God is Gracious

Origin: English

Related names and spelling variations: *Janella,
Janell, Janel*

No foreign version here . . . Janelle's just
another Jane spin-off. And it's lagging
behind its parent name today. After peaking in the late seventies at #186, Janelle has
been declining over the past few decades.
Janelle is still a great choice if you want to
honor a certain Jane, or just want something a bit more feminine.

THIS NAME IN HISTORY

Janell Cannon (author)

Janelle Monáe (singer)

Janel Parrish (actor)

Janelle Wang (TV personality)

Jasmine

Meaning: Jasmine flower

Origin: Persian

Related names and spelling variations:
*Jazmine, Jasminne, Jazminne, Jazmin,
Jasmin, Jessamyn, Yasmin, Yazmin,
Jazmyn, Yasmine, Jaz, Jazz*

Aladdin couldn't have helped this Persian
flower name if it tried. When the animated Disney classic came out, its princess's name was already in the U.S. top 50.

TOP TEN: FEMALE TITANIC SURVIVORS

1. Rhoda ("Rosa" Abott)
2. Kornelia (Theodosia Andrews)
3. Elsie (Edith Bowerman)
4. Charlotte (Appleton)
5. Marjorie (Dutton)
6. Adä (Ball)
7. Mabel (Helen Fortune)
8. Laina (Heikkinen)
9. Amelie (Icard)
10. Violet (Jessop)

Jasmine saw the U.S. charts for the first time in 1973 and was already in the top 50 by 1989. Other popular variations are Jazmin, Jazmine, Jasmin, Yasmin, Jazmyn, and Yasmine.

THIS NAME IN HISTORY

Jasmine (character in Disney's *Aladdin*)

Yasmine Bleeth (actor)

Jasmine Guy (actor)

Jazmine Sullivan (singer)

Jessamyn West (author)

Jenna

Meaning: Blessed, fair

Origin: Celtic

Related names and spelling variations: *Jena*

Jenna's a modern version of Jennifer, a modern version of the name Guinevere, which means "blessed and fair." What a mouthful . . . this name has quite a pedigree! Today's best-known Jenna is Jenna Fischer, star of *The Office* . . . and who doesn't want a relationship—or a wedding—just like Jim and Pam's? Jenna hit the U.S. charts and debuted at #879 in 1971, then shot up in popularity in the early eighties.

THIS NAME IN HISTORY

Jenna Bush (daughter of former president George W. Bush)

Jenna Dewan (actor)

Jenna Elfman (actor)

Jenna Fischer (actor)

Jenna Maroney (character on the TV show *30 Rock*)

Jenna McCorkell (figure skater)

Jenna Morasca (reality TV star)

Jenna Ushkowitz (actor)

Jenna Wade (character on the TV show *Dallas*)

Jennifer

Meaning: White phantom; woman of the people; blessed, fair

Origin: Celtic

Related names and spelling variations: *Gennifer, Genifer, Jenife, Jenny, Guinevere*

Jennifer is the Celtic version of antique Guinevere, Sir Lancelot's belle back in King Arthur's time. The name means "white phantom," "woman of the people," and "blessed and fair." That's a lot for your baby girl to live up to, but we're sure she'll take it all in stride. Jennifer was the most popular U.S. girl's name from 1970 through 1984, but has since dropped out of not only the top spot, but also the top 100. Looking for something a bit more unique? Consider root name Guinevere, which has never ranked in the top 1,000.

THIS NAME IN HISTORY

Jennifer Aniston (actor)

Jennifer Capriati (tennis player)

Jennifer Cavalleri (character from the book and movie *Love Story* by Erich Segal)

Jennifer Connelly (actor)

Jenny Craig (weight loss company founder)

Jennifer Garner (actor)

Jennifer Hudson (actor and singer)

Jennifer Lopez (actor and singer)

Jenny McCarthy (actor and comedian)

Jennifer Warnes (singer)

Jennifer Weiner (author)

"867-5309/Jenny" (song by Tommy Tutone)

Jessica

Meaning: Wealthy; God sees

Origin: Hebrew

Related names and spelling variations: *Jessaca, Jessaka, Jessie, Jess*

Jessica means "wealthy" and "God sees" and has a somewhat uncertain background. What we do know is that Shakespeare used the name in his famous play *The Merchant of Venice* and he may have taken it from the biblical name Iskah (also

Hi, My Name Is

spelled Jesca or Jeska). Regardless of the origin, parents have loved the name ever since. Jessica was in the U.S. top 1,000 in 1880 and started to get really popular in the 1970s, when it positively skyrocketed in popularity. Jessica was the #1 name for ten years during the 1980s and 1990s and has spent a stunning twenty-one years in the top 5. Jessica has been dropping down the list for more than a decade now, but remains in the top 100.

THIS NAME IN HISTORY

Jessica Alba (actor)

Jessica Biel (actor)

Jessica Fletcher (character on the TV show *Murder, She Wrote*)

Jessica Lange (actor)

Jessica Rabbit (character in the movie *Who Framed Roger Rabbit*)

Jessica Simpson (singer)

Jessica Tandy (actor)

Jillian

Meaning: Youthful

Origin: English

Related names and spelling variations: *Jill, Jilly, Gillian*

Jillian is a variation of the name Gillian, a feminine version of Julian, which means "youthful." Today's famous Jillian, the fitness coach and personality on the reality show *The Biggest Loser*, added "hard-ass" to the word's official meaning. (Okay, not

TOP TEN: FIFTIES STARLETS

1. Brigitte (Bardot)
2. Cyd (Charisse)
3. Cleo (Moore)
4. Irish (McCalla)
5. Pier (Angeli)
6. Eva (Marie Saint)
7. Doris (Day)
8. Sandra (Dee)
9. Bettie (Page)
10. Hazel (Court)

officially, but she added it in our minds.) Jillian entered the U.S. charts in 1976 and hasn't moved much since, staying in the top 200 for most of those years. Gillian has been on the charts since 1968, but it hasn't ranked as highly. It peaked at #303 in 1999 and has been dropping since. Let cute nicknames Jill or Gill sell you on either of these great names.

Joanna

Meaning: God is gracious

Origin: Scandinavian; French; German

Related names and spelling variations: *Joanne, Shona, Jo*

Joanna is a Jane with Scandinavian, French, and German roots. Joanna dates as far back as the Bible and has been on the charts since 1880. It gained some ground in the 1970s and even hit the top 100 for two years in the 1980s, but it's mostly been a middle-of-the-pack name. With a regal, sophisticated sound and a lack of overpopularity in its past, this might be the name for your baby girl.

Jocelyn

Meaning: Member of the Goths

Origin: German

Related names and spelling variations: *Jocelynne, Joslyn, Jocelin, Joselyn, Jocelynn*

Don't want your kid hanging out with the wrong crowd? Try another name. Jocelyn is a German name that means "member of the Goths." Okay, not those Goths . . . these were a group who settled in the Roman Empire between the third and fifth centuries. Still, if names have any power, your baby girl will be dressing all in black, chain-smoking cigarettes, and listening to "industrial rock" (what is that, anyway?) by the time she's fifteen. Maybe that image appeals to today's parents. Jocelyn first hit the top 1,000 in 1927, stuck to the middle of the pack until the eighties, then peaked in 2007 at #50.

NAME FACTOID

Jocelyn used to be a boy's name, but is now only used for girls.

1 Michelle (Obama)

2 Hillary (Clinton)

3 Jacqueline (Kennedy Onassis)

4 Eleanor (Roosevelt)

5 Martha (Washington; Jefferson)

6 Elizabeth (Truman; Ford; Monroe)

7 Edith (Roosevelt; Wilson)

8 Abigail (Adams; Fillmore)

9 Julia (Grant; Tyler)

10 Dolley (Madison)

THIS NAME IN HISTORY
Jocelyn Brando (actor)
Jocelyn Enriquez (singer)
Jocelyn Kelley (author)
Jocelyn Moorhouse (director)
Jocelyn Pook (composer)

Josephine

Meaning: God shall add

Origin: English

Related names and spelling variations:
Josefine, Jo, Josie, Joey

Josephine is the female version (and extra-long version) of the boy's name Joseph, which means "God shall add." To the name, that is. Because it's longer than Joseph, you know? Despite its extra length, Josephine had a heyday in the early 1900s . . . but it hasn't been too popular since, and even went through an uncool phase for a few years (can you even imagine? A three-syllable Joe being unpopular). Josephine's slowly climbing back up the charts, maybe aided by its vintage appeal and its boyish nickname, Jo.

1. Bill/William (O'Reilly; Maher; Bennett; Kristol)

2. Joe (Scarborough; Trippi; Klein)

3. Mark (Levin; Shields; Halperin)

4. Chris (Matthews; Hitchens)

5. Rachel (Maddow)

6. Jon (Stewart)

7. Frank (Rich; Luntz)

8. Michael (Barone; Kinsley; Savage)

9. Peggy (Noonan)

10. Paul (Krugman; Begala)

THIS NAME IN HISTORY

Josephine Baker (performer)

Joséphine de Beauharnais (wife of French leader Napoléon Bonaparte)

Josephine Hull (actor)

Josephine "Jo" March (character in Louisa May Alcott's *Little Women*)

Josephine "Joey" Potter (character on the TV show *Dawson's Creek*)

Josephine St. Pierre Ruffin (civil rights activist and suffragist)

Josie and the Pussycats (TV show and movie)

"My Girl Josephine" (song by Fats Domino)

Joy

Meaning: Joy

Origin: Latin

Related names and spelling variations: *Joia, Joie*

Joy's not just a virtue name . . . it's a promise to the world, and one that your daughter will be expected to live up to. Can you imagine? "Man, for a Joy, you're just not that joyful." Better hope she can laugh at the same joke for twenty years. Joy first made the U.S. charts in 1885, gained ground in the twenties, then was a top 200 name through the early 1980s. Joy is a simple and sweet name, and its heart is certainly in the right place. Still, though . . . what a burden.

THIS NAME IN HISTORY

Joy Behar (TV personality)

Joy Bryant (actor)

Julia

Meaning: Youthful

Origin: Latin

Related names and spelling variations:
Giulia, Julie, Juliet, Juliette, Yuliana, Juliana, Julianna, Julianne, Giuliana

Whether you prefer Roberts, Child, Louis-Dreyfus, or Stiles, Julia is well-represented in pop culture. It's a female version of the Latin Julius, which means "youthful." It dates back to the Bible and was a top 50 name in the 1880s through the 1910s. The eighties saw a Julia revival, and by 1996, it was in the top 50 again. Today, Julia shares its popularity with a score of other versions, including Juliana, Julianna, Juliet, Julissa, Julie, Juliette, and Julianne.

Julie Andrews (actor)

Juliette Binoche (actor)

Julia Child (chef and TV personality)

Julianne Hough (TV personality and dancer)

Julia Ward Howe (abolitionist and poet)

Julia Louis-Dreyfus (actor)

Julianna Margulies (actor)

Julianne Moore (actor)

Julia Ormond (actor)

Giuliana Rancic (TV personality)

Julia Roberts (actor)

Julia Stiles (actor)

Julie and Julia (blog, book, and movie by Julie Powell)

Romeo and Juliet (play by William Shakespeare)

Kk

Kaitlyn

Meaning: Pure

Origin: Irish

Related names and spelling variations: *Caitlin, Caitlyn, Katelyn, Katelynn, Kaitlin, Kaitlynn*

Kaitlyn—Caitlyn is the traditional spelling, but that *K* is so much "kooler"—is an Irish form of the name Katherine, which means "pure." Here's another name that can be spelled in any way you choose to put Kate and Lynn together. Some of the more popular versions include Kaitlyn, Katelyn, Caitlyn, Caitlin, Katelynn, Kaitlin, and Kaitlynn. This name is adorable no matter how you spell it. Just don't try to push that idea too far.

THIS NAME IN HISTORY

Caitlin Crosby (singer)

Kaitlyn Lawes (curler)

Kaitlin Olson (actor)

Kaitlynne Postel (former Miss Kentucky)

Kara

Meaning: Wholesome; dear; friend

Origin: Greek; Danish; Italian; Irish Gaelic

Related names and spelling variations: *Cara*

Kara has Greek and Danish roots that mean "wholesome," Irish Gaelic roots that mean "friend," and Italian roots that mean "dear." (Want to say "my dear" in Italian? It's "cara mia.") The Cara spelling was on the U.S. charts in 1880, but didn't hold steady until the 1950s. Kara entered the charts then, too, jumping quickly and making the top 100 in the mid-1980s. This is a choose-your-own-pronunciation name: do you want a "CARE-uh" or a "CAR-uh"? The choice is yours! (And that of anyone else who tries to pronounce your little girl's name.)

THIS NAME IN HISTORY

Cara Black (tennis player)

Kara DioGuardi (TV personality)

Kara Keough (TV personality)

Kara Thrace (character on the TV show *Battlestar Galactica*)

Karen

Meaning: Pure

Origin: Danish

Related names and spelling variations: *Caren, Caron, Caryn, Karina, Karin, Carine, Kerrin*

TOP TEN: POPULAR GIRLS IN HIGH SCHOOL MOVIES

1. Cher (*Clueless*)
2. Veronica (*Heathers*)
3. Sloane (*Ferris Bueller's Day Off*)
4. Corey (*Empire Records*)
5. Claire (*Breakfast Club*)
6. Regina (*Mean Girls*)
7. Bianca (*10 Things I Hate About You*)
8. Amanda (*Can't Hardly Wait*)
9. Summer (*Napoleon Dynamite*)
10. Caroline (*Sixteen Candles*)

A great line from the band Cake—"She's changing her name from Katie to Karen"—really says it all. Karen is the Danish version of the name Katherine—Katie, if you're still following us—which means "pure." But Karen has better trappings than its parent. A bit more sophisticated, a bit more unusual, a bit less overused, this name is just a cut above its mother. Karen didn't really catch on with U.S. parents until 1928, when it got on the charts to stay. In 1938, Karen entered the top 50 and stayed there through 1979 (unusual isn't the same as unpopular!). Another Karen plus: it doesn't have any easy nicknames.

THIS NAME IN HISTORY

Karen Bass (politician)
Karen Brown (author)
Karen Carpenter (singer)
Karen Millen (fashion designer)
Karen Marie Moning (author)

Karina

Meaning: Pure

Origin: Scandinavian; Russian

Related names and spelling variations: *Carina, Kareena, Karena, Karine*

If you thought Karen was one sophisticated gem, check out Karina. A Russian and Scandinavian version of Karen with a super-popular *-ina* ending, this name has more feminine flair than Karen, which makes it more appealing to parents. In the U.S. top 1,000 since 1969, Karina peaked at #108 in 1996 and has been slowly dropping since. *Dancing with the Stars'* Karina Smirnoff has given the name a recent boost.

THIS NAME IN HISTORY

Karina Grimaldi (fashion designer)

Kareena Kapoor (actor)

Karina Lombard (actor)

Karina Pasian (singer)

Karina Smirnoff (dancer and TV personality)

Karla

Meaning: Free man

Origin: German

Related names and spelling variations: *Carla*

Carla is a female version of the name Carl, which means "free man" or "farmer." Carla with a *C* is the more traditional spelling, but Karla with a *K* is the more popular spelling these days. In 2009, Karla ranked #295 while Carla ranked #665. In the 1980s, parents started choosing Karla over Carla and also began switching to the similar name Carly. Other *K* names that have become more popular than the more traditional *C* spellings include Kaitlyn and Kara.

THIS NAME IN HISTORY

Carla Tortelli (character on *Cheers*)

Karla Bonoff (songwriter)

Carla Bruni (singer and wife of French president Nicolas Sarkozy)

Carla Gugino (actor)

Katherine

Meaning: Pure

Origin: Greek

Related names and spelling variations: *Kathryn, Katie, Kate, Kathy, Kitty, Katy, Catherine*

Katherine has Greek roots that mean "pure," but nicknames Katie, Kitty, Kathy, and Kate all have American roots that just mean "fun." And this name's got a vanguard of spokespeople giving it an endless assortment of flavors: Katherine Heigl, Catherine Zeta-Jones, Kate Austen from *Lost*, Kate Gosselin, and the list just goes on . . . pick your favorite and name your daughter after her! Katherine has been a top 100 in the U.S. almost every year since the list began in 1880.

THIS NAME IN HISTORY

Catherine Earnshaw (character in Emily Brontë's *Wuthering Heights*)

Kate Austen (character on the TV show *Lost*)

Kate Beckinsale (actor)

Katie Couric (TV journalist)

Kate Gosselin (TV personality)

Catherine the Great (empress of Russia)

Katherine Heigl (actor)

Katharine Hepburn (actor)

Katherine McPhee (singer)

Kitty Montgomery (character on the
    TV show *Dharma and Greg*)

Kate Moss (model)

Katherine Paterson (author)

Katy Perry (singer)

Kate Winslet (actor)

Catherine Zeta-Jones (actor)

Kathleen

Meaning: Pure

Origin: Irish

Related names and spelling variations:
Cathleen, Kathie, Kathy

"Tip it, Kathleen!" The most famous
Kathleen of recent years—Kathy Griffin—
may have hurt this name a bit through
stories of her mother's love for boxed
wine . . . but the name probably lost some
ground just from being too popular for
its own good. Kathleen was in the U.S. top
100 between 1920 and 1990, even spending a few years in the top 10 in the forties
and fifties. Although this name is past its
prime, it's an old-fashioned gem that still
appeals to parents today.

THIS NAME IN HISTORY

Kathy Bates (actor)

Kathleen Battle (singer)

Kathy Griffin (comedian)

Kathleen Madigan (comedian)

Kathleen Robertson (actor)

Kathleen Turner (actor)

Katrina

Meaning: Pure

Origin: German

Related names and spelling variations: *Katrin,
Katrine, Catrina, Catriona*

Katrina is the German variety of classic
Katherine. It entered the U.S. top 1,000
in 1945, gained popularity in the eighties, and even spent a few years in the top
100. Hurricane Katrina, however, turned
out to be a disaster for the name as well as
for New Orleans, sending Katrina plum-
meting down the charts. Avoid the tragic
association by opting for the feline nickname Kat.

THIS NAME IN HISTORY

Katrina Bowden (actor)

Cat Deeley (TV personality)

Katrina vanden Heuvel (journalist and editor)

Kat Von D (tattoo artist and TV personality)

Katrina (2005 hurricane)

Kayla

Meaning: Crown, laurel; slender

Origin: Arabic; Gaelic

Related names and spelling variations: *Kaylah,
Kaila, Kaela, Cayla*

When Kayla Brady was introduced on
Days of Our Lives, her first name was only
moderately popular, ranking #581 in

TOP TEN: PRESIDENTIAL PETS

1. Nelson (Washington: horse)

2. Billy (Coolidge: pygmy hypo; Grant: pony)

3. Emily (Jackson: horse; Theodore Roosevelt: snake)

4. Juno (John Adams: dog; Hayes: dog)

5. Mason (Fillmore: pony)

6. Millie (G. H. W. Bush: dog)

7. Vicki (Nixon: poodle)

8. Jack (Lincoln: turkey; Theodore Roosevelt: dog)

9. Ofelia (G. W. Bush: longhorn cow)

10. Bo (Obama: dog)

1981. A year after she was introduced, Kayla reached #81. As the character got more popular, the name kept going higher, peaking at #11 in the 1990s. Then when Kayla Brady took a long leave of absence from the show, the name began a slow decline, too, with an emphasis on "slow." With a modern *K* beginning and a super-chic *-a* ending, Kayla is sure to be a favorite over the next few years.

THIS NAME IN HISTORY

Kayla Ewell (actor)

Kayla Brady (character on *Days of Our Lives*)

Kayla Stra (jockey)

Kaylee

Meaning: Slender

Origin: Gaelic

Related names and spelling variations: *Caylee, Cailee, Kailee, Kailey, Kayleigh, Kaylie, Kaleigh, Kayley, Kaley*

Just how many ways can you spell the name "Kay-Lee"? Parents have gotten really creative with this one: Kaylee, Kayleigh, Caylee, Kailey, Kaylie, Cali, Kali, Kailee, Kaleigh, Caleigh, and Kayley. This is a perfect DIY name, too. Want a modern, hip feel? Start with a *K* and wrap it with a *-li* or a *-lee*. Prefer classic styling? Stick with a *Ca* and end with a *-leigh* or *-ley*. Go ahead . . . make *K-ly* yours!

THIS NAME IN HISTORY

Kaylee Frye (character on the TV show *Firefly*)
Kailee O'Sullivan (model)
Kaylee Tankus (Korean fashion design house)
"Kayleigh" (song by Marillion)

Keira

Meaning: Black, dark

Origin: Irish

Related names and spelling variations: *Kira, Kiera, Kierra*

Want your daughter's name to pay tribute to black, the most love-it-or-hate-it color of all time, but don't want to go the medieval "Karen the Black" route? Try Keira instead. The female version of Irish Kieran, a name that means "black, dark," Keira says it all. Besides, Irish girls' names *are* the new black. We have Keira Knightley to thank for her name's rise to power today. In 2000, Keira first entered the charts at #949. In 2006, it peaked at #110. We're willing to bet our last gold doubloon that the first two *Pirates of the Caribbean* movies had something to do with the jump.

THIS NAME IN HISTORY

Keira Knightley (actor)
Keira Morrisette (TV producer)

Kelly

Meaning: Troublesome

Origin: Irish

Related names and spelling variations: *Kelli, Kellie*

Mom and Dad, if little Kelly starts going bad at a young age, you've got nobody to blame but yourselves. Kelly, a classic Irish name that's gotten super-popular in the U.S., means "troublesome." (So don't say we didn't warn you.) Kelly was originally a unisex name, but you don't see too many guys with the name anymore (extreme exception: pro surfer Kelly Slater). The girl's name overtook the boy's name in the fifties—a happening that means trouble for any unisex name—and boy Kelly has been on his way out ever since.

THIS NAME IN HISTORY

Kelly Carlson (actor)
Kelly Clarkson (singer)
Kelly McGillis (actor)
Kelly Osbourne (reality TV star)
Kellie Pickler (singer)
Kelly Preston (actor)
Kelly Ripa (TV personality)
Kelly Rowland (singer)
Kelly Slater (surfer)
Kelli Williams (actor)

Kelsey

Meaning: Fierce island; victorious ship

Origin: English

Related names and spelling variations: *Kelsie*

Here's a warning for you, parents: if you name your daughter Kelsey, she'll almost certainly grow up to be a pirate. Kelsey is an English surname that may mean "fierce island" or "victorious ship," which makes it a great name for boys, chock-full of adventure and danger. Sadly, Kelsey has been predominantly a girl's name for decades (Kelsey Grammer is the big exception, and he's done the name a huge service . . . but seemingly just for girls), dropping off the boys' list entirely after 1996. Girl Kelsey's on her way out, too; after peaking at #23 in 1992, she's been sliding steadily downhill ever since.

THIS NAME IN HISTORY
Kelsey Grammer (actor)

Kendall

Meaning: Kent's valley

Origin: English

Related names and spelling variations: *Kendyl, Kendelle, Kendal*

Kendall might be the only unisex name that'll stay an option for boys *and* girls, at least for a while. Of course, this might just be because neither name is that popular. An English surname that means "Kent's valley," Kendall has been a regular on the U.S. boys' list since 1924 (though it first appeared in 1913). It gained popularity and peaked in the early 1990s. Kendall became a constant on the girls' chart in 1980 and passed Kendall the boy not long after. Girl Kendall has fluctuated a bit in the last few years, but is on a general trajectory up the charts, while boy Kendall is headed the opposite direction.

THIS NAME IN HISTORY
Kendall Cross (actor)
Kendall Farr (stylist)
Kendall Jenner (reality TV star)
Kendall Schmidt (actor)
Kay Kendall (actor)
The Kendalls (music group)
Kendall Jackson (winery)

Kendra

Meaning: Royal power

Origin: English

Related names and spelling variations: *None*

Let's face it—when you think of Kendra, only one face comes to mind. *The Girls Next Door* made Playboy Playmate-turned-reality TV star Kendra Wilkinson first-name famous—on the same plane as Cher, Bono, and Tyra—and all other Kendras just ceased to exist. Her first name had been in the U.S. top 300 for decades, but it soared in popularity when the show premiered. It's lost a lot of ground since (possibly *also* because of Kendra Wilkinson).

THIS NAME IN HISTORY
Kendra Giardi (character on the TV show *Glee*)
Kendra Bentley (reality TV star)
Kendra Shank (singer)
Kendra Wilkinson (reality TV star)

Hi, My Name Is

Kimberly

Meaning: Kimber's meadow

Origin: English

Related names and spelling variations:
Kimberlee, Kimberleigh, Kimberli, Kimberlie, Kimberley

Did you know Kimberly used to be a boy's name, too? Well, you wouldn't . . . when Kimberly the girl hit its top 10 peak in the mid-1960s and stayed there until the late seventies, parents eventually stopped using it for boys and it dropped off the charts entirely in 1980. Oddly, girl Kim didn't wipe itself off the charts from its own soaring popularity. Sure, it fell from its top 10 heights, but never very far. Part of the long-lasting appeal of the name might be its make-it-yours ending. Try Kimberlee, Kimberleigh, Kimberli, Kimberlie, or Kimberley for something a little different.

THIS NAME IN HISTORY

Kim Basinger (actor)

Kim Cattrall (actor)

Kimberly Elise (actor)

Kim Fields (actor)

Kimberly Denise Jones (singer known as Lil' Kim)

Kim Kardashian (reality TV star)

Kim O'Hara (title character in Rudyard Kipling's *Kim*)

Kim Possible (animated TV show)

Kimberly Wyatt (singer)

TOP TEN: BELOVED WOMEN WRITERS

1. Jane (Austen)
2. Charlotte (Brontë)
3. Emily (Brontë; Dickinson)
4. Toni (Morrison)
5. Louisa May (Alcott)
6. Virginia (Woolf)
7. Alice (Walker)
8. Isabel (Allende)
9. Margaret (Atwood)
10. Maya (Angelou)

Kylie

Meaning: Boomerang

Origin: Australian

Related names and spelling variations: *Kylee, Kiley, Kileigh, Kylee, Kyleigh*

Kylie is an Australian name that may have come from the Aboriginal word for "boomerang," but so far in its U.S. history, no comebacks have been necessary. Kylie hit the U.S. charts in 1978, made big leaps in the eighties, and hit the top 100 for the first time in 2001. It's still on its way up, probably fueled by Australian singer Kylie Minogue. This is another winner for creative spellers; other Kylies include Kylee, Kyleigh, and Kiley.

THIS NAME IN HISTORY

Kylie Bax (model)

Kylie Jenner (reality TV star)

Kylie Minogue (singer)

Kylee Russell (actor)

Kylie Travis (actor)

Kyra

Meaning: Lady; king; sun

Origin: Greek; Persian

Related names and spelling variations: *Cyra*

Kyra may sound like the other big *K*s of today—Kylie, Kaylee, Kayla, Kelsey, or Kendra—but the name's roots are deeper and more proper than its kompetitors. Both a Greek name that means "lady" and a Persian one that means "king" or "sun," this name is steeped in class, royalty, and beauty.

Kyra first appeared on the U.S. list of girls' names in 1969. Kyra peaked at #179 in 2005, the same year Kyra Sedgwick's show *The Closer* debuted. It's been dropping since . . . which just means it won't get overused for parents looking for a stylish *K* option.

THIS NAME IN HISTORY

Kyra Davis (author)

Kyra Phillips (news anchor)

Kyra Sedgwick (actor)

LI

Lacey

Meaning: From Lassy

Origin: English

Related names and spelling variations: *Lacy, Laci, Lacie*

Parents, naming your daughter Lacey is sure to confine her to a well-dressed life (not a turnoff for stylish moms and sharp-dressed dads!). Although the English name means "from Lassy" (a place in France), the name brings to mind nothing but ruffles, lace, and fine stitching.

Lacy (note the dropped *e*) was on and off the U.S. charts from 1880 to 1910, then disappeared until 1975. But seventies parents soon decided the *e* made the name—Lacey first entered the charts in 1975, soared up the list, and peaked at #116 in 1984. It's dropped since, but it's still a pretty and modern name, especially with that chic -*ey* ending.

THIS NAME IN HISTORY

Lacey Chabert (actor)

Lana

Meaning: Beautiful, peaceful; afloat

Origin: Irish; Hawaiian

Related names and spelling variations: *Lanna, Lannie*

Lana sounds as modern as Jada or Kylie, but this name is 100 percent vintage. Lana was a steady chart presence starting in 1939, thanks to movie star Lana Turner. It peaked at #188 in 1948, then started a long fall off the charts. *Smallville* character Lana Lang might have brought the name back to vogue; it started to rise again in the early 2000s. Lana's modern sound and vintage pedigree make it a great choice if you're looking for either characteristic.

THIS NAME IN HISTORY

Lana Lang (character from the TV show *Smallville*)

Lana Turner (actor)

Lana Wood (actor)

Laura

Meaning: Laurel

Origin: Latin

Related names and spelling variations: *Lora*

Laura's a Latin name that means "laurel," an ancient symbol of victory and honor, but it's not so victorious these days. Laura's been popular for centuries and was in the top 100 for most of the last century, but classic's not chic these days, and Laura's dropping down the list. Although the name is just too universal to ever sound out of date, if you're looking for an alternative with the same meaning, you might try Daphne.

THIS NAME IN HISTORY

Laura Branigan (singer)

Laura Bush (first lady)

Laura Dern (actor)

Laura Esquivel (author)

Laura Ling (journalist)

Laura Linney (actor)

Dr. Laura Schlessinger (radio personality)

Laura Spencer (character on *General Hospital*)

Laura Ingalls Wilder (author)

Laura Ashley (fashion designer)

Lauren

Meaning: From Laurentium, laurel

Origin: English

Related names and spelling variations: *Loren, Lorin, Lorren, Lorynn, Lauryn, Lorena, Laurel*

Lauren comes from the masculine name Laurence and means "from Laurentium" (an ancient Roman site) and "laurel." The Loren spelling hit the charts first as a boy's name in 1880 (the first year they started keeping track). The Lauren spelling was also on the boys' chart consistently starting in 1913. While Lauren hasn't been on the boys' list since 1989, Loren didn't drop off until 1998. Lauren didn't start getting popular as a girl's name until the 1940s, probably due to the popularity of Lauren Bacall. Today, Lauren has a sophisticated, feminine appeal without being overly girly.

THIS NAME IN HISTORY

Lauren Bacall (actor)

Lauren Conrad (reality TV star)

Lauren Graham (actor)

Lauryn Hill (singer)

Lauren Holly (actor)

Lauren London (model)

Layla

Meaning: Night

Origin: Arabic

Related names and spelling variations: *Laila, Leila, Leyla, Lailah, Laylah*

Layla has Arabic roots and means "night," which may be a reference to dark hair or a dark complexion. The Leila spelling is the one that originally hit the charts in 1880. The Layla spelling was made popular here by Eric Clapton; it hit the U.S. charts in 1972, two years after his band Derek and the Dominoes released their same-name

Hi, My Name Is

hit (about Clapton's unrequited love for George Harrison's wife) and the same year the song actually got popular. Clapton's popularity may have waned a bit since then, but Layla's kept on climbing the charts. Other popular spellings are Laila, Leyla, Lailah, and Laylah.

THIS NAME IN HISTORY

Laila Ali (professional boxer)

"Layla" (song by Eric Clapton)

"Layla and Majnun" (seventh-century Persian poem)

Leila (character in Lord Byron's poem "Don Juan")

Leah

Meaning: Languid

Origin: Hebrew

Related names and spelling variations: *Lia, Lea, Leia*

Leah is a Hebrew name that means "languid"—what a downer—and an Old Testament character from the book of Genesis. Yeah, this name's been around for a while. It has been on the U.S. charts since 1880 and stayed sort of popular for decades, then climbed quickly to the top 100 in the late seventies. This may have been thanks to the Roy Orbison song, but we think *Star Wars* may have had something to do with it, too; Leah is a common alternative to Leia (and can have the same pronunciation—"lay-uhh"—if you wish).

Leah's leapt again in the last few years—perhaps due to Leah Clearwater,

TOP TEN: RADIO PERSONALITIES

1 Howard (Stern)

2 Casey (Kasem)

3 Rush (Limbaugh)

4 Garrison (Keillor)

5 Don (Imus)

6 Ryan (Seacrest)

7 Dick (Biondi)

8 Jonathan (Glass)

9 Laura (Schlessinger)

10 Delilah (Rene Luke)

a werewolf in the *Twilight* series. If Leah's too typical, try alternate spellings Lia, Lea, or Leia.

THIS NAME IN HISTORY
Princess Leia (character in *Star Wars* series)
Leah Clearwater (character in Stephenie Meyer's *Twilight* series)
Leah Remini (actor)
Rashida Leah Jones (actor)
"Leah" (song by Bruce Springsteen)
"Leah" (song by Roy Orbison)

Lena

Meaning: Seductress; sleep

Origin: Latin; Hebrew

Related names and spelling variations: *Lina*

Lena has Latin roots that mean "seductress" and Hebrew roots that mean "sleep." So parents, when teen Lena goes to bed at night, be sure she's doing so alone! Despite its scandalous roots, Lena was big at the end of the prim and proper 1800s. It stayed in the top 100 until 1920, then began a long, slow fall down the list, right into the early 2000s, when it started to turn around. Lena can also be a nickname for names that end with -*lena*, such as Magdalena.

THIS NAME IN HISTORY
Lena Headey (actor)
Lena Horne (singer)
Lena Olin (actor)

Leslie

Meaning: Garden of holly

Origin: Gaelic

Related names and spelling variations: *Lesli, Lesley, Lesleigh, Leslee, Lezlee, Lezlie, Lesly*

Like the name Holly, but don't want the obvious Christmas connection? Consider Leslie. A Scottish name that means "garden of holly," it grew out of the super-Scottish surname Lesslyn. It was also primarily a boys' name (think Leslie Nielsen) until boy Leslie was passed in the ranks by girl Leslie in the 1950s. It hasn't ranked in the boys' list since 1997 but has remained popular as a girl's name. Try variations Lesli, Lesley, Lesleigh, Leslee, Lezlee, Lezlie, or Lesly for added flair.

THIS NAME IN HISTORY
Leslie Bibb (actor)
Leslie Caron (actor and dancer)
Lesley Gore (singer)
Leslie Howard (actor)
Leslie Mann (actor)
Leslie Nielson (actor)
Leslie Patricelli (author)
Lesley Stahl (journalist)
Leslie Ann Warren (actor)
Lisa Leslie (basketball player)

Lila, Lyla

Meaning: Lilac; playful; God's free will

Origin: Persian; Sanskrit; Hindi

Related names and spelling variations: *Lila, Lyla, Lilah*

TOP TEN: RAPPERS

1	The Notorious B.I.G.	**6**	Lil Wayne
2	Tupac	**7**	Nas
3	Eminem	**8**	Outkast
4	Jay-Z	**9**	T. I.
5	Kanye West	**10**	Drake

If you love the name Delilah, but don't want your daughter to be marked for life by the Plain White T's song, try nickname Lila (or Lilah) as a full first. It's a Persian name that means "lilac" and a Sanskrit one that means "playful"—and who doesn't want a playful flower for a daughter? Lila was top 250 material from the end of the 1800s through the mid-1930s, then fell through the 1960s and even dropped off the charts for years. Then when singer Lila McCann got famous in 1997, her first name was back the following year . . . and has been on the rise ever since. If you want a nature-based classic, try Lilac.

THIS NAME IN HISTORY
Lila Downs (singer)
Lila McCann (singer)

Lily

Meaning: Lily

Origin: Latin

Related names and spelling variations:
Lillian, Lilly, Lillie, Lilian, Lilyana, Lilianna, Lilliana, Lilliana, Lillianna, Lilia

Teenagers and twentysomethings might know Lily only as Harry Potter's mum, but for older generations, this name is all about Lily Tomlin. Long before her supporting roles in TV shows *Damages* and *Desperate Housewives,* Tomlin's career took off in seventies comedy. And her name took off along with it; a chart staple until the 1960s, Lily fell off the list entirely until Tomlin pushed the name back into contender status. And it's still on its way up—maybe thanks to *Harry Potter.* Longer version Lillian ranked #27 in 2009.

THIS NAME IN HISTORY

Lily Allen (singer)

Lillian Jackson Braun (author)

Lillian Gish (actor)

Lily Potter (character in *Harry Potter*)

Lily Tomlin (actor)

Linda

Meaning: Pretty

Origin: Spanish

Related names and spelling variations: *Lindy, Lynda*

Linda is a Spanish name that means "pretty," but to today's audience, it translates better to "someone's mom." And that's not wrong: Linda skyrocketed in popularity in the 1940s and sailed right to the top 10, where it stayed through 1965. It's been dropping ever since. That means the Linda count in the older parents and grandparents-to-be categories is way higher than in the young adults and soon-to-be-parents categories. Linda will come back again—it's too pretty not to!—but for now, consider modern version Lindy. Linda can also be a cute nickname

for names with the *-lind* sound, like Belinda or Rosalind.

THIS NAME IN HISTORY

Linda Blair (actor)

Lynda Carter (actor)

Linda Evangelista (model)

Linda Evans (actor)

Linda Hamilton (actor)

Linda Hunt (actor)

Linda Lael Miller (author)

Linda Ronstadt (singer)

Lindsey

Meaning: Linden tree island or Lincoln's island

Origin: English

Related names and spelling variations: *Lindsay*

Believe it or not, Lindsey used to be just for the boys. It started high on the charts in 1880, but fell toward the back of the pack for most of the next century. And when Lindsey made the girls' chart for the first time in the seventies, it was a quick hit, reaching the top 100 by 1980. Lindsey the boy is all but unheard of today; it dropped off the boys' chart in 1988 and hasn't been seen since. Today, Lohan's antics may be killing off her first name; both spellings have lost ground.

THIS NAME IN HISTORY

Lindsey Graham (U.S. senator)

Lindsey Jacobellis (skier)

Lindsay Lohan (actor)

Lindsay Price (actor)

Lindsey Vonn (skier)

Hi, My Name Is

Lisa

Meaning: God is my oath

Origin: Hebrew

Related names and spelling variations: *None*

Lisa is one of a big family of names—Liza, Lizzie, and Beth are examples—derived from the name Elizabeth, which means "God is my oath." Lisa entered the U.S. charts in 1937, was #1 by 1962, and stayed there for the rest of the sixties. Neither Kudrow nor Simpson could restore this name to its former popularity, but Lisa still holds a comfortable spot on the charts.

THIS NAME IN HISTORY

Lisa Bonet (actor)

Lisa Kudrow (actor)

Lisa Leslie (basketball player)

Lisa Ling (journalist)

Lisa Loeb (singer)

Lisa Lopes (singer)

Lisa Marie Presley (musician and daughter of Elvis Presley)

Lisa Rinna (actor)

Lisa Simpson (character on the TV show *The Simpsons*)

Mona Lisa (painting by Leonardo da Vinci)

Lola

Meaning: Sorrows

Origin: Spanish

Related names and spelling variations: *Dolores, Lolita*

Lola sounds modern and chic—an image helped by the spiky-haired lead in the 1998 film *Run Lola Run*—but this name is classic vintage. Lola is an old pet name for Spanish Dolores, which means "sorrows." It hit its peak in the early 1900s, ranking near the top 100, and has been cruising down the charts ever since, despite the saucy song "Whatever Lola Wants" from the 1950s musical *Damn Yankees* and the seventies rock hit "Lola" by the Kinks. Lola fell off the charts completely in 1981, only to reemerge in 2002 and rise through the ranks fast. We're not sure why the name jumped. The Kinks' "Lola" was already thirty years old, and *Run Lola Run* didn't have the box office success to count (although it did become a cult classic). This might just be the era of old vintage names getting brought back into the light.

THIS NAME IN HISTORY

Lola Consuelos (daughter of Kelly Ripa and Mark Consuelos)

Lola Facinelli (daughter of Jennie Garth and Peter Facinelli)

Lola Montez (dancer and mistress of King Ludwig I of Bavaria)

Lola Sheen (daughter of Charlie Sheen and Denise Richards)

"Lola" (song by the Kinks)

Run Lola Run (movie)

"Whatever Lola Wants" (song from the musical *Damn Yankees*)

Lolita (novel by Vladimir Nabokov)

1. Ingrid (Bergman)

2. Lauren (Bacall)

3. Yvonne (De Carlo)

4. Ava (Gardner)

5. Jane (Russell)

6. Lena (Horne)

7. Rita (Hayworth)

8. Veronica (Lake)

9. Hedy (Lamarr)

10. Ella (Raines)

Lorelei

Meaning: Captivating

Origin: German

Related names and spelling variations:
Loralei, Lorelai

"Lorelei, let's liiiiive together!" Anyone? Styx? Best band of the seventies? No . . . okay. Lorelei, a German name that means "captivating," hasn't ever captivated American parents. Since first appearing in 1938, it's spent more time off the charts than on. It was briefly popular in the fifties, when character Lorelei Kilbourne appeared in *Big Town* and Marilyn Monroe played Lorelei Lee in *Gentlemen Prefer Blondes*. The Styx song had no such impact . . . we guess "Mr. Roboto" is the real fan favorite. The name made a comeback in 2004, thanks to Lorelai Gilmore of *Gilmore Girls*, and has been on its way up since.

THIS NAME IN HISTORY

Lorelai Gilmore (character on the TV show *Gilmore Girls*)

Lorelei Lee (character in *Gentlemen Prefer Blondes*)

Lorelei Kilbourne (character in *Big Town*)

Lucy

Meaning: Light

Origin: English

Related names and spelling variations:
Luci, Lucie, Lucille, Lucia, Luciana, Lucienne, Lucetta

Everybody sing it: Lucy in the sky with diamonds! The song is just so catchy. It didn't help the name, though; after being a top 100 name from 1880 to 1924, Lucy started a fall that lasted all the way through the seventies. But it's on its way back. (Why? Lucy Liu? Lucy Lawless? We don't know.) Like Violet and Sophie, Lucy is riding on today's rage for vintage names. Want extra vintage? Try Lucille.

THIS NAME IN HISTORY

Lucille Ball (actor)

Luciana Barroso (wife of actor Matt Damon)

Lucille Clifton (poet)

Lucy Lawless (actor)

Lucy Liu (actor)

Lucy Pevensie (character in the *Chronicles of Narnia* book series)

Lucy van Pelt (character from Charles Schulz's *Peanuts*)

"Lucy in the Sky with Diamonds" (song by the Beatles)

Luna

Meaning: Moon

Origin: Latin

Related names and spelling variations: *None*

Luna's a Latin name that means "moon," but after Luna Lovegood, a favorite from the *Harry Potter* craze, it took on a new character: bashful and bookish but fiercely loyal. The name had been in the middle of the pack since the late 1800s, then dropped off the charts entirely for almost ninety years. But it rose like the moon after 2003. If outer space is your thing, but the moon isn't, try Celeste ("celestial") or Stella ("star").

THIS NAME IN HISTORY

Luna Lovegood (character in J. K. Rowling's *Harry Potter* series)

Diego Luna (actor)

Lydia

Meaning: Woman from Lydia

Origin: Greek

Related names and spelling variations: *Lidia*

Lydia is a location name—it was a kingdom in Asia Minor (located in present-day Turkey) dating back to 700 B.C.E. Although Lydia has never fallen lower than the 300s since 1880, it's been on an upswing since the late seventies. It's on an upswing now probably because of the popularity of old-fashioned sounding names. Here's the best part about this old beauty for full-namer parents: no available nicknames!

THIS NAME IN HISTORY

Lydia (biblical figure)

Lydia Bennet (character in Jane Austen's *Pride and Prejudice*)

Lidia Bastianich (celebrity chef)

Lydia Cornell (actor)

Lydia Pense (singer)

Lydia Sigourney (poet)

Lydia Sokolova (ballet dancer)

Lydia Deetz (character in *Beetlejuice*)

Mm

Mackenzie

Meaning: Son of the fair one

Origin: Gaelic

Related names and spelling variations:
Mackenzy, Makenzy, Mckenzy, Mckenzie, Makenzie, Kenzie

Mackenzie is a Gaelic surname that means "son of the fair one." Mackenzie didn't make the U.S. top 1,000 until 1976. Mackenzie Phillips starred in the TV show *One Day at a Time*, which debuted in 1975, so the name's initial popularity is likely tied to her. The name continued to gain popularity and peaked at #40 in 2001. It has dropped a few spots since then. Mackenzie is a sassy name that sounds a bit boyish, which should appeal to you if you like unisex names (Mackenzie hasn't appeared on the boy's chart since 2001).

THIS NAME IN HISTORY
Mackenzie Phillips (actor)
Mackenzie Rosman (actor)
Mackenzie Blue (series of books by
    Tina Wells)

Macy

Meaning: From Massey

Origin: French

Related names and spelling variations:
Macey, Maci, Macie

Devout shopaholics might express their love of department stores by naming their daughters Macy, but we prefer to think of Macy Gray: a moody and bluesy R&B singer. Macy is a French name that means "from Massey," which could refer to several places in the country . . . so just think of it as "from France." After dropping off the charts for eighty years, Macy reappeared in 1990 at #641, and its popularity has only risen since.

THIS NAME IN HISTORY
Macy Gray (singer)
Macy's (department store)

Madeline

Meaning: Woman from Magdala

Origin: French

Related names and spelling variations:
Madeleine, Madalynn, Madalynne, Madelyn, Madilyn, Madalyn, Madelynn, Madilynn

TOP TEN: CHILD STARS

1. Shirley (Temple)
2. Michael (Jackson)
3. Macaulay (Culkin)
4. Drew (Barrymore)
5. Thora (Birch)
6. Soleil Moon (Frye)
7. Abigail (Breslin)
8. Elijah (Wood)
9. Hayley/Haley (Mills; Joel Osment)
10. Dakota (Fanning)

Madeline is a spelling variation of Madeleine, which is the French form of Magdalene and comes from a place-name that means "woman from Magdala." Magdalene is a reference to the biblical figure Mary Magdalene. Madeline has been on the charts since 1880 and has been the most popular spelling in the U.S. overall. It made a huge leap in popularity in the mid-1980s, and like other old-fashioned sounding names, it has continued to gain popularity. Creative spellers have put quite a few versions of the name into the top 1,000, including Madelyn, Madilyn, Madeleine, Madalyn, Madelynn, Madalynn, and Madilynn.

THIS NAME IN HISTORY

Madeline Albright (former secretary of state)
Madelyn "Maddie" Hayes (character on the TV show *Moonlighting*)
Madeleine L'Engle (author)
Madeline Kahn (actor)
Madeline Stowe (actor)
Madeline (series of books by Ludwig Bemelmans)
madeleines (French cookies)

Madison

Meaning: Maud's son

Origin: English

Related names and spelling variations: *Maddison, Madisyn, Madyson*

Is your name Maude? Do you like keeping names in the family? Try Madison, a name that means "Maud's son" (but daughter works just as well). When the mermaid in 1984's *Splash* chose the name Madison for herself—after seeing the Madison Avenue street sign in New York—America chose it, too. It hit the charts for the first time one year later, got to #222 by the end of the eighties, hit the top 10 in 1997, and remains popular today. Alternate spellings include Maddison, Madisyn, and Madyson. This name isn't just for Maudes anymore.

THIS NAME IN HISTORY

Madison (character in the movie *Splash*)

Madison Keys (tennis player)

James Madison (U.S. president)

Madison Avenue (iconic street in New York City)

Maeve

Meaning: Intoxicating

Origin: Irish

Related names and spelling variations: *None*

Maeve might seem prim and proper to today's audience, but it's an Irish name that means "intoxicating." What a title to stick your daughter with as she enters the world! The name's been around for centuries, but it just hit the U.S. charts for the first time in 1997 (meaning this is the cubic zirconium of vintage names—not a bit legit . . . but don't worry, we won't tell your classy friends).

THIS NAME IN HISTORY

Maeve Binchy (author)

Maeve Quinlan (actor)

Makayla

Meaning: Who is like God?

Origin: Hebrew

Related names and spelling variations: *Makaila, Mckayla, Micaela, Mikaela, Mikayla, Michaela, Micaela*

"Who is like God?" No, don't answer, it's kind of a rhetorical question. It's also the meaning (yes, the meaning itself is a question) of the name Makayla, a variation of older Michaela, the female version of Michael. Michaela has been on the U.S. charts since the 1960s, but made a big leap when *Dr. Quinn, Medicine Woman* debuted in the early nineties. The show's main character was Dr. Michaela Quinn, but people called her Mike . . . a nickname we don't recommend for baby Michaela. Makayla, similar to ultra-popular Kayla, is a better-liked spelling than the original today, but Michaela's hanging in there, too. Variations popular today are Mikayla, Michaela, Mikaela, and Mckayla.

Hi, My Name Is

1. Will (Ferrell)
2. Andy (Samberg)
3. Amy (Poehler)
4. Tina (Fey)
5. Tim (Meadows)
6. John (Belushi)
7. Molly (Shannon)
8. Chris (Farley)
9. Dana (Carvey)
10. Mike (Myers)

THIS NAME IN HISTORY
Michaela Conlin (actor)
Michaela "Mike" Quinn (character on the TV show *Dr. Quinn, Medicine Woman*)
Michaela Watkins (actor)

Malia

Meaning: Bitter; drop of the sea

Origin: Hawaiian

Related names and spelling variations: *Maliyah, Malea, Maliah, Maleah*

Hawaiian Malia, like Irish Molly, is a version of Mary, so all three names mean "bitter" or "drop of the sea." Although many had never heard the name before, Malia was already getting big among new parents when Barack Obama entered the Oval Office. First Daughter Malia has given the name a serious boost, and Maliyah isn't far behind.

THIS NAME IN HISTORY
Malia Obama (daughter of U.S. president Barack Obama)

Mallory

Meaning: Unlucky

Origin: French

Related names and spelling variations: *Mal, Mallary*

Mallory comes from a French name that means "unlucky." Tough break, Mals of the world. But the name's no-luck meaning hasn't stopped parents from picking it. Mallory entered the U.S. charts in 1983 and jumped to #83 in 1986—with a little help from the character Mallory on *Family Ties*. It's dropped a lot in the last few years, further proof that, in names as in music, what gets big must soon go out.

THIS NAME IN HISTORY

Mallory Keaton (character on the TV show *Family Ties*)

Mallory Pike (character in Ann M. Martin's *The Baby-Sitters Club* series)

Mallory Snyder (model)

Margaret

Meaning: Pearl

Origin: Hebrew

Related names and spelling variations: *Maggie, Meg, Peg, Peggy, Madge, Marge, Daisy, Meggie, Margarita, Marguerite, Margie*

Margaret is a Hebrew word that means "pearl." And like Elizabeth, it's the basis of endless nicknames and spinoffs: Maggie, Meg, Peg, Peggy, Madge, Marge, Meggie, Margarita, Marguerite, Margie, and even Daisy (where did that come from? Marguerite. It's the French version of Margaret, but also a word for daisy). While a few of its more modish nicknames have become names in their own right, Margaret is still holding its own.

THIS NAME IN HISTORY

Margaret Atwood (author)

Margaret Cho (comedian)

Maggie Gyllenhaal (actor)

Margaret Mead (anthropologist)

Margaret Mitchell (author)

Marguerite Moreau (actor)

Meg Ryan (actor)

Maggie Simpson (character on *The Simpsons*)

Dame Maggie Smith (actor)

Margaret "Maggie" Thatcher (former British prime minister)

"Maggie May" (song by Rod Stewart)

Mariah

Meaning: Bitter; drop of the sea

Origin: Latin

Related names and spelling variations: *None*

Don't be fooled by its chic sound—Mariah is just another Mary. This one's a version of Maria, the Latin Mary, and means "bitter" or "drop of the sea." Mariah took on a life of its own when Mariah Carey got big. When the singer hit the airwaves in 1990, the name was already #259, but the very next year it hit #69. Although the name has had rises and falls in popularity since, it's still top 100 material.

THIS NAME IN HISTORY

Mariah Carey (singer)

Mariah Fredericks (author)

Mariah Stewart (author)

Marissa

Meaning: Sea; bitter; drop of the sea

Origin: Latin; Italian

Related names and spelling variations:
Maris, Marisa

Marissa is a version of the name Maris, which may mean "sea," and a version of Maria, which means "bitter" or "drop of the sea." The traditional spelling is Marisa and its first appearance on the U.S. charts was in 1956. Marissa showed up a few years later and has taken over as the most popular spelling. It started to really gain ground in the late 1970s and entered the top 100 in 1989. Marissa stayed there through 2005 and has dropped a few spots since then. Marissa is a very pretty name that should appeal to water-lovers and parents who like names without nicknames.

THIS NAME IN HISTORY
Marissa Miller (model)
Marisa Tomei (actor)

Marley

Meaning: Pleasant meadow

Origin: English

Related names and spelling variations:
Marlea, Marleigh, Marlee, Marlie

Marley is an English surname that meant "pleasant meadow" until Bob Marley came along and switched it to "pleasant mellow." Marley's new trappings include

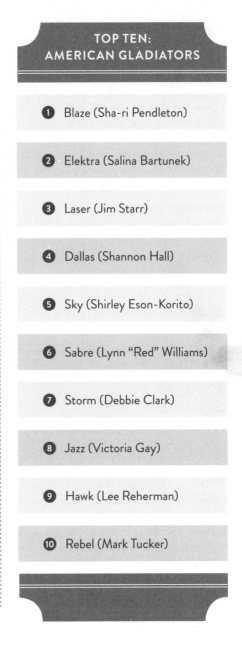

TOP TEN:
AMERICAN GLADIATORS

1. Blaze (Sha-ri Pendleton)
2. Elektra (Salina Bartunek)
3. Laser (Jim Starr)
4. Dallas (Shannon Hall)
5. Sky (Shirley Eson-Korito)
6. Sabre (Lynn "Red" Williams)
7. Storm (Debbie Clark)
8. Jazz (Victoria Gay)
9. Hawk (Lee Reherman)
10. Rebel (Mark Tucker)

peace-loving, love-worshipping, and some strong political views. And for dog lovers, the 2005 book (and subsequent 2008 movie) *Marley & Me* changed the name's image again . . . to a big, goofy, bad-mannered dog. Whatever meaning you attach to the name, it's incredibly popular these days. It appeared on the girls' chart in 1994, and showed up on the boys' chart in 2008. Maybe this unisex pair, like so few others, will get along in peace.

THIS NAME IN HISTORY

Marlee Matlin (actor)

Marley & Me (book and movie by John Grogan)

Marley Shelton (actor)

Bob Marley (singer)

Jacob Marley (character in Charles Dickens's *A Christmas Carol*)

Martha

Meaning: Lady

Origin: Aramaic

Related names and spelling variations: *Marty, Marta, Martina*

Martha is an Aramaic name that means "lady" . . . a meaning that has been well-maintained by its holders, from Martha Washington to Martha Stewart. Maybe because the lady meaning has been so well-guarded, the name hasn't been too popular in recent years. After staying in the top 50 from 1880 through 1954, it's been losing ground ever since. This is one vintage name that isn't coming back this decade.

THIS NAME IN HISTORY

Martha Graham (dancer and choreographer)

Martina Hingis (tennis player)

Martha MacCallum (news anchor)

Martina McBride (singer)

Martina Navratilova (tennis player)

Martha Plimpton (actor)

Martha Stewart (entrepreneur)

Martha Washington (first lady)

Mary

Meaning: Bitter; drop of the sea

Origin: Hebrew

Related names and spelling variations: *Maria, Maree, Mariam, Miriam, Mariana, Mariella, Marilyn, Marilla, Marie, Mariyah, Mariela, Mia, Molly*

Mary may seem like the mother of all *M* names (fitting, since she was Jesus's mother in the Bible)—Maria, Malia, Mariah, Molly, and so on—but it's just another version of the real Mama M, the Hebrew name Miriam. Of all Miriam's offspring, Mary has historically been the most popular. It topped the charts at #1 for more than seventy years, first between 1880 and 1946, then between 1953 and 1961 (and it spent that seven-year gap at spot #2), making it by far the most dominant female name of the last 130 years. But thanks to its prim-and-proper purity and its near century at the top, Mary's on her way back down, and Latin twist Maria has finally surpassed her in the ranks.

Hi, My Name Is

TOP TEN: SILENT MOVIE STARS

1. Charlie (Chaplin)
2. Greta (Garbo)
3. Buster (Keaton)
4. Lon (Chaney Sr.)
5. Rudolph (Valentino)
6. Lillian (Gish)
7. Roscoe (Arbuckle)
8. Wallace (Reid)
9. Bebe (Daniels)
10. Pola (Negri)

If you want something with a bit more flair, you could try Mariella, Marilla, or Mariana.

THIS NAME IN HISTORY

Queen Maria I and Queen Maria II (queens of Portugal)

Maria (character on the TV show *Sesame Street*)

Maria (character in the musical *West Side Story*)

Marie Antoinette (Queen of France)

Mary J. Blige (singer)

Mary Cassatt (painter)

Maria Menounos (TV personality)

Maria Montessori (founder of the educational method)

Mary Tyler Moore (actor)

Mary-Kate Olsen (actor)

Mary-Louise Parker (actor)

Mary Robinson (Ireland's first female prime minister)

Mary Shelley (author)

Maria Shriver (journalist)

Mary Stuart (Queen of Scots)

Maria von Trapp (matriarch of the family that inspired *The Sound of Music*)

Mary Poppins (movie and book series by P. L. Travers)

Maya

Meaning: God's creative power; mother; great

Origin: Hindi; Greek; Latin

Related names and spelling variations: *Maia, Miyah, Miya, Mya, Myah*

Maya's a great every(wo)man name. Maya has Hindi roots meaning "God's creative power" and is also related to the Roman goddess Maia (the goddess of spring, who gave her name to the month of May). And with Greek roots that mean "mother," you're bound to get those grandkids we know you really want. Maya first made the list in the early seventies and has now made it all the way to the top 100.

THIS NAME IN HISTORY

Maya Angelou (poetess)

Mýa Marie Harrison (singer)

Maya Lin (architect and sculptor)

Maya Plisetskaya (ballerina)

Maya Ritter (actor)

Maya Rudolph (actor)

Maya and Miguel (TV show)

Maya (people of Central America)

Megan

Meaning: Pearl

Origin: Welsh

Related names and spelling variations: *Meghan, Meaghan, Meagan, Meaghann, Meighan, Meg, Meggie, Meggin*

Brunette bombshell Megan Fox just changed this name from a sweet classic to a saucy choice. But she hasn't sent her name flying back up the charts (not that it has that much further to go). Megan entered the U.S. charts in the early fifties and had its heyday in the eighties and the nineties, when it stayed in the top 15. But despite Megan Fox's presence, it's dropped some since. Megan is a Welsh name (something you don't see a lot of in this list) that means "pearl."

THIS NAME IN HISTORY

Meggin "Meg" Cabot (author)

Megan Fox (actor)

Meaghan Jette Martin (actor)

Megan McArthur (astronaut)

Megan Mullally (actor)

Meg White (musician)

Melanie

Meaning: Black, dark

Origin: Greek

Related names and spelling variations: *Melany*

Can Melanie still be riding the wave of popularity it got from *Gone with the Wind*? Nah—its current rank probably has more to do with Melanie Griffith—but the name got big when the movie *Gone with the Wind* premiered and hasn't gone away since. Melanie didn't hit the U.S. charts until 1886, then disappeared almost immediately until it came back in 1938. When *Gone with the Wind* came out, the name made a huge leap, and more popularity surges came in the seventies and eighties. Melanie has Greek roots that mean "black, dark," but this name is as sweet as can be. And as old; it goes back centuries and was popular during the Middle Ages.

THIS NAME IN HISTORY

Melanie Brown (singer)

Melanie Chisholm (singer)

Melanie Griffith (actor)

Melanie Lynskey (actor)

Mélanie Watt (children's book author and illustrator)

Melanie Wilkes (character in Margaret Mitchell's novel *Gone with the Wind*)

Melissa

Meaning: Bee

Origin: Greek

Related names and spelling variations: *Melessa, Melesa, Missy, Mel, Melisa*

Melissa might be a Greek word for "bee," but your baby girl won't sting—in fact, we bet she'll be sweet as honey, especially with cute boyish nickname Mel or girly Missy. Melissa has been a first name for centuries and hit the charts in 1880. After dropping off for a few decades, it gained some momentum from the mid-1960s to the mid-1980s. Despite fan favorites like Etheridge and Joan Hart, the name's been slowly slipping since.

THIS NAME IN HISTORY

Melissa de la Cruz (author)

Missy Elliott (singer)

Melissa Etheridge (singer)

Melissa George (actor)

Melissa Gilbert (actor)

Melissa Joan Hart (actor)

Missy Higgins (singer)

Melissa Manchester (singer)

Melissa J. Morgan (author)

Melissa "Missy" Reeves (actor)

Melissa Rivers (TV personality)

Melody

Meaning: Music, singing of songs

Origin: Greek

Related names and spelling variations: *Melodie*

There's no hidden meaning here—Melody means just what you think it means. Not only is this Greek name rooted in music, like Harmony or Lullaby (when is that name going to hit the charts? It's genius!), it's as singsongy and melodic as names get. It's been flighty in popularity, peaking in 1960 (#153) and fading in and out ever since. Melody's back near the top now, but she's likely to drift back out again. Don't expect the world to get sick of this one—it never sticks around long enough!

THIS NAME IN HISTORY

Melody Gardot (singer)

Melody Thomas Scott (actor)

Melody Thornton (singer)

My Melody (Hello Kitty product line)

Meredith

Meaning: Splendid lord

Origin: Welsh

Related names and spelling variations: *None*

All the splendid lords in your town will be flocking to your Meredith . . . but they won't know why. Meredith is a Welsh name that may mean "splendid lord"—that's why, boys—but this one's as lady-like as they get! It wasn't always; it hit the U.S. boys' chart for a few years at the end of the 1800s and became a consistent boy's name in the 1900s, before dropping off entirely in the 1950s. Girl Meredith made her appearance in 1910, made big waves in the late sixties, and peaked in 1980 and 1981 at #140. Never trendy, this name's consistently pretty and dependably elegant.

THIS NAME IN HISTORY

Meredith Baxter (actor)

Meredith Brooks (musician)

Meredith Grey (character on the TV show *Grey's Anatomy*)

Meredith Salenger (actor)

Meredith Vieira (TV personality)

James Meredith (civil rights figure)

Mia

Meaning: Bitter; drop of the sea; mine

Origin: Scandinavian; Italian

Related names and spelling variations: *Mea, Miya, Miah*

Oh, mamma mia! Don't worry, your daughter Mia's not destined to be a teen mom . . . it's an Italian interjection, their version of "Good golly!" Mia has roots in a couple different origins. It comes from the Mary family of names and means

"bitter," or "drop of the sea" and it's also Italian for "mine." Mia hit the charts for the first time in 1964; Mia Farrow was probably to thank for the name's popularity at this time. It stuck in the middle of the pack for the next few decades and then started to gain ground in the late 1990s. Look for this name to stay near the top of the charts in the near future. Mia is short and sweet and parents have fallen in love with it.

THIS NAME IN HISTORY

Mia Hamm (soccer player)

Mia Farrow (actor)

Mia Kirshner (actor)

Mia Michaels (dancer and choreographer)

Mia Sara (actor)

"Mamma Mia" (song by ABBA)

Michelle

Meaning: Who is like God?

Origin: French

Related names and spelling variations: *Michele, Mechelle, Mechele, Me'Shell, Meechelle, M'chelle*

"Michelle, ma belle!" Let the Beatles' song "Michelle" remind the world that your baby daughter is *your* belle! The French female version of Michael, Michelle has been on the U.S. charts since 1938, hit the top 100 in the fifties, and got into the top 5 the year after the Beatles' song came out. It stayed there for nearly a decade and only fell out of the top 100 in 2008—the end of

Hi, My Name Is

a 54-year stay at the top of the charts. First Lady Michelle Obama might cause a second coming of this still-great name.

THIS NAME IN HISTORY
Michelle Branch (singer)
Michelle Kwan (figure skater)
Michelle Obama (first lady)
Michelle Pfeiffer (actor)
Michelle Phillips (singer)
Michelle Rodriguez (actor)
Michelle Williams (actor)
Michelle Yeoh (actor)
"Michelle" (song by the Beatles)

Miley

Meaning: None

Origin: American

Related names and spelling variations: *Mylee, Mylie*

If you're looking for names with history, look the other way. As legend has it, Miley Cyrus (born Destiny Hope Cyrus) was nicknamed Miley—short for "Smiley"—because she was such a happy kid. When she got big in 2007, her name shot up the charts, from completely unknown to #128 in two years. This name was 100 percent invented by the Cyrus family . . . but if that doesn't bother you, it's a fun and fashionable firstie!

THIS NAME IN HISTORY
Miley Cyrus (singer and actor)
Miley Stewart (character in the TV show *Hannah Montana*)

TOP TEN: SOAP STAR HEARTTHROBS

1. Alison Sweeney (*Days of Our Lives*)
2. Peter Reckell (*Days of Our Lives*)
3. Susan Lucci (*All My Children*)
4. Rebecca Herbst (*General Hospital*)
5. Cameron Mathison (*All My Children*)
6. Kristian Alfonso (*Days of Our Lives*)
7. Brandon Beemer (*The Bold and the Beautiful*)
8. Maura West (*As the World Turns*)
9. Eddie Cibrian (*The Young and the Restless*)
10. Stephanie Gatschet (*Guiding Light*)

TOP TEN: SONG TITLES WITH NAMES

1. Gloria (Van Morrison)
2. Billie Jean (Michael Jackson)
3. Suzanne (Leonard Cohen)
4. Sweet Caroline (Neil Diamond)
5. My Sharona (The Knack)
6. Come on Eileen (Dexys Midnight Runners)
7. Lucy in the Sky with Diamonds (The Beatles)
8. You Can Call Me Al (Paul Simon)
9. Angie (Rolling Stones)
10. Mandy (Barry Manilow)

Miranda

Meaning: Wonderful, admirable

Origin: Latin

Related names and spelling variations: *None*

Whether you know the name from Shakespeare's *The Tempest* (he invented the name from a Latin word that means "wonderful" or "admirable") or from *Sex and the City*, Miranda is the kind of gal who keeps her head up and gets what she wants. It was on the U.S. charts for a few years near the end of the 1800s, then dropped off until 1957. It rose through the seventies, made the top 100 in 1991, then began falling slowly. Miranda's cute enough to be the life of the party and sophisticated enough to shine on a résumé.

THIS NAME IN HISTORY

Miranda (character in William Shakespeare's *The Tempest*)

Dr. Miranda Bailey (character on the TV show *Grey's Anatomy*)

Miranda Cosgrove (actor)

Miranda Hobbes (character on the TV show *Sex and the City*)

Miranda Kerr (model)

Miranda Lambert (singer)

Miranda Richardson (actor)

Hi, My Name Is

Molly

Meaning: Bitter; drop of the sea

Origin: Irish

Related names and spelling variations: *Mali, Maili, Maile, Mailsi, Mollie, Mary*

Ever heard of "The Unsinkable Molly Brown"? She was a *Titanic* passenger lucky enough to snag a spot on a lifeboat, then convinced her boat mates to turn around and look for other survivors. It turns out nobody called her Molly (she went by Maggie) until long after her death in 1932, but here's the point: Molly itself is just as unsinkable! A pet name for Mary, Molly has been around since the 1700s. Since entering the U.S. charts in 1880, the name's only gone up. It hovered around the 300s and 400s for decades, gained popularity in the 1960s, and has been hanging around the 100s since the mid-1980s. Most names fall down the lists after long periods of popularity, but Miss Molly has real staying power.

THIS NAME IN HISTORY

Molly Bloom (character in James Joyce's *Ulysses*)

Margaret "Molly" Brown (*Titanic* survivor known as "The Unsinkable Molly Brown")

Molly Ivins (columnist)

Molly Maguires (secret Irish-American organization)

Molly Malone (Irish figure)

Molly McIntire (American Girl character)

Molly Parker (actor)

Molly Ringwald (actor)

Molly Shannon (comedian)

Molly Sims (model and actor)

Molly Weasley (character in J. K. Rowling's *Harry Potter* series)

"Good Golly, Miss Molly" (song by Little Richard)

Monica

Meaning: Counselor

Origin: Latin

Related names and spelling variations: *Monique*

Thanks to Monica Geller in *Friends*, Monica sounds a little nineties these days. Its heyday was actually twenty years before that (which, based on *Friends'* twentysomething characters, makes perfect sense!). Monica may have Latin roots in a word that means "counselor." Monica is as old as the fourth century C.E. and has been on the U.S. charts for all but two years since 1880, but the highest it ever climbed was to #39 in 1977. Despite the popularity of the *Friends* character, the name's been on a steady decline ever since.

THIS NAME IN HISTORY

Mo'Nique (actor)

Monica Bellucci (actor)

Monica Geller (character on the TV show *Friends*)

Monica Keena (actor)

Monique Lhuillier (fashion designer)

Monica Potter (actor)

Monica Seles (tennis player)

Nn

Nadia

Meaning: Hope

Origin: Russian

Related names and spelling variations: *Nadja, Nadija, Nadya*

When Olympian Nadia Comăneci made the world scene in 1976, her first name made the American one, making the U.S. girls' list for the first time and rising ever since. It peaked at #178 in 2005 and has been dropping for the past few years. Nadia is a Russian name that means "hope," and just like hope, we doubt Nadia will ever quite die.

THIS NAME IN HISTORY

Nadia Ali (singer)

Nadia Bjorlin (actor)

Nadia Boulanger (composer)

Nadia Comăneci (gymnast)

Nadia Petrova (tennis player)

Nadya Suleman (Octomom)

Nadia Townsend (actor)

Naomi

Meaning: Pleasantness

Origin: Hebrew

Related names and spelling variations: *Noemi, Noémie*

Naomi has a totally unique name noise: a long *a* followed by a long *o*. We dare you to find it anywhere else! (Peony comes close, but isn't nearly as charming.) Even though it sounds cute and sweet—which fits its Hebrew meaning, "pleasantness," perfectly—Naomi hasn't ever been super popular. It's been in the 100s and 200s for most of the years since 1880, but hasn't even broken into the top 100. Naomi's been rising recently, suggesting that this cutie might finally get her big day out . . . or she could sink back to her familiar old post.

THIS NAME IN HISTORY

Naomi Campbell (model)

Naomi Judd (singer)

Naomi Klein (journalist)

Naomi Novik (author)

Naomi Watts (actor)

Naomi Wolf (author)

Natalie

Meaning: Born on Christmas

Origin: French; Russian

Related names and spelling variations:
Natalia, Nataly, Natalee, Nathalie, Natalya, Nathaly, Nathalia, Nat

Parents, there's a lot of name-trickery going on these days. Take Natalie, for example. As the French version of Russian Natalia, it means "born on Christmas." We're willing to bet that only a small fraction of U.S. baby girls are *actually* born on Christmas, but this old favorite made it to spot #13 in 2008. We're not pointing fingers here, Natalie Portman, and we sure don't want to accuse anyone of lying, Natalie Imbruglia, but *someone's not telling the truth.* Fortunately for America's future, the problem is taking care of itself; although Natalie's been gaining popularity since the mid-1970s, it's finally showing signs of falling.

THIS NAME IN HISTORY

Natalie Angier (journalist)

Natalie Cole (singer)

Natalie Coughlin (swimmer)

Natalie Imbruglia (singer)

Natalia Linichuk (ice dancer)

Natalia Livingston (actor)

Natalie Maines (singer)

Natalie Merchant (singer)

Natalie Portman (actor)

Natalie Wood (actor)

"Natalia" (song by Van Morrison)

Natasha

Meaning: Born on Christmas

Origin: Russian

Related names and spelling variations: *Tasha*

Natasha started life as a nickname for Natalia, which means "born on Christmas," but the name got much darker, more devious and—well, dimwitted—in the sixties. *The Rocky and Bullwinkle Show* began in 1959 and introduced the show's villains, Boris Badenov and Natasha Fatale, agents of Pottsylvania who would stop at nothing to . . . to stop Moose and Squirrel. It didn't make sense then, either, but America loved it. Natasha entered the U.S. charts in 1965 at #930 and was in the top 100 by 1980. It was popular through the eighties, peaking at #70, but has been on the decline since (now that Rocky and Bullwinkle are too old to even be retro). Natasha comes equipped with cute nickname Tasha.

THIS NAME IN HISTORY

Natasha Bedingfield (singer)

Natasha Fatale (character on the
    TV show *The Rocky and Bullwinkle Show*)

Natasha Henstridge (model)

Natasha Richardson (actor)

Tasha Smith (actor)

Natasha Zvereva (tennis player)

Nevaeh

Meaning: No meaning

Origin: American

Related names and spelling variations: *Neveah*

The name Nevaeh sounds like something you've heard before, maybe something from the Bible . . . but you haven't, and it's not. It has no real history and its origin is totally American. Just spell it backward and you'll understand where it comes from. Got it? Great. Nevaeh came out of nowhere in 2001 and hit #266 after musician Sonny Sandoval used the name for his daughter a year earlier. Nevaeh continues to rise, while misspelling Neveah—possibly just because it mirrors the spelling of names like Leah—recently made the charts. Nevaeh attracts religious and creative types alike . . . and might start a deep fountain of brand new, totally made-up names! Try these out: Lufyoj, Detirips, Ykcul, and Ronoh. We just might have something with Ronoh.

THIS NAME IN HISTORY

Nevaeh Sandoval (daughter of Sonny Sandoval)

Nicole

Meaning: People's victor

Origin: Greek

Related names and spelling variations: *Nichole, Niccole, Nikole, Nicola, Nicolette, Nicky, Nicki, Colette, Nicolina*

Nicole, a female version of the Greek name Nicholas, means "people's victor." This meaning itself is a winner; give your girl this name and she'll always get what she wants . . . she'll make sure of it. Look at Kidman and Richie's careers: both worked for what they wanted and made it big. And as soon as Nicole entered the girls' chart in 1942, it fought its way tooth and nail to the top. It gained a lot of ground in the 1960s and got into the top 100, then made its way to the top 15 between 1972 and 1994. Then in the nineties, Nicole beat a hasty retreat, dropping quickly back down the charts. If you're looking for something a little more colorful, try stylish Nicola or sassy Nicolette.

THIS NAME IN HISTORY

Nicky Hilton (socialite)

Nicole Jordan (author)

Nicole Kidman (actor)

Nicole Miller (fashion designer)

NiCole Robinson (actor)

Nicole Richie (reality TV star)

Nicole Scherzinger (singer)

Nicolette Sheridan (actor)

Nicole Sullivan (comedian)

Nina

Meaning: Girl

Origin: Spanish

Related names and spelling variations: *Nena*

Want your baby girl to be a real girly girl? Think she'll burp daintily, spit up cutely, and soil herself sweetly? Well, flaunt it—give her the name Nina, a Spanish word that actually means "girl." The name itself may have had its origins as a nickname for names with a *-nina* ending (like Antonina), but it's a full name in its own right now. Short, sweet, and a little sassy, Nina's been on the U.S. charts since 1880 . . . and has floated mostly between #150 and #250 the entire time. It peaked in 1887 at #115 and has fallen since, but it's never too far out of its familiar spectrum. That means Nina's a familiar name without being a terribly popular one . . . a perfect medium!

THIS NAME IN HISTORY

Nina Dobrev (actor)

Nina Garcia (fashion expert
and TV personality)

Nina Ricci (fashion designer)

Nina Simone (singer)

Noelle

Meaning: Birthday, Christmas

Origin: French

Related names and spelling variations: *Noëlle, Noella, Noel*

Noelle may sound like it's all about Christmas, but it actually translates to "birthday." As in the birthday of Christ. So yeah, you were right . . . it's about Christmas. Noelle has been on the U.S. charts since 1964 and has always been right in the middle of the pack. This makes Noelle a perfect pick if you like familiar names, but not common ones, or if you absolutely *love* Christmas. Or

1. Tina Brown (*The New Yorker, Vanity Fair*)

2. Graydon Carter (*Vanity Fair*)

3. Anna Wintour (*Vogue*)

4. Jane Pratt (*Jane, Sassy*)

5. Jann Wenner (*Rolling Stone*)

6. Clay Felker (*New York magazine, Village Voice*)

7. Helen Gurley Brown (*Cosmopolitan*)

8. Gloria Steinem (*Ms.*)

9. Osborn Elliott (*Newsweek*)

10. Briton Hadden (*Time*)

birthdays. Whichever. If you want a name with today's super-chic *-ella* ending, try Noella.

THIS NAME IN HISTORY

Noelle Beck (actor)

Noelle Oxenhandler (author)

Noelle Parker (actor)

Noelle Pikus-Pace (skeleton racer)

Nora

Meaning: Honor

Origin: Irish

Related names and spelling variations: *Norah*

Nora sounds a bit serious, and its meaning—an Irish version of the names Honor and Honora, which both mean "honor"—is meant to be taken as seriously as it sounds. Nora is also a nickname for names with the *-nora* ending like Eleanora or Leonora. Nora's been on the list for as long as the list has been around . . . but was really in its prime back in the late 1800s, and it's been heading downhill ever since. But like so many other classic names, it's coming back into fashion today. So if vintage Violet or antique Audrey are too bright and cheerful, just get serious . . . and stick with Nora.

THIS NAME IN HISTORY

Nora Ephron (writer and director)

Norah Jones (singer)

Nora Kaye (ballerina and choreographer)

Norah O'Donnell (news anchor)

Nora Roberts (author)

Oo

Olivia

Meaning: Olive tree

Origin: Latin

Related names and spelling variations: *Livia, Oliveah, Alivia, Alyvia, Olive, Oliva*

Olivia may come from a Latin word that means "olive tree," but Shakespeare may very well have made the name up just to use it in his play *Twelfth Night*. And today's parents, it seems, are all Shakespeare fans; after enjoying only modest popularity for most of the twentieth century, Olivia made a serious climb to the top 10 in 2001 has stayed up there since. Too popular for you? Try Olive, a top 100 name at the end of the 1800s that's only #588 today, or Italian Oliva, which hasn't seen the charts since 1894.

THIS NAME IN HISTORY

Olivia (children's book series by Ian Falconer)

Olivia d'Abo (actor)

Olivia de Havilland (actor)

Olivia Newton John (singer and actor)

Olivia Palermo (reality TV star)

Olivia Wilde (actor)

Pp

Paige

Meaning: Page, servant

Origin: English

Related names and spelling variations:
Page, Payge

You don't see many occupational girl's names these days. No Butlers, Lawyers, Baristas, or Clerks . . . even Chandler, an old word for a candle maker, didn't really come into vogue, even after *Friends* introduced Chandler Bing. But Paige is the exception—it's an old English name that used to refer to a page or servant. And for the last part of the twentieth century, parents loved calling their kids servants. After making the charts in 1952, the name shot up in popularity and has been in the top 100 for nearly twenty years. Although Paige Davis of *Trading Spaces* gave the name a bit of a boost, Paige is heading back down the list. Paige is short, cute, and a little boyish, so it should appeal to you if you aren't looking for a unisex name, but you don't want a Daisy, either.

Pamela

Meaning: No meaning

Origin: Invented by Sir Phillip Sidney for his poem "Arcadia"

Related names and spelling variations: *Pam*

When William Shakespeare makes up a name, like Olivia or Miranda (really—they're both his!), he at least bases it on Latin roots. When Sir Philip Sidney makes up a name, he just *makes up a name*. And you have to give the guy credit . . . he's good at it! Pamela, a name the poet created for his poem "Arcadia," first hit the charts in 1925, climbed to the top 50 in the next twenty years, then stayed there for another twenty years. It even had one solid year in the #10 spot—1953. It's been on a fairly rapid decline since. Maybe parents found out about its dirty (lack of) history . . . or maybe the world finally got sick of Pamela Anderson.

THIS NAME IN HISTORY

Pamela Anderson (actor)

Pamela Bach (actor)

Pam Beesly (character on the TV show *The Office*)

Pam Dawber (actor)

Pam Grier (actor)

Patricia

Meaning: Patrician, nobleman

Origin: Latin

Related names and spelling variations: *Pat, Patsy, Patty, Tisha, Tricia, Trish, Patrice, Patrizia, Patti*

Patricia just exudes class (despite nicknames like Patty or Trish). It's the feminine version of the Latin name Patrick, which means "patrician, nobleman." Patricia made the U.S. charts in 1886, gained popularity fast, and spent almost forty years in the top 10, from 1929 to 1966. And thanks to that long reign at the top, the name's been on a steady downhill course ever since. The name's due for a comeback someday, but most of today's parents are politely looking the other way.

THIS NAME IN HISTORY

Patricia Arquette (actor)

Pat Benatar (singer)

Patricia Clarkson (actor)

Patsy Cline (singer)

Patricia Cornwell (author)

Patty Duke (actor)

Patty Griffin (musician)

Patricia Heaton (actor)

Patricia Highsmith (author)

Patti LaBelle (singer)

Trisha Yearwood (singer)

Penelope

Meaning: Weaver; duck

Origin: Greek

Related names and spelling variations: *Penny*

Many parents will pick Penelope for its pretty little nickname, Penny . . . but consider the full name itself, a beautiful one from Greek mythology that, oddly, may mean "duck" or "weaver." And best of all, it has the same *-ope* ending as Calliope, another Greek classic. Despite its beauty, Penelope has spent more time off the charts than it's spent on them. It started another comeback in 2001, and has been shooting up recently. But it's still far from being a common name, and America's interest in it might drop again, so jump aboard this bandwagon before you forget it even exists. Again.

THIS NAME IN HISTORY

Penélope Cruz (actor)

Penny Marshall (director and actor)

Penelope Ann Miller (actor)

"Penny Lane" (song by the Beatles)

Peyton

Meaning: Paega's estate

Origin: English

Related names and spelling variations: *Payton, Paityn, Payten*

Sorry to break this to you, Peyton Manning, but in about twenty years, your name's almost certain to be as girly as Taylor is today. An English surname that means "Paega's estate," Peyton was on the boys' top 1,000 for a handful of years in the 1800s, then came back in 1989, racking up a considerable backing of Peyton-happy parents. Three years later, it hit the girls' list, too, which usually spells trouble for boys' names. But it hasn't happened yet—Peyton is still holding his own on the boys' list.

THIS NAME IN HISTORY

Peyton Manning (football player)

Peyton Sawyer (character on the
TV show *One Tree Hill*)

Elizabeth Peyton (artist)

Peyton Place (novel, movie, and TV show)

Phoebe

Meaning: Bright, radiant

Origin: Greek

Related names and spelling variations: *None*

Phoebe is a name from Greek mythology that means "bright, radiant," but since *Friends* became one of the biggest shows of the nineties, Phoebe just means "quirky." But the world *loved* the Phoebe of *Friends* fame, and when the show debuted, they loved this name, too. After being popular from 1880 to 1956, the name faltered and fell off the charts for several years until 1989. It was still only #816 when *Friends* debuted in 1994. The following year it had jumped to #582, and it's been climbing steadily ever since. So while *Friends'* Phoebe may have cheapened her name's meaning, she certainly repaid it in popularity.

THIS NAME IN HISTORY

Phoebe Buffay (character on the
TV show *Friends*)

Phoebe Cates (actor)

Phoebe Caulfield (character in
J. D. Salinger's *Catcher in the Rye*)

Piper

Meaning: Pipe player

Origin: English

Related names and spelling variations: *None*

Piper is another occupational name that means "one who pipes" . . . or pipe player, if you want to be that way. Piper didn't even appear on the list until 1999, but it's flown up the ranks since then. A cute, quirky, and musical name (a modern relative of Melody?), Piper's a great choice if you prefer something a little less girly.

THIS NAME IN HISTORY

Piper Laurie (actor)

Piper Perabo (actor)

Priscilla

Meaning: Ancient

Origin: Latin

Related names and spelling variations: *Cilla, Prissy*

Priscilla wants to be a contender for coolness—it's got that *-lla* ending that everyone loves, it's got cool nicknames like Cilla and Pris, and it's an old vintage classic with its last heyday in the forties—but today's audience just hasn't caught on. A Latin name that means "ancient," Priscilla just feels . . . old. And sort of spooky, or cold, or something. And while today's parents sure dig "old," they're not big fans of "spooky" or "cold." The name had a resurgence in the eighties, but it's been declining ever since.

THIS NAME IN HISTORY

Priscilla Barnes (actor)

Priscilla Presley (actor)

The Adventures of Priscilla, Queen of the Desert (movie)

TOP TEN: SUPERHEROES

1. Clark (Superman)
2. Peter (Spider-Man)
3. Diana (Wonder Woman)
4. Logan (Wolverine: X-Men)
5. Reed (Mr. Fantastic: Fantastic Four)
6. Scott (Cyclops: X-Men)
7. Raphael (Teenage Mutant Ninja Turtle)
8. Bruce (Batman)
9. Anthony (Iron Man)
10. Ororo (Storm: X-Men)

Rr

Rachel

Meaning: Ewe

Origin: Hebrew

Related names and spelling variations:
Rachael, Racheal, Rachell, Rachele, Rachelle, Rachil, Raquel

Rachel? Eww. Oh wait, that's "ewe," an outdated word for "female sheep"! A Hebrew word that means "ewe," (the "bahhh" kind, not the "blahhh" kind), Rachel goes all the way back to the Book of Genesis. It hit the U.S. charts in the 1880s and has stayed remarkably popular; its lowest rank was #202 in 1951. It's been in the top 100 since the late 1960s and broke into the top 10 for one year in 1996, thanks to the lovable character from *Friends*. It's been on the decline—as much as Rachel's *ever* been on the decline—in recent years . . . but if history has anything to say about it, this name's not going anywhere.

THIS NAME IN HISTORY

Rachel (biblical figure)

Rachel Bilson (actor)

Rachel Carson (environmentalist)

Rachael Leigh Cook (actor)

Rachel Green (character on the TV show *Friends*)

Rachel Hunter (model)

Rachel Maddow (TV anchor)

Rachel McAdams (actor)

Rachel Portman (composer)

Rachael Ray (celebrity chef)

Rachel Weisz (actor)

Raquel Welch (actor)

Reagan

Meaning: Impulsive; angry; queen

Origin: Irish

Related names and spelling variations:
Raegan, Regan

No, parents, this name does not mean "president." In fact, it didn't become a popular girl's name until the 1990s, years after the Ronald's presidency ended. Before that, though, Linda Blair's creepy character (actually the related name Regan) in the 1973 horror flick *The Exorcist* is probably what gave the name the boost it needed to enter the charts for the first time the year after the movie's debut . . . and the character fits the name's description to a tee. Reagan has Irish roots and may mean "impulsive, angry," and "queen." After *The Exorcist*, we can add "creepy" to that list. The name's received a bit of attention for the boys, too—while Reagan the girl remains popular among parents, which is usually enough to kill most unisex names for boys, Reagan the boy is still hanging in there, although it's much less popular than its female counterpart.

THIS NAME IN HISTORY

Regan (character in the movie *The Exorcist*)
Reagan Gomez-Preston (actor)
Reagan Pasternak (actor)
Ronald Reagan (U.S. president)

Rebecca

Meaning: God's servant; knotted cord

Origin: Hebrew

Related names and spelling variations:
Rebbecca, Rebecka, Rebeckah, Rebekah, Beck, Becky, Becka, Becca

Rebecca's a strange case. It's been in use for centuries and hasn't ever fallen below #185, yet it never seems dated or overused. A variation of the Hebrew name Rebekah, the name may mean both "God's servant" and "knotted cord," so you can pick whichever definition you want. (And good luck explaining that "knotted cord" thing to the in-laws.) Rebecca hit its heyday in the seventies, when it was in the top 10 for two years . . . but it hasn't fallen that far. Both the Rebecca and Rebekah spellings remain popular today.

TOP TEN: SUPERMODELS

1. Gisele (Bündchen)

2. Naomi (Campbell)

3. Heidi (Klum)

4. Helena (Christensen)

5. Adriana (Lima)

6. Christy (Turlington)

7. Tyson (Beckford)

8. Cindy (Crawford)

9. Yasmeen (Ghauri)

10. Marcus (Schenkenberg)

Rebecca De Mornay (actor)

Rebecca Gayheart (actor)

Rebecca Howe (character on the
TV show *Cheers*)

Rebecca Romijn (actor and model)

Becky Thatcher (character in Mark Twain's
The Adventures of Tom Sawyer)

Rebecca (novel by Daphne du Maurier;
movie by Alfred Hitchcock)

Rebecca of Sunnybrook Farm (novel
by Kate Douglas Wiggin)

Regina

Meaning: Queen

Origin: Latin

Related names and spelling variations: *Reggy,
Régine, Reggie*

Regina is a Latin word that means "queen,"
and it's ruled the charts since 1880. It fluctuated between the 100s and 200s until
it hit the top 100 in 1961 and peaked at
#80 in 1967. But the fame was too much
for this regal girl—it's taken a sharp blow
in the last decade. Only time will tell if
Regina will fight for its right to rule or if it
will be a royal has-been. But if boyish nicknames like Sam or Jo are your thing, then
Reggie will be right up your alley.

THIS NAME IN HISTORY

Regina Belle (singer)

Regina George (character in the movie
Mean Girls)

Regina King (actor)

Regina Spektor (singer)

Renee

Meaning: Reborn

Origin: French

Related names and spelling variations: *Renée,
Rene, Renata*

Renee is the French version of Latin
Renata and its brother Renatus. All three
mean "reborn," so they've been favored
by Christians, who've associated it with
baptism. Today the name is all about
creativity. From actor Renée Zellweger to
philosopher René Descartes, this name
has brains and expresses them in unique
ways. After hitting the girls' chart in 1905,
Renee gained popularity, reached the top
100 in 1960, and peaked at #62 in 1967.
Rene the boy has been on the U.S. charts
since 1881, hit its highest rank at #257 in
1983, and has never gone too far down
since. Rene has managed to stay slightly
ahead of Renee in the past few years, one
of the rare cases of a boy name edging out
its girl version. For a change, consider
root name Renata—it hasn't been on the
list since 1981.

THIS NAME IN HISTORY

René Descartes (philosopher)

Renée Fleming (opera singer)

René Magritte (artist)

Rene Russo (actor)

Renee Walker (character on the TV show *24*)

Renée Zellweger (actor)

Rihanna

Meaning: Queen, nymph, witch

Origin: Celtic

Related names and spelling variations:
Rianna, Rhianna, Rhiannon

Rihanna is straight-up supernatural! A respelling of Rhianna, which is itself a modern version of Celtic mythology name Rhiannon, this name means "queen, nymph, witch," a winning trio for fantasy fans and any parents looking for just a bit of magic. But we can't discuss this name without discussing the singer; Rihanna didn't even appear on the list until the singer, known only by her first name (Aaliyah-style), made it big in the mid-2000s. Rihanna has been on the charts since 1998, but has never been as popular as its misspelled sister.

THIS NAME IN HISTORY
Rihanna (singer)
Rhiannon (Celtic mythological figure)

Riley

Meaning: Rye clearing; courageous

Origin: English; Irish

Related names and spelling variations: *Reilly, Reilley, Rilee, Rileigh, Rylee, Ryley*

Riley is originally a surname with English and Irish roots that means "rye clearing" or "courageous," but today it's a modern-sounding and fun-loving firstie. It's been a staple on the boy's chart since 1880, but

TOP TEN: SUPREME COURT

1. Antonin (Scalia)
2. Potter (Stewart)
3. Clarence (Thomas)
4. Ruth (Bader Ginsburg)
5. Pierce (Butler)
6. Morrison (Waite)
7. Smith (Thompson)
8. Sandra Day (O'Connor)
9. Wiley (Blount Rutledge)
10. Sonia (Sotomayor)

parents started liking the name for their daughters in 1990 and a little over a decade later it was more popular for girls than it was for boys. The name is trendy for both genders right now, with Riley the girl slightly ahead of Riley the boy . . . and that kind of dual popularity can't last. Watch the gap get bigger in years to come.

THIS NAME IN HISTORY

Riley Cooper (football player)

Riley Keough (model and daughter of Lisa Marie Presley)

Hudson "Riley" Hawk (skateboarder and son of Tony Hawk)

Rose

Meaning: Rose; horse; famous

Origin: Latin; German

Related names and spelling variations: *Rosie, Rosa, Roselle, Rosita, Rosetta, Roísín, Rosalie, Roselyn*

Rose is a Latin name that nods to the flower, of course . . . but it also comes from a German one that may mean "horse" or "famous." Other definitions aside, it's the most recognizable flower name, leading a class that includes Ivy, Lily, Lilac, and Daisy. But after fifty years (1880–1943) in the top 50, it no longer outranks all its sisters. It stayed in the top 100 through the 1950s, but it's been on a slow decline since. Its many related names still aren't beating their source, though—Rose still outranks Rosa, Rosemary, Roselyn, and Rosalie (keep your eye on this one in the near future—any name with a *Twilight* character attached to it becomes super-popular in a matter of years!).

THIS NAME IN HISTORY

Rosalie (character in Stephenie Meyer's *Twilight* series)

Rose Byrne (actor)

Rosalynn Carter (first lady)

Rose McGowan (actor)

Rosie O'Donnell (TV personality)

Rosa Parks (civil rights activist)

Rosie Perez (actor)

Rosie the Riveter (World War II icon)

Ruby

Meaning: Ruby, red

Origin: Latin

Related names and spelling variations: *Rubi*

Ruby sounds super-mod, but its top 100 status in the 1890s and the first half of the 1900s makes it super-vintage, too. It dropped down the charts after its heyday, but it's back again, thanks in part to Tobey Maguire and Jennifer Meyer naming their daughter Ruby Sweetheart (+10 cute points!).

THIS NAME IN HISTORY

Ruby Sweetheart Maguire (daughter of Jennifer Meyer and Tobey Maguire)

Ruby Henson (daughter of Charlotte Church and Gavin Henson)

Ruby Dandridge (radio actor)

Ruby Dee (actor)

"Ruby, Don't Take Your Love to Town" (song by Kenny Rogers and the First Edition)

"Ruby Tuesday" (song by the Rolling Stones)

Ruth

Meaning: Compassionate

Origin: Hebrew

Related names and spelling variations: *Ruthie*

Ruth is a Hebrew name that means "compassionate" and belongs to one of only two women (along with Esther) in the Bible who have books named after them. Ruth was a top 100 name between 1880 and 1950 and a top 10 champion between 1892 and 1930, but it's dropped some since then. Today, Ruth isn't out of favor, but not quite popular. It sounds a bit outdated today, but Ruth has all the ingredients of a likeable name—it's short, it's sweet, and it's got a great meaning.

NAME FACTOID

Relatively few women are named in the Bible (compared to the number of men). Parents looking for biblical options should consider these pretty options: Tabitha, Tirzah, Naomi, Hannah, Dinah, and Lydia.

THIS NAME IN HISTORY

Ruth (Biblical heroine)

Ruthie Camden (character on the TV show *7th Heaven*)

Ruth Gordon (actor)

Ruth Reichl (food expert and author)

Ruth Rendell (author)

Ss

Sabrina

Meaning: Princess; Severn River

Origin: English; Celtic

Related names and spelling variations: *Sabreena*

Sabrina, a name from Celtic mythology, means "princess." Since the nineties, it's also meant "teenage witch." Sabrina had been popular before—it entered the charts when the Audrey Hepburn movie *Sabrina* came out in 1954, then climbed the charts through the 1970s—but it got a huge boost in the nineties, when *Sabrina, the Teenage Witch* debuted. Sabrina's dropped several spots since then, but remains a popular name among parents.

THIS NAME IN HISTORY

Sabrina Jeffries (author)

Sabrina Sato (TV personality)

Sabrina (1954 movie and 1995 remake)

Sabrina, the Teenage Witch (TV show)

Sadie

Meaning: Princess

Origin: Hebrew

Related names and spelling variations: *Saidie, Saydie, Saidey*

Mom and Dad, you really had it coming—your daughter's name Sadie is a nickname for the Hebrew name Sarah, which means "princess." So don't be surprised when she acts like one. Sadie has been on the U.S. charts since 1880 and reached its peak at #67 in 1889. It declined in popularity afterward, even dropping off the list for a few years, but it's been on its way up in today's vintage-crazy era. Good luck finding a nickname for this former nickname. Sadie should appeal to you if you want people to call your daughter by the name you gave her.

THIS NAME IN HISTORY

Sadie Tanner Mossell Alexander (first African-American woman to receive a Ph.D. in the U.S.)

Sadie Frost (actor)

Sadie Hawkins (character in the comic strip *Li'l Abner*)

Sadie Sandler (daughter of Adam Sandler)

Sadie Hawkins (dances)

"Sexy Sadie" (song by the Beatles)

Sage

Meaning: Learned, wise

Origin: Latin

Related names and spelling variations: *Saige*

Hi, My Name Is

Sage is both a word that means "learned and wise" and an herb. Both a plant-based nature name and a virtue name, this one's got a wide audience. Sage hit the girls' chart in 1993 and peaked in 2004 at #360. It's been on the boy's chart since 1991, too, but lately it's been more popular for girls. Sage isn't too trendy, isn't too upbeat, isn't too girly, and isn't so connected with one gender that it's a not-so-unisex-anymore name. In short, it's a great choice for today's parents.

THIS NAME IN HISTORY
Sage Steele (sportscaster)

Samantha

Meaning: God has heard

Origin: Hebrew

Related names and spelling variations:
Sammantha, Semantha, Sam, Sammy, Sammie

Samantha's not a unisex name, but nickname Sam certainly is. Samantha is the female version of the Hebrew name Samuel, which means "God has heard." It was on the charts in the late 1890s and very early 1900s—then again in 1958—but it never stuck. Then in 1965, the year after *Bewitched* debuted with main character Samantha Stephens, the name saw a huge boost and started climbing. And thanks to Samantha Micelli from *Who's the Boss?*, Samantha's been in the girls' top 15 since the late 1980s. Beat that, Samuel!

**TOP TEN:
THIRTIES STARLETS**

1 Marlene (Dietrich)

2 Ginger (Rogers)

3 Jean (Harlow)

4 Carole (Lombard)

5 Toby (Wing)

6 Vivien (Leigh)

7 Joan (Blondell, Crawford)

8 Sonja (Henie)

9 Lupe (Vélez)

10 Thelma (Todd)

Samantha Bee (comedian)

Samantha Bond (actor)

Samantha Fox (singer)

Samantha Mathis (actor)

Samantha Micelli (character on the TV show *Who's the Boss?*)

Samantha Stephens (character on the TV show *Bewitched*)

Samantha Who? (TV show)

Sandra

Meaning: Mankind's defender

Origin: Greek

Related names and spelling variations: *Sandy, Sondra, Saundra, Sandrine*

Sandra's a beautiful, classic name, but it's already had its century. It hit the charts in 1913 and quickly rose to top 100 fame, holding its place there from 1934 through 1984 and peaking at #5 in 1947. It's been on the decline ever since, despite Sandra Bullock's recent career upswing. And after such a long period of popularity, we doubt this name will be on the rise again anytime soon. Sandra is related to the name Alexandra and its Italian version Alessandra, and it means "mankind's defender," which is a big meaning to place on your baby girl's shoulders. For something with a little less recent history, consider Sandrine or root name Allesandra.

THIS NAME IN HISTORY

Sandra Bullock (actor)

Sandra Dee (actor)

Sandy Duncan (actor)

Sandra Lee (celebrity chef)

Sandra Day O'Connor (Supreme Court justice)

Sandra Oh (actor)

Sarah

Meaning: Princess

Origin: Hebrew

Related names and spelling variations: *Sara, Sarai, Sari, Suri*

Sarah's a Hebrew name that means princess, and it's had the princess treatment ever since it graced the charts in 1880. It's been in the top 100 for all but a handful of years, was a top 10 name between 1978 and 2002, and remains popular today. Sara's been a popular spelling, too, but Sarah's always been the favorite. Watch out, parents—Sarah's a spoiled name; don't let your Sarah be a spoiled kid.

THIS NAME IN HISTORY

Sara Bareilles (singer)

Sara Evans (singer)

Sarah Ferguson (Duchess of York)

Sarah Michelle Gellar (actor)

Sarah Hughes (figure skater)

Sarah McLachlan (singer)

Sara Moulton (author and TV chef)

Sarah Palin (politician)

Sarah Jessica Parker (actor)

Sarah Silverman (comedian)

Sarah Vaughan (singer)

"Sara Smile" (song by Hall & Oates)

Sasha

Meaning: Mankind's defender

Origin: Russian

Related names and spelling variations: *Sacha*

Even though Obama has a daughter with this pretty name, another face comes to mind when you think of it: Sacha Baron Cohen. A fully absorbed character actor and top-notch comedian (as well as a reigning lord of gross-outs and gawkable moments), Cohen certainly brought the name into popular culture. But most likely it is Sasha Obama who has given this name a big boost in recent years for girls. Sasha is a Russian nickname for either Alexander or Alexandra, both of which mean "mankind's defender." It entered the U.S. girls' chart in 1972, sputtered for a long time, then rose and peaked at #147 in 1988. Sacha, as Cohen demonstrates, is also a boy's name . . . but it's never ranked on the U.S. boys' top 1,000.

THIS NAME IN HISTORY

Sasha Obama (daughter of U.S. president Barack Obama)

Sasha Alexander (actor)

Sacha Baron Cohen (actor)

Sasha Vujaãiç (basketball player)

Savannah

Meaning: Grassy plain

Origin: Spanish

Related names and spelling variations: *Savanah, Savanna, Vanna*

Parents can treat this one as a location name—one that denotes Savannah, Georgia, or maybe the savannah in Africa—but that's not its origin. It comes from a Spanish word that means "grassy plain," a meaning that paints a brilliant picture in parents' minds and does partial justice to the beauty of the African savannah. The name has swept the chart in recent years. After a long period of rising and falling popularity, this never-famous name has risen to the top 50 since 1996. Savannah is stylish and has that chic *V* that parents are desperately seeking, so it's no surprise that it's all the rage today.

THIS NAME IN HISTORY

Savannah Jane Buffett (daughter of Jimmy Buffett)

Savannah Mahoney (daughter of Marcia Cross and Tom Mahoney)

Savannah Walker (actor)

Vanna White (TV personality)

SS *Savannah* (first steamship to cross the Atlantic Ocean in 1819)

Savannah (a cat breed)

Savannah Smiles (movie)

Scarlett

Meaning: Scarlet; fabric dryer

Origin: Latin

Related names and spelling variations: *Scarlet*

Believe it or not, Scarlett is an occupational nickname for a fabric dyer . . . as well as, of course, a deep shade of red. Despite the renown of *Gone with the Wind*'s

Scarlett O'Hara, this name didn't catch on in the forties (although it did grace the charts for a few years). Not until the nineties did the name really get started in the charts, around the same time that actor Scarlett Johansson's career got started with *North*. And in 2006, when Johansson's career *really* took off—*The Black Dahlia*, *The Prestige*, *The Nanny Diaries*, *The Other Boleyn Girl*, *He's Just Not That into You*, and *Iron Man 2* in rapid succession—Scarlett caught a ride into the 200s and upward. Look for this name to catapult to fame in the next decade . . . and let your daughter go along for the ride!

THIS NAME IN HISTORY

Scarlett Johansson (actor)

Scarlett O'Hara (character in Margaret Mitchell's *Gone with the Wind*)

Scarlett Pomers (actor)

The Scarlet Letter (novel by Nathaniel Hawthorne)

Serena

Meaning: Serene

Origin: Latin

Related names and spelling variations: *Rena, Sirena*

Serena is a Latin name that means "serene" . . . about as calm and soothing of a definition as you can hope for, and the last word you'd choose to describe tennis pro Serena Williams on the court. Serena may be calm, but Williams is *fierce*, chasing down each return like it's her last. (We guess that's how you get to Wimbledon.) So whether you like tranquil names or strong ones, give Serena a go. A Latin name that's been around for millennia, Serena has never been too common. It was on and off the charts for most of the last century, but was never quite popular until recent years. Serena doesn't really have any of the elements parents are looking for in super-cool names today, but who knows . . . it still might make a splash in the next decade. Try shortened Rena for a change.

THIS NAME IN HISTORY

Rena Sofer (actor)

Serena Williams (tennis player)

Shannon

Meaning: Old, venerable; God is gracious

Origin: Irish

Related names and spelling variations: *Shannen*

Shannon, a river in Ireland, means "old, venerable" and is also a feminine version of Sean, the Irish version of John, which means "God is gracious." In short, Shannon is the Irish Jane . . . and it's been as popular. Shannon entered the charts in 1937, rose fast to the top 100, and stayed there between 1968 and 1997. It's dropped since, but it's still hanging on today. Shannon is a boy's name, too, but it hasn't ranked in their top 1,000 since 2006 . . . probably because it's such a prominent girl's name.

THIS NAME IN HISTORY

Shannon Bahrke (skier)

Shannon Brown (basketball player)

Shannen Doherty (actor)

Shannon Elizabeth (actor)

Sharon

Meaning: Field

Origin: Hebrew

Related names and spelling variations: *Charon, Sherri, Sherry*

Despite Sharon Osbourne's enormous popularity today, her name is on its way out. Names that were super-popular in the last century tend to have this problem, and Sharon was the cream of the crop—it hit the girl's chart in 1925 and was a top 100 name a decade later, even maintaining a spot in the top 10 between 1943 and 1949. And then it started falling . . . and hasn't stopped since.

THIS NAME IN HISTORY

Sharon Case (actor)

Sharon Gless (actor)

Sharon Osbourne (TV personality)

Sharon Stone (actor)

Sharon Tate (actor)

Shelby

Meaning: Sheltered town

Origin: Norse

Related names and spelling variations: *Chelby*

Shelby, an English surname that means "sheltered town," doesn't have much baggage to carry these days. It made big waves after Barbara Stanwyck's movie *The Woman in Red* came out in 1935 (skyrocketing from #848 to #178 in one year!), but it fell back down the chart just as quickly, so it doesn't seem dated or vintage. In fact, the name never held a top spot on the charts until 1991, when it hit the top 50 and stayed there through most of the next decade. It's been on the decline since. If you're looking for a name that isn't religious, isn't nature-based, isn't vintage, isn't old-fashioned, isn't outdated, isn't . . . well, anything, really . . . then Shelby's a great pick.

THIS NAME IN HISTORY

Shelby Blackstock (son of Reba McEntire)

Shelby Lynne (singer)

Shelby Steele (author)

Sienna

Meaning: Red-brown

Origin: Italian

Related names and spelling variations: *Siena*

Sienna's an Italian color name, a rich reddish-brown. Spelled with one less *n*, it's also an Italian city. So for lovers of color, locations, or Italy itself, this is a great catchall name. Sienna entered the charts for the first time in 1995, was moderately popular over the next decade, then made a big leap in 2005 thanks to Sienna

Miller. The Siena spelling has been on the charts only since 2005.

THIS NAME IN HISTORY

Sienna Miller (actor)

Siena, Italy

Sierra

Meaning: Mountain range

Origin: Spanish

Related names and spelling variations: *Cierra, Ciara*

Sierra is a Spanish word that means "mountain range" that comes from the Latin word *serra* for "saw," and this name isn't dull. With connections to the Sierra Nevada mountain range (and to famous conservation society the Sierra Club), Sierra's a pretty nature name and a natural hit for outdoorsy parents. It appeared on the charts in 1978, had jumped to the top 100 by 1993, and peaked at #49 in 1999.

THIS NAME IN HISTORY

Ciara (singer)

Sierra Adare (author)

Sierra Fisher (daughter of Brooke Burke)

Sierra Leone (African country)

Sierra Nevadas (mountain range)

Skye

Meaning: Sky, cloud

Origin: Norse

Related names and spelling variations: *Sky, Skyla*

Hi, My Name Is

Want a beautiful nature name like Sky, but don't want to just name your poor kid after the sky? No problem, just make it Norse. Skye's an old Norse word that means, of course, "sky" and "cloud," but it's never rocketed skyward. It hit the charts in 1987 and has been in the middle of the pack ever since, peaking at #400 in 2004. For nature lovers, Skye's not as out-there as Rainbow, but not as ordinary as Rose . . . a good choice for a bit of flair!

THIS NAME IN HISTORY

Skye Edwards (singer)

Sky Masterson (character in the musical *Guys and Dolls*)

Skye Sweetnam (singer)

Skylar

Meaning: Scholar, schoolteacher

Origin: Dutch

Related names and spelling variations: *Schuyler, Skyler*

Skylar is a spelling variation of the Dutch name Schuyler, which means "scholar." Academic types and those with scholarly goals for their children may be attracted to this meaning. Sklyar entered the U.S. girls' chart in 1990 at #563 and has grown in popularity. It got a huge boost in 1998—the year after *Good Will Hunting* debuted with Minnie Driver's character named Skylar. The name peaked a year later at #131. It has dropped a few slots since then, but remains stylish. The Schuyler spelling has shown up on the boys' chart

for a handful of years since 1900, but has never been popular. The Skylar spelling has been on the boys' chart since 1981. It peaked in 2000 at #356, but has been on a decline lately.

THIS NAME IN HISTORY

Schuyler Fisk (singer)

Schuyler Frances Fox (daughter of Tracy Pollan and Michael J. Fox)

Skylar Neil Foundation (founded by Vince Neil in memory of his daughter)

Sonia

Meaning: Wisdom

Origin: Russian

Related names and spelling variations: *Sonja, Sonya*

Sonia, a Russian version of Sophia, means "wisdom"—and sure enough, just like with Sage, any bearer of this name will sound wise beyond her years. Sonia started life as a nickname, but it's now a full-fledged first in its own right. It's been on the charts since 1909 and has cycled up and down since. It peaked at #165 in 1976, declined afterward, but perked up just recently, probably thanks to newly appointed U.S. Supreme Court justice Sonia Sotomayor.

THIS NAME IN HISTORY

Sônia Braga (actor)

Sonia Sanchez (poet)

Sonja Sohn (actor)

Sonia Sotomayor (Supreme Court justice)

Sonia Kashuk (cosmetic line)

1. Madeleine (Albright)

2. George (H. W. Bush)

3. Vernon (Walters)

4. Henry (Cabot Lodge Jr.)

5. James (Wadsworth; Wiggins)

6. Alejandro (Daniel Wolff)

7. Zalmay (Khalilzad)

8. Jeane (Kirkpatrick)

9. Herschel (Johnson)

10. Anne (Patterson)

Sophia

Meaning: Wisdom

Origin: Greek

Related names and spelling variations:
Sofia, Sophie

Sophie's Choice doesn't seem like the type of movie to drive a name up the charts, but there's just no other explanation for Sophia's enormous popularity recently. Well, except one: it might just be one of those vintage-sounding names that parents are looking for today. A Greek name that means "wisdom," Sophia got a boost—apparently—from *Sophie's Choice* in the 1980s, then just kept rising higher and higher. It's been in the top 10 since 2006. Even its sister names, Sofia and Sophie, are big these days.

THIS NAME IN HISTORY

Queen Sofia (queen of Spain)
Sophie Blackall (children's book illustrator)
Sophia Bush (actor)
Sofia Coppola (director)
Sophia Hawthorne (painter)
Sophia Loren (actor)
Sofia Vergara (actor)
Sophia Western (character in
   Henry Fielding's *Tom Jones*)
Sophie's Choice (movie and novel
   by William Styron)

Hi, My Name Is

Stacy

Meaning: Resurrection

Origin: Greek

Related names and spelling variations: *Stacey*

Is it strange that the song "Stacy's Mom" didn't drive this old favorite name through the roof? We guess not—the song wasn't really flattering to its character Stacy . . . just to her mom. Stacy is probably rooted in Greek Anastasia, which means "resurrection," a religious meaning, for sure, but religious parents aren't exactly flocking to this one. Nonetheless, Stacy was a top 100 name in 1966 and stayed there through the mid-1980s before it dropped down—far down—the list. (Maybe "Stacy's Mom" had a *negative* effect on the name.) Stacey's doing worse; it hasn't appeared in the top 1,000 since 2006. For a little more appeal, go with the original: Anastasia. Stacy can always be this old beauty's catchy nickname.

THIS NAME IN HISTORY

Stacey Dash (actor)

Stacy "Fergie" Ferguson (singer)

Stacy Keach (actor)

Stacey Keibler (wrestler and actor)

Stacy London (fashion consultant and TV personality)

Stella

Meaning: Star

Origin: Latin

Related names and spelling variations: *Estelle, Estella*

Stella's had a rough few decades . . . but ever since 1998, the name's finally got its groove back! A Latin word that means "star," Stella wasn't a name at all until Sir Philip Sidney made it one for a group of sonnets. (Hey, at least this one's based on a Latin word. Pamela, another Sidney creation, doesn't seem to be based on anything at all!) It was a top 100 name between 1880 and 1923 (vintage cred!) and peaked at #55 in 1889. Then it fell far, dropping out of the top 1,000 altogether in the late eighties. But in 1998, when *How Stella Got Her Groove Back* premiered, the name got its groove back, too.

THIS NAME IN HISTORY

Estelle (singer)

Stella Kowalski (character in Tennessee Williams's *A Streetcar Named Desire*)

Stella McCartney (fashion designer)

Stella Stevens (actor)

Estella Warren (actor)

Stephanie

Meaning: Crown

Origin: Greek

Related names and spelling variations:
Stefanie, Stephany, Stephenie, Stef, Steffi, Steph, Stevie

Stephanie is the female version of the boy's name Stephen, which means "crown." And it crowned the girls' list for years—it had a top 20 run between 1969 and 1996, spending many of those years in the top 10. But despite author Stephenie Meyer's influence, we may be seeing the twilight (get it?) of the Stephanie years. Stephanie's been gradually dropping down the charts for the last decade. It's still a catchy name with great nickname potential (Steph? Stephy?), but turbo-popularity may have killed this queen.

THIS NAME IN HISTORY

Princess Stéphanie (Princess of Monaco)

Stefanie Maria "Steffi" Graf (tennis player)

Stephenie Meyer (author)

Stephanie "Stevie" Nicks (singer)

Stephanie Plum (character in a series of books by Janet Evanovich)

Stephanie Seymour (model)

Stephanie Zimbalist (actor)

Summer

Meaning: Summer

Origin: English

Related names and spelling variations: *None*

Even though it's the second best-liked season name (Autumn still reigns supreme), Summer might be over. Summer entered the charts in 1971 and peaked at #119 in 1977. It had a brief turnaround in the nineties (Summer Sanders?), then started to fall again, although it hasn't strayed far. Maybe summer time will be back soon!

THIS NAME IN HISTORY

Summer Phoenix (actor)

Summer Sanders (swimmer)

Donna Summer (singer)

Susan

Meaning: Lily

Origin: Hebrew

Related names and spelling variations:
Sue, Sukie, Susie, Suzi, Suze, Sookie

In an era of Skyes, Roses, and Violets, parents just don't have patience for a name that just *means* Lily . . . even if it's one as pretty and classic as Susan. Susan is a form of Susanna, which comes from the Hebrew name Shoshana and means "lily." Most parents today are skipping the middle man and just naming their daughter Lily. Oh, Susan had its day in the sun—it was in the top 100 for several years in the late 1880s, then made the top 10 from 1945 through 1968. But even quirky nicknames Suzie and Sukie (where did *that* come from?) can't save this name from its own former fame. (Or from its disguised meaning. Just come right out and say it!)

Susan B. Anthony (women's rights activist)

Susan Boyle (singer)

Sue Grafton (author)

Susan Lucci (actor)

Suze Orman (financial advisor and
TV personality)

Susan Sarandon (actor)

Sookie St. James (character on the
TV show *Gilmore Girls*)

Susan G. Komen for the Cure
(breast cancer awareness organization)

Sydney

Meaning: Wide meadow

Origin: English

Related names and spelling variations: *Sidney, Sidnee, Sydnee, Sid*

Sydney is an English name that means "wide meadow," but today this one's a location name, celebrating Sydney, Australia. For parents who want to suggest that their girl just may be from down under, Sydney's a great choice. It was huge in '96, hitting the top 40 for girls and peaking at #23 a few years later. The TV show *Alias* and superspy Sydney Bristow didn't get the name to peak again, but it didn't hurt it, either. Try boyish nickname Syd on for size!

THIS NAME IN HISTORY

Sydney Bristow (character on the TV
show *Alias*)

Sydney Penny (actor)

Sydney Pollack (director)

Sidney Poitier (actor)

Sydney Poitier (daughter of Sidney Poitier)

Tt

Tabitha

Meaning: Gazelle

Origin: Aramaic

Related names and spelling variations: *Tabby*

Tabitha is apparently related to the Greek name Dorcas. We don't know how Tabitha and Dorcas fit together, but we agree—Tabitha's a much better name. (Dorc's not a nickname any girl wants to have.) Tabitha appeared in the New Testament, but doesn't have that religious-name ring to it, making it a great choice for Christian and non-Christian parents alike. After years of middling-to-zero popularity, *Bewitched* brought the name into the light. The show debuted in 1964, the name hit the charts again in 1966, and it peaked at #126 in 1978. Even though Sarah Jessica Parker and Matthew Broderick named one of their twins Tabitha in 2009, this name is on its way out, falling down the charts. Nicknames like Tab or Tabby might sell this one in a way that Dorc just wouldn't.

THIS NAME IN HISTORY

Tabitha Broderick (daughter of Sarah Jessica Parker and Matthew Broderick)

Tabitha King (author)

Tabitha Soren (MTV VJ)

Tabitha Stephens (character on the TV show *Bewitched*)

Tania

Meaning: Fairy queen

Origin: Russian

Related names and spelling variations: *Tanya, Tatiana, Tatyana, Taniya, Taniyah*

Tania is a U.S.-acceptable nickname for foreign-sounding Russian Tatiana, which means "fairy queen." Tania hit the U.S. charts in 1960, peaked at #314 in 1976, and has been sliding downhill ever since. Meanwhile, full version Tatiana's actually the more stylish version these days. So much for U.S.–acceptable nicknames . . .

THIS NAME IN HISTORY

Tatyana Ali (actor)

Tania Raymonde (actor)

Tanya Roberts (actor)

Tanya Tucker (singer)

Tara

Meaning: Hill

Origin: Gaelic

Related names and spelling variations: *None*

The show *United States of Tara* doesn't seem to be doing much for its main character's name. Maybe it just couldn't undo the damage done by Tara Reid. In any case, Tara is a has-been—it was a top 100 name through the seventies and eighties, peaking at #35 in 1977, but it's been dropping ever since. With Gaelic roots that mean "hill," Tara is nature-y, pretty, and accessible, but its own fame may have already knocked it from the top tier of names for a long time.

THIS NAME IN HISTORY

Tara Conner (actor)

Tara King (character on the TV show
    The Avengers)

Tara Reid (actor)

Tara (plantation owned by the O'Hara family
    in Margaret Mitchell's *Gone with the Wind*)

United States of Tara (TV show)

Tatum

Meaning: Tate's homestead; cheerful

Origin: English; Norse

Related names and spelling variations: *None*

Tatum is a surname that means "Tate's homestead" and can also be considered the feminine form of the name Tate, which means "cheerful"—one of the best name definitions you'll find. Tatum first made the U.S. charts in 1994. Since the early 2000s, Tatum has held fairly steady, hovering in the 300s. Even though Tatum is the feminine version of Tate, it still has a very boyish feel. That may be the reason

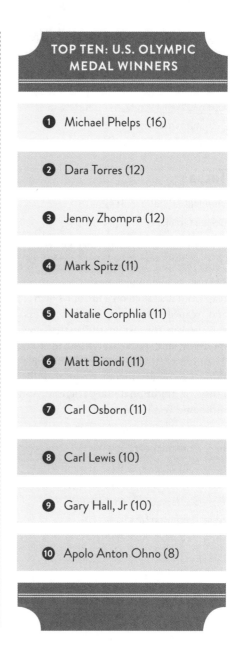

TOP TEN: U.S. OLYMPIC MEDAL WINNERS

1. Michael Phelps (16)
2. Dara Torres (12)
3. Jenny Zhompra (12)
4. Mark Spitz (11)
5. Natalie Corphlia (11)
6. Matt Biondi (11)
7. Carl Osborn (11)
8. Carl Lewis (10)
9. Gary Hall, Jr (10)
10. Apolo Anton Ohno (8)

why it's started to appeal to parents lately, as unisex names become more and more popular for girls.

THIS NAME IN HISTORY

Tatum O'Neal (actor)

Art Tatum (musician)

Channing Tatum (actor)

Tessa

Meaning: To harvest, reap

Origin: Greek

Related names and spelling variations: *Tess*

Tessa started life as a nickname for Theresa, which may mean "to harvest, reap." But it's taken on a life of its own . . . and reaped a serious fan base. Tessa sprouted in the list in the sixties, grew modestly, and peaked at #190 in 2007. Tessa is a great choice if you want something feminine, but not super-girly like Daisy or traditional like Theresa. And nickname Tess is a winner!

THIS NAME IN HISTORY

Tessa Dare (author)

Tessa Dunlop (journalist)

Tessa Horst (reality TV star)

Tessa Sanderson (javelin thrower)

Tessa Thompson (actor)

Tessa Virtue (ice dancer)

Tess of the d'Urbervilles (novel by Thomas Hardy)

Tiffany

Meaning: God's appearance; epiphany

Origin: Greek

Related names and spelling variations: *Tiffani, Tifani, Tiff*

Do you know why Tiffany sounds so eighties today? Here are some hints: it can't be Tiffany & Co., around since 1837, and it's not from *Breakfast at Tiffany's*, a 1961 movie based on a 1958 book (and the Deep Blue Something song came out too late, in 1995). Oh, that's right: Tiffany was an eighties singer who tore up the charts, and you didn't remember her because, well . . . what did she sing, anyway? Tiffany is a Greek name that means "God's appearance" or "epiphany." It hit the charts in 1962, but didn't really take off until the Tiffany-crazy eighties, when it peaked at #13 for a few years. It's been dropping ever since. Even though it's still catchy—and comes with great nickname Tiff—it just feels hopelessly dated today.

THIS NAME IN HISTORY

Tiffany (singer)

Tiffani-Amber Thiessen (actor)

Tiffany Thornton (actor)

Tiffany & Co. (jeweler)

Breakfast at Tiffany's (novella by Truman Capote and movie)

Trinity

Meaning: Triad

Origin: Latin

Related names and spelling variations:
Trinidad

Trinity lives a double life. The name means "triad" and refers most often to Christianity's belief that God has three forms: the Father, the Son, and the Holy Ghost. But since *The Matrix* came out in 1999, the name's gone cyberpunk. Trinity today is as likely to bring to mind bug-eyed black shades and a long leather jacket as it is a holy *anything*. The name was already popular, at #209, when the movie came out in 1999, then it jumped to #74 the next year. Whether you tend toward the religious or the rebellious, Trinity seems like a likely pick.

THIS NAME IN HISTORY

Trinity (character in *The Matrix*)

TOP TEN: VAMPIRES

1. Edward Cullen (*Twilight*)
2. Carlisle Cullen (*Twilight*)
3. Alice Cullen (*Twilight*)
4. Bill Compton (*True Blood*)
5. Lestat (*Interview with a Vampire*)
6. Selene (*Underworld*)
7. Victor (*Underworld*)
8. Damon Salvatore (*The Vampire Diaries*)
9. Stefan Salvatore (*The Vampire Diaries*)
10. Orlock (*Nosferatu*)

Valerie

Meaning: Strong, healthy

Origin: Latin

Related names and spelling variations: *Valeria, Val*

Valeria and Valerie both come from the Latin boy's name Valerius—"strong, healthy," both great meanings—but Valerie was historically the more popular name. Then, in 2004, Valeria took over. Still-popular Valerie stayed in the 100s while Valeria kept climbing. (Parents love *-a* endings today.) Both come standard with cute nickname Val.

THIS NAME IN HISTORY

Valerie Bertinelli (actor)

Valeria Golino (actor)

Valeria Messalina (Roman empress)

Valeria Bruni Tedeschi (actor)

Vanessa

Meaning: No meaning

Origin: invented by Jonathan Swift for *Cadenus and Vanessa*

Related names and spelling variations: *Van, Venesa, Venessa, Nessa*

Vanessa sounds like a Greek goddess. And it's not. Jonathan Swift actually created the nickname for his friend Esther Vanhomrigh, then used it in his 1726 poem *Cadenus and Vanessa*. And literary parents ever since have put it on the map. Vanessa hit the U.S. charts in 1950, then came into its real vogue in the eighties, when it peaked at #41 in 1988. It's fallen slightly from its prime loft, but is still a terribly popular name today. Thank you, Vanessa Hudgens.

THIS NAME IN HISTORY

Vanessa Brown (actor)

Vanessa Bell Calloway (actor)

Vanessa Carlton (singer)

Vanessa Hudgens (actor and singer)

Vanessa Minnillo (actor)

Vanessa Redgrave (actor)

Vanessa Williams (singer)

Veronica

Meaning: Bringer of victory; true image

Origin: Greek; Latin

Related names and spelling variations: *Ronnie, Veronika*

Sorry, *Veronica Mars* fans—your favorite show didn't really do anything for its titular name. Veronica is a Greek word that means "bringer of victory" and is related to a Latin phrase that means "true image." On the U.S. charts since 1880, Veronica hovered between the 100s and 200s in the early 1900s before getting boosted both by Archie's sultry love-interest Veronica Lodge and by movie star Veronica Lake. Veronica kept climbing in the seventies and stayed in the top 100 between 1972 and 1992, but it's dropped some spots since then.

THIS NAME IN HISTORY

Veronica Lake (actor)

Veronica Lodge (character in *Archie* comic book series)

Veronica Mars (TV show)

Victoria

Meaning: Victor

Origin: Latin

Related names and spelling variations:
Viktoria, Tori, Vickie, Vicky

Here's a clue for you, sleuths: Victoria's meaning hides in plain sight. Victoria's the female version of the name *Victor*, and both mean—what, did you give up already? We'll tell you later. Queen *Victori*a gave this name its regal air, but it was always a *winner*. It's never fallen outside the 200s since the 1880s, and it's spent quite a bit of time up top . . . in fact, it's been in the top 100 since 1981. *Victori*a Beckham hasn't given

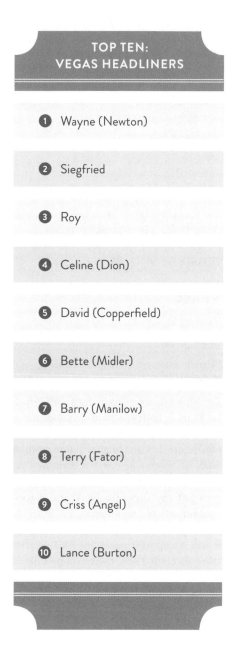

**TOP TEN:
VEGAS HEADLINERS**

1 Wayne (Newton)

2 Siegfried

3 Roy

4 Celine (Dion)

5 David (Copperfield)

6 Bette (Midler)

7 Barry (Manilow)

8 Terry (Fator)

9 Criss (Angel)

10 Lance (Burton)

her name the *victory* it's been after—that coveted top 10 spot. Nicknames Vicki and Tori shrug off some of that nose-in-the-air *Victor*ian attitude, but still carry the same meaning, which is—okay, okay—"Victor." Of course. Come on.

THIS NAME IN HISTORY
Queen Victoria (queen of England)
Victoria Beckham (singer)
Victoria de los Ángeles (opera singer)
Victoria Principal (actor)
Victoria "Tori" Spelling (actor)
Victor Victoria (movie)
Victoria's Secret (lingerie company)

Violet

Meaning: Violet

Origin: Latin

Related names and spelling variations: *Vi, Violette, Viola*

Shy Violet deserves to be far more popular than it is. It's a nature name. It's a flower name. It's a color name. It's a vintage name. It's a character name from *A Series of Unfortunate Events, Charlie and the Chocolate Factory,* and *The Incredibles.* It's even got the super-trendy *V* and a too-cool-for-school nickname, Vi. And it hasn't been too terribly popular recently; it was a top 100 name in 1901, stayed there through 1926, then dropped like a petal, leaving the charts entirely for most of the seventies, eighties, and nineties. It came back with a . . . comeback . . . in

1998, but it's not top 100 yet. All aboard, parents—this one's going straight for the top 10, whether she likes it or not.

THIS NAME IN HISTORY
Violet Affleck (daughter of Jennifer Garner and Ben Affleck)
Violet Beaudelaire (character in Lemony Snicket's *A Series of Unfortunate Events*)
Violet Beauregarde (character in Roald Dahl's *Charlie and the Chocolate Factory*)
Violet Parr (character in the movie *The Incredibles*)

Virginia

Meaning: Virgin; staff-bearer

Origin: Latin

Related names and spelling variations: *Ginny, Virginie*

Meet Virginia. It's the feminine form of the Latin name Virgil—"virgin, staff-bearer"—a name you don't see nearly enough of on the boys' chart today. Virginia spent most of its time between 1880 and the 1960s lounging around the top 100, even gracing the top 10 between 1916 and 1928, but has been falling since. Sure, it's a bit old-fashioned, and it's the name of a state, but it's got classic appeal and a ready-made nickname, Ginny. So if you're looking for classic names, location names, or southern gal names, consider Virginia.

THIS NAME IN HISTORY
Virginia Madsen (actor)
Virginia Woolf (author)

Hi, My Name Is

TOP TEN: VIDEO GAME HEROES

1 Super Mario	**6** Duke Nukem
2 Link (*The Legend of Zelda*)	**7** Pac Man
3 Ryu (*Street Fighter*)	**8** Kirby (*Kirby's Adventure*)
4 Cloud (*FFVII*)	**9** Lara Croft (*Tomb Raider*)
5 Samus Aran (*Metroid*)	**10** Kratos (*God of War*)

Vivian

Meaning: Lively, full of life

Origin: Latin

Related names and spelling variations: *Vivienne, Vivianne, Vivien, Viviana*

Vivian—like related words *viva, vive, vivacious,* or *revive*—is chock-full of life. A Latin name that means just that, this definition is perfect for any newborn. Although Vivian was once fitting for boys, it's all for the girls today. It's been on the girls' chart since 1880, was most popular in the 1920s (it peaked at #64), and only recently started up the charts again. This might be because Vivienne joined Maddox, Zahara, Shiloh, Pax, and Knox as Official Jolie-Pitt Names . . . a free pass to Coolsville. The Vivienne spelling hadn't been on the charts since 1930, but reemerged in 2009 at #532.

THIS NAME IN HISTORY

Vivienne Jolie-Pitt (daughter of Angelina Jolie and Brad Pitt)

Vivien Leigh (actor)

Vivienne Tam (fashion designer)

Vivian Vance (actor)

Vivienne Westwood (fashion designer)

Ww

Wendy

Meaning: Fair, blessed ring

Origin: Welsh

Related names and spelling variations: *Gwendolen*

Wendy was invented by J. M. Barrie for *Peter Pan,* but can also be a nickname for Welsh Gwendolyn, which means "fair, blessed ring" (and comes with super-cute nickname Gwen!). The fairy dust has worn off this great name, and Wendy is starting to lose her power to fly. Wendy has been on the U.S. charts since 1936, peaked in 1970 at #28, and has been slowly falling since then. Although Wendy's slow plummet doesn't seem to be stopping, its current lack of popularity might appeal to some parents. For a less popular (and far older) name, consider Gwendolyn.

THIS NAME IN HISTORY

Wendy Darling (character in J. M. Barrie's *Peter Pan*)

Wendy Testaburger (character in the TV show *South Park*)

Wendy Wasserstein (Pulitzer-Prize-winning playwright)

Wendy Williams (TV personality)

Wendy's (restaurant)

Whitney

Meaning: White island

Origin: English

Related names and spelling variations: *Whit*

They say that nobody is an island, but that doesn't mean the idea can't have some appeal. Whitney, an English name that means "white island," has been appealing to parents for decades. It hit the charts in 1962, grew in popularity for the next few years, and saw its time in the limelight just as Whitney Houston did in the eighties. Whitney peaked at #32 in 1986 and 1987 and has been on the decline since. But perhaps thanks to Whitney from MTV shows *The Hills* and *The City*, it's been seeing some improvement recently.

THIS NAME IN HISTORY

Whitney Houston (singer)

Whitney Port (reality TV star)

Whitney Young (civil rights leader)

Eli Whitney (inventor)

Willow

Meaning: Willow

Origin: English

Related names and spelling variations: *None*

The movie *Willow* came out in 1988, but the name of its titular character didn't even the make the list until a decade later, a year after *Buffy the Vampire Slayer* debuted with a same-name character. (Sorry, Ron Howard—Joss Whedon has more impact on pop culture than you do.) Willow has climbed up the charts quickly. If you like nature names—especially tree names—this one's a keeper.

THIS NAME IN HISTORY

Willow (character on the TV show *Buffy the Vampire Slayer*)

Willow Smith (daughter of Jada Pinkett Smith and Will Smith)

Willow (movie)

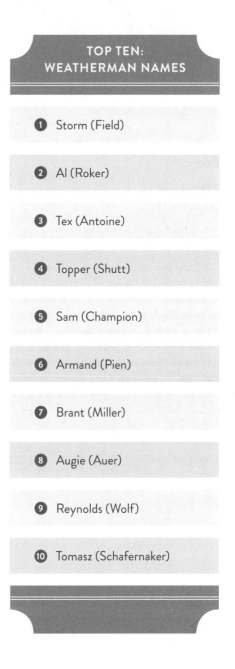

TOP TEN: WEATHERMAN NAMES

1. Storm (Field)
2. Al (Roker)
3. Tex (Antoine)
4. Topper (Shutt)
5. Sam (Champion)
6. Armand (Pien)
7. Brant (Miller)
8. Augie (Auer)
9. Reynolds (Wolf)
10. Tomasz (Schafernaker)

Zz

Zoe

Meaning: Life

Origin: Greek

Related names and spelling variations: *Zoey, Zooey, Zoie, Zoë*

We'd tell you that this name's popularity stems from actors Zooey Deschanel and Zoe Saldana, or even from J. D. Salinger's famous character Zooey Glass . . . but we know it probably comes from the character on *Sesame Street*. More accessible than Kermit or Elmo and more pronounceable than Snuffleupagus, Zoe's a great pick for the young at heart. A Greek name that means "life," Zoë (note the two dots, they tell you to pronounce the *e* separately from the *o*) has been in use since ancient Greece, so this name has serious history. It was a semi-popular name in the late 1800s, then dropped off the charts entirely until 1983. Zoe finally returned to the top 100 in 2000. Zoe's an attractive name for little girls and sophisticated adults alike, and it's brought to you by the letter *Z*.

THIS NAME IN HISTORY

Zoe (character on the TV show
   Sesame Street)

Zoe Caldwell (actor)

Zooey Deschanel (actor)

Zooey Glass (character in *Franny and Zooey*
   by J. D. Salinger)

Zoë Heller (author)

Zoe Saldana (actor)

Names Index

Hi, My Name Is

H

K

Kaden, 73
Kadin, 73
Kadyn, 73
Kaeden, 73
Kaela, 275–76
Kaiden, 73
Kaila, 275–76
Kailee, 276–77
Kailey, 276–77
Kaitlin, 272
Kaitlyn, 272
Kaitlynn, 272
Kaleb, 73
Kaleigh, 276–77
Kaley, 276–77
Kalvin, 74
Kameron, 75
Kamila, 229
Kamilla, 229
Kamille, 229
Kamren, 75
Kamron, 75
Kara, 272
Kareena, 273–74
Karen, 272–73
Karena, 273–74
Karin, 272–73
Karina, 272–74
Karine, 273–74
Karl, 75
Karla, 274
Karlee, 229–30
Karleigh, 229–30
Karley, 229–30
Karli, 229–30
Karlie, 229–30

Karly, 229–30
Karol, 75
Karoline, 231
Karolyne, 231
Karson, 76
Karter, 76
Kasey, 76–77
Kassandra, 231
Kassidy, 231–32
Kate, 274–75
Katelyn, 272
Katelynn, 272
Katherine, 274–75
Kathie, 275
Kathleen, 275
Kathryn, 274–75
Kathy, 274–75
Katie, 274–75
Katrin, 275
Katrina, 275
Katrine, 275
Katy, 274–75
Kayden, 73
Kayla, 275–76
Kaylah, 275–76
Kaylee, 276–77
Kayleigh, 276–77
Kayley, 276–77
Kaylie, 276–77
Keira, 277
Keith, 136
Kell, 136–37
Kellan, 136–37
Kellen, 136–37
Kelli, 277
Kellie, 277
Kellin, 136–37
Kelly, 277

Kelsey, 277–78
Kelsie, 277–78
Ken, 137
Kendal, 278
Kendall, 278
Kendelle, 278
Kendra, 278
Kendyl, 278
Kenneth, 137
Kennith, 137
Kenny, 137
Kenzie, 290
Kerrin, 272–73
Kerstin, 234–35
Kev, 138
Keven, 138
Kevin, 138
Khloe, 234
Khloey, 234
Kiera, 277
Kierra, 277
Kileigh, 280
Kiley, 280
Kimberlee, 279
Kimberleigh, 279
Kimberley, 279
Kimberli, 279
Kimberlie, 279
Kimberly, 279
Kira, 277
Kitty, 274–75
Klay, 81
Klayton, 81
Kloe, 234
Kodie, 81–82
Kody, 81–82
Kolby, 82–83
Kole, 83

Hi, My Name Is

Nathanial, 155
Nathaniel, 155
Nathen, 155
Neal, 155–56
Ned, 100
Neil, 155–56
Nell, 243–44
Nelly, 243–44
Nena, 307
Nessa, 336
Nevaeh, 305–6
Neveah, 305–6
Niall, 155–56
Niccole, 306–7
Nicholas, 156
Nichole, 306–7
Nick, 156
Nicki, 306–7
Nickolas, 156
Nicky, 306–7
Nico, 156
Nicola, 306–7
Nicolas, 156
Nicole, 306–7
Nicolette, 306–7
Nicolina, 306–7
Niko, 156
Nikoas, 156
Nikolai, 156
Nikolas, 156
Nikole, 306–7
Nina, 307
Noah, 156–57
Noel, 157–58, 307–8
Noël, 157–58
Noella, 307–8
Noelle, 307–8

Noëlle, 307–8
Noemi, 304
Noémie, 304
Nolan, 158
Nolen, 158
Nollan, 158
Nolyn, 158
Nora, 308
Norah, 308

O

Oliva, 309
Olive, 309
Oliveah, 309
Oliver, 159
Olivia, 309
Olivier, 159
Ollie, 159
Ondrea, 215
Orien, 159–60
Orion, 159–60
Orlando, 174
Oscar, 160–61
Oskar, 160–61
Osker, 160–61
Ostin, 63
Owain, 161
Owen, 161
Owin, 161

P

Pablo, 162–63
Padraic, 162
Page, 310
Paige, 310
Paityn, 312
Pam, 310–11
Pamela, 310–11

Pat, 162, 311
Patrice, 311
Patricia, 311
Patrick, 162
Patrik, 162
Patrizia, 311
Patryk, 162
Patsy, 311
Patti, 311
Patty, 162, 311
Paul, 162–63
Paulo, 162–63
Payge, 310
Payten, 312
Payton, 312
Pearce, 164–65
Pedro, 163
Peg, 294
Peggy, 294
Penelope, 311
Penny, 311
Pete, 163
Peter, 163
Peyton, 312
Phil, 163–64
Philip, 163–64
Phillip, 163–64
Phoebe, 312
Pierce, 163, 164–65
Pierre, 163
Piers, 163, 164–65
Piper, 312
Pres, 165
Preston, 165
Priscilla, 313
Prissy, 313
Prudence, 30

Hi, My Name Is

S

Sabreena, 320
Sabrina, 320
Sacha, 323
Sadie, 320
Sage, 320–21
Saidey, 320
Saidie, 320
Saige, 320–21
Sam, 178, 321–22
Samantha, 321–22
Sammantha, 321–22
Sammie, 321–22
Sammy, 178, 321–22
Samuel, 178
Sandra, 210, 322
Sandrine, 322
Sandy, 322
Sara, 322
Sarah, 322
Sarai, 322
Sari, 322
Sasha, 323
Saul, 178–79
Saundra, 322
Savanah, 323
Savanna, 323
Savannah, 323
Sawyer, 179–80
Saydie, 320
Scarlet, 323–24
Scarlett, 323–24
Schuyler, 327
Scot, 180
Scott, 180
Scottie, 180
Scotty, 180
Séamas, 122–23

Sean, 180
Seb, 180–81
Sebastian, 180–81
Sebastien, 180–81
Semantha, 321–22
Serena, 324–25
Seth, 181
Shamus, 122–23
Shane, 182
Shannen, 325
Shannon, 325
Sharon, 325
Shaul, 178–79
Shaun, 180
Shawn, 180
Sheena, 264
Sheila, 232–33
Shelby, 325–26
Sherri, 325
Sherry, 325
Shlomo, 183–84
Shona, 268
Shyanne, 234
Si, 183
Sid, 331
Sidnee, 331
Sidney, 331
Siena, 326
Sienna, 326
Sierra, 326
Silas, 183
Simeon, 183
Simon, 183
Sinéad, 264
Sisley, 232–33
Sky, 326–27
Skye, 326–27
Skyla, 326–27

Skylar, 327
Skyler, 327
Sofia, 328
Sol, 178–79, 183–84
Solly, 178–79, 183–84
Solomon, 183–84
Sondra, 322
Sonia, 327
Sonja, 327
Sonya, 327
Sophia, 328
Sophie, 328
Spence, 184–85
Spencer, 184–85
Spenser, 184–85
Spensor, 184–85
Stacey, 214, 329
Stacy, 214, 329
Stasia, 214
Stef, 330
Stefan, 185
Stefanie, 330
Steffi, 330
Stella, 329
Steph, 330
Stephanie, 330
Stephano, 185
Stephany, 330
Stephen, 185
Stephenie, 330
Steve, 185
Steven, 185
Stevie, 185, 330
Sue, 330–31
Sukie, 330–31
Summer, 330
Suri, 322
Susan, 330–31

Hi, My Name Is

General Index

acknowledgments

Still need a name for your imminent little one? Maybe pick from the top 10 people who helped with this book: Amanda Barden (baby name researcher extraordinaire); our crack team of writers: Jennifer Hughes, Samuel Warren, or pinch-hitter Brian Fairbanks; our persevering editors at Chronicle, Jodi Warshaw and Laura Lee Mattingly; our list masters, Lauren De Luca and Trish Halpin; proofreader Andrea Roxas; or even we two humble Babble editors, Jack Murnighan and Sarah Bryden-Brown (oops, I guess, like the amplifier in *Spinal Tap*, we go to 11). This has been a collaborative effort in the best of senses, and we thank you all and the many other people who lent a hand in the process.